The Workless

The Workless

Stigma, Unpaid Labour and the Myth of Economic Inactivity

James Morrison

Bristol, UK / Chicago, USA

First published in the UK in 2026 by
Intellect, The Mill, Parnall Road, Fishponds, Bristol, BS16 3JG, UK

First published in the USA in 2026 by
Intellect, The University of Chicago Press, 1427 E. 60th Street,
Chicago, IL 60637, USA

EU GPSR Authorised Representative
LOGOS EUROPE, 9 rue Nicolas Poussin, 17000,
LA ROCHELLE, France
E-mail: Contact@logoseurope.eu

A catalogue record for this book is available from the British Library.

Copy editor: Sarah Johnson
Cover designer: Natalie Thomas
Cover images: smartboy10, iStock 960333052 and 1324246375
Production manager: Rebecca Hedger
Typesetter: Newgen Knowledge Works

Hardback print ISBN: 978-1-83595-318-1
Paperback ISBN: 978-1-83595-374-7
ePDF ISBN: 978-1-83595-320-4
ePUB ISBN: 978-1-83595-319-8

To find out about all our publications, please visit our website.

There you can subscribe to our e-newsletter, browse or download our current catalogue and buy any titles that are in print.

www.intellectbooks.com

To all those who have been labelled 'economically inactive' –
workless of the world, unite!

Contents

Figures and Tables

Figures

Tables

Abbreviations

ADHD	attention deficit hyperactivity disorder
ATD	All Together in Dignity Fourth World
BES	brown envelope syndrome
CA	Carer's Allowance
CAB	Citizens Advice Bureau
CDA	critical discourse analysis
CPS	Centre for Policy Studies
CPAC	Child Poverty Action Group
CSJ	Centre for Social Justice
CSV	Community Service Volunteers
DIY	do it yourself
DLA	Disability Living Allowance
DPhil	Doctorate of Philosophy
DWP	Department for Work and Pensions
EDI	equality, diversity and inclusion
ESA	Employment and Support Allowance
ESRC	Economic and Social Research Council
GDP	gross domestic product
GP	general practitioner
GRIPP	Growing Rights Instead of Poverty Partnership
HB	housing benefit
IB	incapacity benefit
IFS	Institute for Fiscal Studies
IMPRESS	independent monitor of the press
IPPR	Institute for Public Policy Research
IPSO	Independent Press Standards Organization
JRF	Joseph Rowntree Foundation
JSA	Jobseeker's Allowance
LFS	Labour Force Survey
LHA	Local Housing Allowance

MOT	Ministry of Transport certificate
NEET	not in education, employment or training
NHS	National Health Service
NUJ	National Union of Journalists
OBR	Office for Budget Responsibility
OECD	Organisation for Economic Cooperation and Development
Ofcom	Office of Communications
ONS	Office for National Statistics
OT	occupational therapist
Oxbridge	Oxford and Cambridge
PIP	Personal Independence Payment
PLC	public limited company
UC	Universal Credit
UK	United Kingdom
WCA	Work Capability Assessment

Acknowledgements

Writing this book would have been impossible without the benefit of the incisive, moving and, above all, expert input of the dozen or more individuals kind enough to make time in their busy lives to share their personal (hi)stories and experiences – and their perspectives on Britain's febrile ongoing debate about economic inactivity. Contrary to ill-informed popular myths circulating about people designated 'inactive' or 'workless', almost everyone I spoke to was, by almost any standards, extremely time-poor. Far from living lives of infinite leisure, theirs were tales of continual, demanding disabled labour: complex, physically and emotionally draining (and occasionally painful) daily routines, punctuated by periods of much more intense pressure, whether associated with medical procedures, form-filling or benefit reassessments. This is to say nothing of those with hectic unpaid care schedules, responsible for children and/or other dependants – partners, parents, siblings and multiples thereof – often while managing their own illnesses and disabilities. Although my interviewees are all quoted here under aliases, they will know who they are. These stories, experiences and expert insights belong to them, as living exemplars of Britain's great and growing army of hardworking 'active inactives'.

The process of contacting, approaching and arranging to meet people online was facilitated by partners at four key charities, without whose encouragement and willingness to circulate my appeal for interviewees I would have struggled hugely. Thanks especially to Diana Skelton at ATD Fourth World (who also gave her own time for an interview), and to Aishah Sidiqqa at Heard, Bethany Sikes and Debbie Maltman at Volunteer Scotland, and Laura Robertson at the Poverty Alliance. I would also like to thank academic colleagues who have done most to support me (and egg me on) as the book has evolved. Chief among them are Steven Harkins at Stirling and Rachel Broady at Liverpool John Moores University.

Finally, I want to acknowledge my debt to many people I have met in my own life – some dear to me – who have direct lived experience of disability, mental ill health, unpaid caregiving, and (in many cases) the stigma of being labelled 'workless'. Many years ago, I spent some months working as a voluntary care-worker through the Community Service Volunteers (CSV) programme at the National Star

Centre for Disabled Youth near Cheltenham. As I researched this book, I couldn't help wondering how many of the young people I met back then – some managing the severest forms of physical disability – must have been impacted by the relentless onslaught of benefit cuts, wider 'welfare reforms' and accompanying stigma and negativity that has typified the UK's so-called national conversations about work, worklessness and the welfare state over the intervening 30-plus years. It is to these people, and everyone like them, that I dedicate this book.

Introduction: Corralling the 'Workless' – Contemporary Policy Debates in Perspective

Britain's latest moral panic about the evils of 'worklessness' came of age in an airless seminar room at the Centre for Social Justice, in London's Smith Square, on 19 April 2024. Twenty years after its launch by Iain Duncan Smith (later work and pensions secretary and architect of the most swingeing cuts to Britain's welfare state since its inception), grave-faced prime minister Rishi Sunak chose his right-wing think-tank as a platform to call time on the 'sick-note culture' bedevilling the country – a tabloid trope that met the nodding approval of IDS himself (Sunak 2024). The task of 'reforming welfare to give everyone who can the best possible chance of returning to work', argued the soon-to-be ex-premier, was nothing less than a 'moral mission': to empower people 'to contribute, to belong, to overcome feelings of loneliness and social isolation'; end the 'over-medicalizing' of 'everyday challenges and worries of life'; and arrest the 'irresponsible burden' of a 'spiralling increase in the welfare bill' on 'this and future generations of taxpayers'.

By invoking a moral lens to frame his binary distinction between 'hardworking taxpayers' and the 'economically inactive' – a grouping consistently cast in conservative circles as 'workless' and (by inference) worthless (Lawford and Butcher 2024) – Sunak set a tone that would cast a long shadow across Britain's body politic over the ensuing months of pre- (and post-) election campaigning. In the sub-heading to its cutting critique of Sir Keir Starmer's Labour Party Conference speech that September – delivered two months after he had safely ensconced himself in Downing Street – *The Guardian* posed this pointed question: 'Serving working people, but what about others?' The paper noted the newly elected prime minister's rhetorical efforts to engender 'a public morality' guaranteeing 'collectively funded support for the employed rather than the unemployed' (and, by extension, everyone out of work) (*The Guardian* 2024b: n.pag.). Starmer had done so by asserting his 'cultural and economic affiliation with working people' and vowing to 'prioritize the interests of those in work over other sections of society' – a nexus of allegiances most heavily symbolized in his disingenuous peroration eliding his twin goals of tackling the disparate evils of 'benefit fraud' and 'worklessness' (Starmer 2024a).

Precise definitions of moral panic differ in terms more of wording than of substance, but one of the most widely accepted is that of sociologists Erich Goode and Nachman Ben-Yehuda, who famously characterized it as a scare about 'a threat or supposed threat from deviants or "folk-devils" ' (Goode and Ben-Yehuda 2009: 2). The threat, in this case, was the latest iteration of that most morally corrosive and abject of figures, 'the scrounger' (Morrison 2019): a storied social construct repeatedly revived by politicians and the media as an object of discursive distraction, blame and ridicule at times of widespread economic hardship. In this case, the parlous backdrop was provided by the combined impact of a household 'cost-of-living crisis' (Francis-Devine et al. 2024) and the soaring debt-to-GDP ratio bequeathed by a perfect storm of fiscal shocks – from Brexit to the pandemic to the now-notorious 'mini-budget disaster' that sent shockwaves through the money markets under short-lived 2022 Prime Minister Liz Truss (Islam 2023).

At the time Sunak stood up to deliver his 'sick-note culture' speech, the latest available labour market data from the Office for National Statistics (ONS) certainly made grim reading. According to these statistics, the number of working-aged adults classified as 'economically inactive' – those 'not in employment', who had 'not been seeking work in the last four weeks' and who were 'unable to start work within the next two weeks' (ONS 2021: n.pag.) – had risen by 850,000 since the economic quarter immediately before the pandemic (December 2019 to January 2020), taking the total to 9.4 million. Between December 2023 and February 2024 some 22.2 per cent of the working-aged population – more than a fifth of all 16- to 64-year-olds – were recorded as 'inactive' (Powell 2024). Most significantly, the latest spike in 'inactivity' was found to be 'driven by an increase in the number of people who are unable to work due to long-term sickness' – which hit a 'record high' of 2.8 million that quarter.

As one politician after another lined up to emphasize, this not only left Britain languishing beneath its competitors in terms of economic growth but also put it in an OECD league table position that was, if anything, even more ignominious: as the country with the lowest post-pandemic 'workforce participation rate' of all G7 economies (Partington 2023: n.pag.). Sunak's response was blunt: 'people are not three times sicker than they were a decade ago', and, while anyone 'feeling anxious or depressed' should 'of course' receive support and treatment needed to 'manage' their conditions, this did not mean we should assume they 'can't engage in work' (Sunak 2024: n.pag.). As for the right-wing press, the only logical explanation was that too many people had got so used to furloughs, lockdowns and being allowed to work from home during the pandemic that they had succumbed to what the *Daily Telegraph* and *Daily Mail* respectively dubbed 'workshy Britain' (Warner 2023) and 'sicknote Britain' (Merriman 2024) – a state of collective indolence *The Times* crystallized even more balefully as a 'British disease' of 'worklessness' (*The Times* 2024a).

A measure of the extent to which this narrative became normalized over ensuing months was its growing prominence as an accepted truth in even the more studiously neutral and impartial corners of the media. In a July 2024 edition of his BBC Radio 4 *Political Thinking* podcast, the corporation's former political editor, Nick Robinson, persistently quizzed then newly installed Labour Work and Pensions Secretary Liz Kendall about her party's attitude towards alleged 'scroungers', before posing this question:

> Here's what I think is going on – you tell me if I'm wrong. What the Tories do is give quite a lot of help and support to people, but produce headlines saying they're attacking scroungers, and what you do is produce policies that *are* tackling scroungers but have headlines about helping people. You're not, in reality, that different. It's all about spin.
>
> (*Political Thinking* 2024)

As it transpired, Robinson's incisive diagnosis (robustly denied by Kendall at the time) proved alarmingly prescient. Once he was in office, Starmer's very particular imaginary of a 'Labour' government would be confected to combine its loud and repeated disdain for 'Tory' labels like 'scrounger' and 'shirker' with a determination to slash disability benefits that was, if anything, even more ruthless than what had come before.

The worship of work

The seeds of this tortuous double-think were sowed in the earliest stages in the life of Starmer's administration. Whereas his 2024 conference speech undoubtedly channelled the essence of Sunak's moralizing discourse, other senior Labour figures had hitherto adopted a subtly different response to what the Centre for Cities and others had long-since branded Britain's unfolding 'economic inactivity crisis' (Quinio 2023: n.pag.). For a party whose very name enshrines its reverence for the virtues of honest toil, it was perhaps unsurprising that the moral dichotomy Labour drew between 'work' and 'worklessness' was less about denying (or drastically downplaying) the existence of work-limiting disability, mental illness or long-term health conditions than about romanticizing the dignity of labour itself.

In her widely publicized speech heralding the publication of party elder statesman Alan Milburn's 'Pathways to Work' report – a 'deep dive' study into the drivers, experiences and potential solutions for 'economic inactivity' in Barnsley (Milburn 2024a) – Kendall spoke solemnly of the 'dignity and self-respect' work could offer people, and reeled off an over-lexicalized list of benefits she ascribed to it, from 'pride, fulfilment, relationships and connections' to 'a sense of purpose, values, and control' (Kendall 2024). Shortly afterwards, in a more personal contribution to the debate – an op-ed for the *Mail on Sunday* heralding the unveiling of Labour's long-awaited 'Get Britain Working' white paper – Starmer himself adopted a similarly misty-eyed approach. Here he drew on personal anecdote to recall how his first humble job, onerously slaving to 'clear out stones' from a local farmer's field, had left him with 'the feeling of independence and achievement that comes with earning a living' (Starmer 2024b: n.pag.).

Labour's escalating emphasis on reframing the 'economic inactivity' debate in moralistic terms would reach its apotheosis in March 2025, in the immediate run-up to a dual policy event surrounded by near-hysterical levels of media anticipation. This was the publication, within days of each other, of a much-heralded (and, for many, long-dreaded) 'Pathways to Work' green paper on the future of disability and incapacity-related benefits and an ominously presented spring economic statement from Chancellor Rachel Reeves, in which she set out plans to match the Tories' pre-election pledge to slash £6 billion from the welfare budget. Interviewed on BBC Radio 4's *Today* programme on 5 March, in the days leading up to the green paper announcement, then Justice Secretary Shabana Mahmood adopted the role of outrider, suggesting that there was 'a moral case' for 'making sure that people who can work are able to work' (*Today* 2025a). Later that same day, Cabinet Office Minister Ellie Reeves (the chancellor's sister) told BBC2's *Politics Live* that ministers had 'a moral obligation' to provide work for the 'lost generation' of one million young people not in education, training or employment (*Politics Live* 2025), rather than 'incentivizing' people to remain out of work. This was an allusion to Milburn's criticism that 'perverse incentives' for people to claim disability-related support are baked into a system that 'rewarded' them more than the unemployed (Milburn 2024a: 22).

Over the coming days these arguments would be reheated by numerous Labour politicians – including loyalist backbench MP Mike Tapp, who told Radio 4 the government had a 'moral duty' to get people back to work (*Today* 2025b). It only fell to Starmer himself to set the seal on this twin-pronged approach with a no-holds-barred address to the Parliamentary Labour Party on 10 March, in which he decried the present welfare state as sowing the seeds for 'a wasted generation' of young people not in education, employment or training ('NEETS') – a situation, he declared, that 'runs contrary to those deep British values that if you can work, you should'. 'This is the *Labour* party', he added, before invoking those oft-romanticized tribal shibboleths of 'the dignity of work' – and a belief in 'the dignity of every worker' (quoted in Elgot and Butler 2025: n.pag.).

Yet somewhere in this heady rhetorical brew there also lurked a decidedly neoliberal conceptualization of morality: one driven as much by the cold, hard logic of fiscal realpolitik as any principled sense of fairness (whether concerning inactive people themselves or the burden they heaped on taxpayers). In expanding on his 'dignity of labour' mantra, Starmer painted a picture of a frayed social 'safety net' that no longer always gave those 'who really need' it 'the dignity they deserve' – a situation that 'people feel...in their bones' was 'unsustainable, indefensible and unfair' (Elgot and Butler 2025: n.pag.). Coming as his intervention did amid alarming predictions of global recession, following US president Donald Trump's imposition of widespread tariffs on imports and withdrawal of military support for Ukraine (a decision leaving a gap in defence spending to be compensated by the UK and European Union), there was no mistaking the meaning he attached to the economistic term 'sustainability' – or to his imaginary of 'the people'. The message was clear: the UK and its hallowed moral majority, or virtuous in-group ('working people'), could no longer afford its welfare state to be a soft touch for anyone who was not in gainful employment and *should* be (that deviant out-group, 'the workless').

Between Labour and Tories, then, a bipartisan consensus had been reached around the concept of disability benefit reform (for which read 'cuts') as a moral mission – with only minor variations to distinguish one party's position from the other's. The Conservatives' emphasis was unambiguously on the immorality of allowing people who (in truth) were well enough to work to continue exploiting the generosity of hardworking taxpayers. Labour strained to adopt the contorted position of both extolling Starmer's moralizing case that 'those who can work should work' while also stressing the morality of incentivizing and enabling sick and disabled people who 'want' to work but face barriers preventing them from doing so. But in buying into the neoliberal argument that the primary obstacle consigning disabled people to the scrapheap was not prejudiced employers, inflexible working conditions or chronically underfunded health and care services but a Byzantine, disempowering benefits system, they accepted (and amplified) what sociologist Tracey Jensen terms the 'doxa' of 'welfare commonsense' (Jensen 2014: n.pag.).

Missing from both the Tories' and Labour's moralistic paeans to a narrowly defined imaginary of intrinsically virtuous, rewarding graft – a rose-tinted portrayal here conceptualized as the 'worship of work' – was any recognition of the value of forms of endeavour and social contribution that do not offer even nominal financial reward. Implicit in both was a denial of the soullessness, pointlessness and precarity of much of what qualifies as paid work in the contemporary neoliberal economy – and the many meaningful (if less fiscally measurable) contributions made by numerous people coldly categorized as 'workless' and 'inactive' but who nonetheless work, unpaid, as caregivers and volunteers. The failure to acknowledge such contributions – and the omission of anyone not in *conventional* employment (or self-employment) from the hallowed ranks of those performatively revered as 'working' people – evoked sociologist George Gerbner's concept of 'symbolic annihilation'. This is an 'absence' from discourse that has the effect of denying individuals' (or groups') very 'social existence' (Gerbner and Gross 1976: 182).

As another sociologist, David Frayne, argues in his excellent *The Refusal of Work*, domestic labour, 'along with certain forms of artistic, intellectual or care work', often sits 'uncomfortably on the fringes of what society is prepared to categorise as actual "work" ' – especially 'in cases where the value of these activities cannot be explained in terms of any measurable social or economic contribution' (Frayne 2015: 18–19). Or, to return to the language of morality, as political scientist Deborah Stone argued in *The Disabled State* (still a seminal work of disability studies four decades after its publication): 'Why should not child-rearing, creative but unpaid endeavors, or voluntary labor count in the grand tally of moral worth?' (Stone 1986: 176).

It is this simple proposition that forms the premise for this book: the argument that Britain's increasingly narrow and judgmental political, media and wider public discourse around what constitutes 'work', value and meaningful 'activity' (economic or otherwise) is long overdue a fundamental rethink. In an age when unpaid carers in England and Wales alone save UK taxpayers £445 million a day (Carers UK 2024) – by plugging gaping holes in an overstretched, underfunded National Health Service, welfare state and social care system – it is surely untenable to continue denying their economic contributions. More importantly, how can we continue to tolerate narratives that glibly frame people who give so *much* of their time as caregivers or volunteers as 'inactive' or 'workless', when analysis of the latest English and Welsh census shows the number of people providing 50 hours or more of unpaid care a week rose by 152,000 between 2011 and 2021, to 1.5 million (Carers UK 2023), while three out of five adult carers in Scotland had similar-sized workloads (The Scottish Government 2023)? Then there is the widely ignored fact that the same ten-year period saw a rise in the number of unpaid carers living with *their own* disabilities – the biggest increase being among the youngest age group. ONS figures show that, between 2011 and 2021, the number of carers aged 5 to 17 who were disabled themselves leapt from 9.4 and 9.5% to 23.6 and 20.9% in England and Wales respectively. Caregivers are also more likely than non-carers to have their own disabilities (Eley 2023). Significantly, even the government-endorsed 'Pathways to Work' report acknowledged that 22 of the 37 Barnsley residents it profiled were managing both caring pressures *and* health conditions (Milburn 2024a).

The symbolic annihilation of these hugely important segments – and the many unrecognized, highly *active* individuals among them who would doubtless be classed as *in*active, according to today's prescriptive dominant definitions of 'work' – brings us to another of the book's key aims. This is to recognize the complex and (more often than not) intersectional challenges and inequalities faced by many 'inactive' people – from caregivers and those with work-limiting disabilities to others who are simply too physically and/or mentally unwell to undertake conventional structured employment (let alone the more erratic, insecure work patterns associated with the 'gig economy' and 'zero-hours contracts'). These inconvenient realities are discursively annihilated by the moralizing tropes of 'sick-note Britain', 'workshy Britain' and the supposed 'British disease' of 'worklessness'. And, I will argue, just as pernicious in their way are functionalist bureaucratic terms like 'economic inactivity' itself: a clinical officialese that notes the price of everything and the value of nothing. Significantly, this term was rightly called out as a 'terrible' way to describe 'real human beings' by Kendall, in one of her more progressive comments in office, addressing the Work and Pensions Select Committee (Wilcock 2024).

But it is not merely symbolic annihilation that is at play in the popular construction of economic inactivity. When not being ignored, negated, annihilated, through their *absence* from media and political discourse, people classified as inactive are subject to another, perhaps even more dehumanizing, form of symbolic violence: stigma. As defined by sociologist Erving Goffman in his seminal work of the same name, stigma can best be conceptualized as a form of 'spoiled identity' that acts to undermine an individual's 'social acceptance' and, in many cases, render them 'deviant' in the eyes of those who encounter and behold them (Goffman 1990: ix–x). What identity can be considered more 'spoiled' in today's ableist, transactional, materialistic age – an era so singularly and universally obsessed with the acquisition and performative display of capital, image and status – than that of the 'inactive', 'workless' and/or disabled person? In one of his book's defining passages, Goffman describes the process by which stigma is ascribed to individuals through the person of the newly encountered 'stranger'. He argues:

> When a stranger comes into our presence, first appearances are likely to enable us to anticipate his category and attributes, his 'social identity' – to use a term that is better than 'social status' because personal attributes such as 'honesty' are involved, as well as structural ones, like 'occupation'.
>
> (Goffman 1990: x)

By applying the social signifiers we habitually use to divine an individual's honesty (or trustworthiness) and their occupation (a quality of intrinsic relevance in the context of economic in/activity), we can discern 'evidence' as to whether the stranger possesses 'an attribute that makes him different from others in the category of persons available for him to be, and of a less desirable kind – in the extreme, a person who is quite thoroughly bad, or dangerous, or weak'. Should such evidence be discernible – for the economically inactive, through the person's careworn or impoverished appearance, embarrassed manner or cagey reply to an innocent ice-breaker question such 'so what do you do?' – 'they are thus reduced in our minds from a whole and usual person to a tainted, discounted one' (Goffman 1990: x).

At the heart of this book is a dual concern with these twin sociological concepts – symbolic annihilation and stigma – and, specifically, how we talk and think about other (often more vulnerable) *people*: to quote Kendall, 'real human beings'. Specifically, the book is concerned with the question of how politicians, the news media and the public(s) at large talk (and, by inference, *think*) about disability, long-term sickness, mental ill health and neurodiversity – and, more importantly, the individuals these affect. It is not a book *about* disability or work-limiting health conditions themselves – or even how these are defined. Similarly, it is not *about* carers, volunteers or definitions of what constitutes caring or voluntary work. Since the 1980s the field of disability studies has grown rapidly, and there is an expansive literature unpacking and contesting everything from the nature and efficacy of medical versus social diagnoses and labels (Bunbury 2019) to the prevalence of ableist norms – both in terms of social attitudes (and prejudices), and in relation to how society conditions and frames issues around access to/participation in the worlds of home, leisure and work (Bogart and Dunn 2019). Equally, the nature of care – and, in particular, unpaid/voluntary caregiving – has latterly come in for increasing academic scrutiny. As with disability, the charitable/third sector itself has produced a growing body of high-quality research exploring the practical, financial and emotional challenges carers face, and the valuable contributions they make (e.g. Sempick and Becker 2013) – often drawing on individuals' lived experiences (Rainer et al. 2024).

Where this book *is* concerned about people with disabilities, long-term illnesses and caring responsibilities – facets often present in *the same individual* (as we shall see) – it is less with questions about the objective scale of these issues as drivers of economic inactivity than how these often intersecting groups are *constructed* and *portrayed* in the political public sphere (Habermas 2022). Moreover, in the extended discursive 'moment' that forms the backdrop for this book, these constructions and portrayals are conceived through the prism of the febrile post-pandemic debate about 'economic inactivity' and that often interchangeably used term, 'worklessness'. To this extent, if there is a focal discursive object at the centre of our concerns, it is not so much disability, illness, caregiving or other factors inhibiting an individual's ability to enter or remain in the world of paid labour *in themselves*, but dominant *conceptions* of what is (or is not) an acceptable reason for someone *not* working – as well as the nature of how society *defines* 'work' and its supposed equal and opposite, 'worklessness'. This is, then, a book that seeks to unpack – primarily through its analysis of public discourse – those barriers or challenges that are presented as sufficiently valid to 'justify' people being *unable* to work (in the conventional sense); 'choosing' not to; or either falling or opting out of the workplace. Bound up with all of this is a secondary focus: on the discursive distinctions media, political and wider public narratives draw between disabilities, illnesses and other barriers to work they judge to be *genuinely* disabling and those they consider to be exaggerated, even fraudulent. This focus entails not only examining how society seeks to construct hierarchies of deservingness *in the present*, but diving back through history to encounter age-old imaginaries around 'fake' injury, sickness and disability, from 'false mendicants' to 'sturdy beggars' to 'palliards', 'Clapperdudgeons', 'counterfeit cranks' and other fabular folk-devils of antiquity and early modern times (Row-Heyveld 2018).

Just as this is not a book *about* disability or work-limiting illness, neither is it about the various factors that lead working-aged people to become 'economically inactive' – from the decisions to retire early taken by a wave of what might be termed 'new inactives' during the later stages of the pandemic to the conscious rejection of work by a small minority who opt out of the labour market entirely, or the circumstances that drive 'discouraged workers' to simply give up trying to find jobs, consigning them to the ranks of a 'hidden' unemployed (Leaker 2009: 52–55). For an exploration of the motives of those who chose to leave the labour market early during the late-COVID period, there is much to be learned from *The Great Resignation: The New Refusal of Work* by sociologist Francesca Coin. For incisive sociological critiques of the structural problems and inequities inherent in the neoliberal workplace – and the Protestant work ethic underlying it – look no further than Frayn's aforementioned *The Refusal of Work* and Kathi Weeks's *The Problem of Work*.

Above all else, the book is most concerned with examining, and querying, societal conceptions of 'deservingness'. With this in mind, its primary preoccupation is the question of what constitute deserving versus undeserving forms of 'inactivity' and/or reasons for being 'inactive': challenges society deems manageable while making oneself available for work versus those judged sufficiently inhibiting to legitimately prevent this availability. In doing so, it opens up questions around the relative levels of deservingness attributed to people who are 'inactive' owing to disability, illness, caring responsibilities and/or other barriers to work, versus those deemed to be 'workless' out of *choice*. At this point, a note: as it will be necessary to use phrases like 'economic inactivity' and 'worklessness' repeatedly from here on, the book would be labouring the point (so to speak) were it to continue overtly problematizing them by using inverted commas on each occasion they are mentioned. For this reason, the reader is asked to take as read that inverted commas remain *implied* whenever they appear from now on.

In using Britain's hysterical current (and likely ongoing) media-political debate about economic inactivity as a prism through which to explore public conceptions of societal value and worth – not least of a sizeable proportion of our fellow citizens – this book seeks to build on classic studies that have previously addressed debates about deservingness, particularly in the context of social security and the UK's (and other) welfare state(s). In particular, like my earlier book *Scroungers*, it draws on sociologists Peter Golding's and Sue Middleton's seminal *Images of Welfare*, to whose keen historical sensibilities and respect for the origins, evolution and (dis)continuities in conceptualizations of authentic versus fraudulent illness, disability and (un)fitness for work it owes a particular debt. It also draws heavily on ideas in political scientist Deborah Stone's *The Disabled State* – most notably her argument that, while concerns about fake or fraudulent disability may often be the focus of accusatory media narratives, people judged to be *genuinely* disabled have come to occupy a position of particular 'political privilege' in latter-day welfare states. Genuine disability 'is a political privilege', Stone argues, 'because, as an administrative category, it carries with it permission to enter the need-based system' (i.e. entitling people to state-funded social protection without any expectation that they will put into the pot themselves, by working and paying taxes). This exempts them from 'the work-based system' to which everyone else is subject – which allocates resources according to contribution, rather than need (Stone 1986: 28).

Stone's arguments are important because the privileged exemption from work she ascribes to disabled people in countries like Britain (to the extent this still exists, following successive recent waves of 'welfare reform' that have made it ever harder to prove one's disabilities are serious enough to stop one working) is implicitly founded on contracts of trust. Disabled people are (or have been) exempt from the 'work-based system', and entitled to social protection solely on the basis of their financial and physical/mental needs – provided, that is, their disabilities are judged to be both genuine and chronic. This question of social trust, as we shall see, is intrinsically important to contemporary media and political discourses problematizing people out of work owing to disability, long-term sickness and/or mental ill health, as it is feelings of *distrust* that are activated by narratives portraying inactive people as 'scroungers' and 'shirkers'. Distrust is also the sentiment underpinning many of the sceptical (and, in some cases, hateful) comments posted by newspaper readers online, with numerous posters drawing on anecdotes about fake disabled people living off the largesse of the state whom they have supposedly encountered or observed in their daily lives – dubious characters this author has previously conceptualized (drawing on Gerbner and others) as 'familiar strangers' (Morrison 2016).

It is with both these core concepts in mind – relative measures of deservingness and discourses of (dis)trust – that we begin our journey in Chapter 1. This opening chapter focuses on the historical evolution of cultural and media representations of what would today be labelled 'inactivity' – with a particular focus on popular portrayals of those claiming to be incapable of work, owing to disability, disease, mental illness and (very often) intersections between two or more of these. In Chapter 2, we return abruptly to the present, to begin unpacking the ways in which economic inactivity is conceived and depicted in Britain today, in both mainstream media and political narratives. We do this through a critical discourse analysis of national and regional newspaper articles, Hansard records (parliamentary debates) and comment threads posted beneath press content online around a series of key discursive events or moments during the life cycle of the panic over 'sick-note culture'.

After this point, we turn to what is perhaps the book's main focus: putting these dominant narratives to the test in the first of three chapters exploring the extent to which prevailing discourses about inactivity bear any resemblance to the lived experiences of people classified as economically inactive. In Chapter 3, we focus on unpacking the multiple, often intersecting factors that can contribute to individuals' being or becoming inactive – from work-limiting disabilities and chronic health conditions to mental illness and full-time caring responsibilities. These strands are then further developed in Chapter 4, in which the emphasis pivots towards considering the plight of what might be termed 'workless workers' (or 'active inactives'): individuals classified as inactive yet very far from idle, on account of their caregiving duties and/or other contributions to the common good through volunteering, charity work, campaigning and/or community organizing. Finally, we round off this trilogy of chapters exploring the lives of inactive people themselves by switching the focus towards a particular grouping of individuals that have come under the spotlight increasingly since the advent of COVID-19. These are the growing number of 'elective' or 'new inactives' who have voluntarily opted out of the labour market since the pandemic – whether to spend more time caring for family, to slow down and 'downsize', or to enjoy the benefits of early retirement, such as opportunities for travel, increased leisure time or improved quality of life generally.

But before we embark on any of this, we must first begin by setting the scene for the peculiar moral panic about inactivity that has erupted since the pandemic – the context and detail of which forms the backdrop for this book. In doing so, we will frame discussion around a handful of questions. What exactly *is* (or was) the scale of inactivity in the UK two or three years out from the pandemic, and how did it compare to both pre-COVID rates and those of other (comparable) countries? Which are/were the main demographics affected, and what were the principal factors fuelling their withdrawal from the labour market? Perhaps most importantly, in considering the media-political response through the analytical lens of moral panics, how rational and proportionate were the discursive and policy tools deployed to characterize and contain any 'surge' in activity?

In opening in this vein, the book seeks to question and (where it can) contest a host of popular tropes – about idleness, laziness, fraudulence and, above all, worklessness. Above all, it aims to challenge, and perhaps reject, one of the defining fallacies of our times: the myth of economic inactivity. Whatever we might like to call people who are not in conventional paid employment or self-employment, in truth precious few of them are genuinely workless, let alone inactive. The large majority of individuals classed as such tend to subsist on such low incomes that they cannot afford to save and have no choice but to spend what little they have. If anything, then, they are highly economically *active*, and perhaps more so than many other people, as what little money they have is ploughed straight back into the system – contributing (however modestly) to economic growth. Moreover, as we shall see, many so-called inactive people spend much or all of their lives toiling, unpaid and unrecognized, in valuable ways that are nonetheless rendered invisible – or symbolically annihilated – in the hegemonic discourse around what constitutes work.

Anatomy of a 'sick-note' panic

The UK's much-publicized moral crusade against 'sick-note culture' began life in the context of what was widely (though not entirely accurately) reported as an unprecedented rise in working-aged economic inactivity in the shadow of the pandemic. The late stages of COVID-19 witnessed a blizzard of papers from policy think-tanks (Boileau and Cribb 2022; Williams 2023), executive agencies (Murphy et al. 2022) and quangos (Office for Budget Responsibility 2023) puzzling over what appeared to be a significant (if ultimately short-lived) surge in middle aged and older workers opting for early retirement – a phenomenon quickly popularized by the news media as the 'Great Resignation' (Kamal 2022; Knapton 2022; Iarcurci 2023) or 'Great Retirement' (Wallace 2023).

Though early official analyses were sober – with both the ONS and Office for Budget Responsibility recording the uptick with concerned but clinical detachment – 2022 and 2023 saw an escalating sense of alarmism, most notably among free market think-tanks on the political Right. 'Why is this happening?' was the exasperated question from Karl Williams, senior researcher with a prominent right-wing think-tank, as he pondered why Britain had become 'an international outlier', with '516,000 more inactive people aged 16–64 than was the case pre-pandemic', in his polemical March 2023 paper *Where are the Workers?* (Williams 2023: 4). Williams's speculative policy paper was a product of the Tufton Street-based Centre for Policy Studies: a Petri dish for fundamentalist free-market thinking ever since its foundation, in 1974, by one Margaret Thatcher and her mentor, Keith Joseph – perhaps the single most influential of a long line of post-war 'moral missionaries' on issues around employment and welfare (Morrison 2019: 84–85). While younger inactive people, suggested Williams (channelling Joseph), largely needed sticks to force them *into* the workplace – a heady conservative cocktail of benefit cuts, sanctions and patronizing pep-talks about responsibility and resilience – older workers tempted to quit employment to sample the spoils of early retirement needed carrots to incentivize them to *stay*. Chief among these, he argued, was an increase or abolition of the amount of money individuals were allowed to withdraw from their pension pots prior to retirement without being taxed – the so-called lifetime allowance (LTA) or 'pension cap' (Williams 2023: 28). Significantly, these decidedly uneven-handed recommendations for tackling Britain's inactivity spike were to end up forming a key plank of outgoing Conservative Chancellor Jeremy Hunt's then-upcoming spring Budget.

It was in this unfolding context that, back in August 2022, a recording had been leaked to *The Guardian* of soon-to-be Tory Prime Minister (and friend of Tufton Street) Ms Truss disparaging Britons from areas outside London as lacking the 'mindset or attitude' to put in the 'hard graft' or 'skill and application' typically found in foreign migrant workers (Crerar 2022). Truss's off-the-cuff remarks to supporters (back in 2019) carried clear echoes of arguments she had made in the 2012 book *Britannia Unchained*, which infamously mocked the British as 'among the worst idlers in the world' – a people 'more interested in football and pop music' than work (quoted in Wintour 2022).

While the initial focus of politicians' concern might have centred on premature retirees and/or older workers leaving the labour market for health reasons (including 'long COVID'), by early 2024 attention had shifted decisively towards a second – for many, more concerning – demographic. Far from being driven by opt-outs in older age groups (generation X and the last of the post-war 'boomer' generation), inactivity of the post-pandemic variety had settled into what the Resolution Foundation conceptualized as a 'U-shaped legacy' – with people aged 16–24 and 50–64 accounting for 'nine-tenths of the rise in economic inactivity among working-age adults since the end of 2019' (Murphy 2024: n.pag.). Suddenly it was rising rates of mental ill health, neurodivergent conditions and (for some) caring responsibilities among the former segment – the oft-labelled 'NEETs' – that were held to be driving the upward trend in inactivity as much as any ongoing increase among middle-aged and older workers. 'The U-shaped nature of this problem is especially worrying', observed foundation chief economist Louise Murphy, because, while 'any spell out of work due to ill health can be damaging to an individual's well-being and living standards', these risks were 'even greater for young people at the start of their working lives' (Murphy 2024: n.pag.). Meanwhile, concern about the older workers who accounted for the second 'arm' of Murphy's 'U-shape' curve had shifted away from voluntary downsizers and early retirees (many of whom, in any case, had been forced back to work during the unfolding 'cost-of-living crisis') towards those reluctantly joining the ranks of sickness benefit claimants as they queued for delayed NHS treatment for musculoskeletal disorders and other age-related complaints that had emerged or worsened during the pandemic.

By the time Murphy reached her diagnosis, the overall number of inactive working-aged adults had topped 9 million. While this inflated figure included several groups no one expected to be in or seeking full-time work – notably full-time university students – more disquieting was the fact that 2.7 million (and that number was rising) were out of work owing, at least partly, to long-term sickness. Even more concerning for ministers was the fact that Murphy's figures showed how, by December 2023, more than a third of people receiving Universal Credit had a health condition or disability affecting their ability to work, while new claims among working-aged adults in England and Wales for the main non-means-tested disability benefit, Personal Independence Payment (PIP), had leapt by 68% in the four years leading up to early 2024. Crucially, the number of new PIP claims for 16- to 17-year-olds and 18- to 24-year-olds had surged by 138 and 77% respectively (Murphy 2024: n.pag.).

This significant increase in disability-related claims caused sufficient alarm for the Resolution Foundation to argue that governments in the 2020s 'should be wary about having an increasingly strict unemployment benefits system (where claimants are subject to high levels of benefit conditionality), since this may be acting to encourage more people to claim health-related benefits instead' (Murphy 2024: n.pag.). Building on this theme, Labour grandee Alan Milburn's 'Pathways to Work' Commission Report observed that 'some point to perverse incentives in the benefits system whereby claimants get higher weekly payments if they claim incapacity on the basis of poor mental health than if they are able to actively seek work' – a carefully hedged observation that steered perilously close to suggesting vulnerable people were gaming the system (Milburn 2024a: 22). The implication of both interventions was clear: because disability-related benefits were more generous than those received by the unemployed, and recipients of the former generally came under less pressure from job coaches than the latter to actively seek work, many adults who lost jobs or fell out of the 'habit' of working during COVID had taken the rational decision to pursue the better deal. Added to this, the usual in-person fitness-for-work tests had largely been suspended throughout the pandemic, to be replaced by a mix of paper-based applications and telephone appointments – making it 'easier' (in theory at least) for new claimants to qualify for sickness benefits.

These arguments did, however, ignore a colossal elephant in the room. This was the fact that, if there were any 'perverse incentives' in the system encouraging out-of-work adults to claim *disability* rather than unemployment benefits, it was not so much that the former were over-generous, but that payments received by jobseekers had plunged to such an historic low. Analysis by the Institute for Public Policy Research (IPPR) published in October 2023 highlighted the inconvenient truth that unemployment-related benefits had been worth 20.1 per cent of median pay in 1971, but were projected to plummet to barely half that value by 2030 (IPPR 2023). Perhaps more importantly, for the many long-term sick and disabled adults genuinely unable to work, and with no choice but to rely on social security, the prospect of their benefits being *cut*, rather than those for the unemployed *raised*, began to cause mounting fear – especially when allied to tabloid-stoked rumours that the new Labour government was planning to toughen and make more frequent their re-assessments (Pring 2025).

If statistics emphasizing the supposed surge in sickness benefit claims appeared baleful enough when couched in the dry statistical jargon of grey literature, by the time they had passed through the filter of Britain's right-wing commentariat, they looked apocalyptic. 'It's not an honour to which any nation would aspire but Britain can now boast of being the sick note capital of the West', declared Charlotte Lytton in *The Telegraph* in April 2024, atop an article claiming that GPs were now too intimidated (and overworked) to 'say no' to requests from belligerent people asking to be signed off work (Lytton 2024: n.pag.). But it took more unapologetically outspoken commentators to voice what others seemed to be thinking. 'Where these questions point, commentators and politicians apparently fear to tread, so let this commentator rush in', veteran *Times* columnist Matthew Parris had ventured some eight months prior to Lytton's intervention, adding:

> Are we really facing a pandemic of these conditions, or are we facing a pandemic of people reporting them as part of a claim for benefits? Every one of the list [James] Kirkup cites will contain a core of individuals who suffer horribly from the stated condition, many finding it genuinely impossible to make a full, or any, economic contribution. But surrounding this core, could there be a large and growing cohort of those who have persuaded themselves, their bosses or their benefits officers that their employability is restricted but who, were they living a decade or two ago, would have soldiered on?
>
> (Parris 2023: n.pag.)

Through a succession of ensuing comment pieces – and the flurry of letters to the editor and talk-show phone-ins they provoked – Parris became (for a time) the standard-bearer for commentators willing to say the unsayable about inactivity. Just as public deliberation over earlier moral panics had played out across the letters pages of the popular press – not least during the early 1970s law-and-order panic around 'mugging' that was the subject of cultural theorist Stuart Hall et al.'s classic *Policing the Crisis* (Hall et al. 1978) – so, too, was this one of the primary fields in which the 'sick-note panic' unfolded. 'Sir, Matthew Parris's thoughtful article underlines the growing number of the population who believe government has to solve their issues whether it be obesity, energy bills, mortgage support and now an inability to work', began Jeremy Preston from Northamptonshire, two days after the columnist's opening salvo of 4 August 2023 (Preston 2023: n.pag.). His sentiments were broadly echoed by consultant psychiatrist Andrzej Wilski, from Hertfordshire, who observed how 'work can be a great healer of morbid unhappiness', while 'sloth and inaction can drive one to despair' – albeit with the caveat that these healing properties rested, in part, on having 'warm and sympathetic' employers and colleagues (Wilski 2023: n.pag.).

But it would take until November 2024, and the perceived failure of the first Labour Budget in fifteen years to enact a tough enough crackdown on working-aged inactivity, for the flood of conservative copycats to cross the line into near-hate speech levels of vitriol. In one breathless broadside, Isabel Oakeshott, self-styled doyenne of the Reform-supporting Right, reeled out a string of stereotypical tropes about 'scroungers' on Rupert Murdoch-owned online channel TalkTV. Oakeshott's over-lexicalized tirade accused Chancellor Rachel Reeves of siding with 'parasites', who

> frankly, can't be bothered to get out of bed and get themselves out, whether it's to an office or to any kind of job, and prefer to just sit on the sofa and order their Deliveroo and drive their Motability free vehicle and take everything that the state can offer.
>
> (Jackson 2024: n.pag.)

While few would have been surprised by the response of such a notorious right-wing controversialist, ministerial spins on the issue were scarcely less judgmental (if marginally more circumspect) – at least up to the point of the July election. In perhaps the single most widely quoted intervention, Conservative Work and Pensions Secretary Mel Stride had used a March 2024 interview with *The Telegraph* to condescendingly mull on the feebleness of young people unable to cope with 'the normal ups and downs of life' (Gutteridge 2024a: n.pag.).

> If they go to the doctor and say I'm feeling rather down and bluesy, the doctor will give them on average about seven minutes and then, on 94 per cent of occasions, they will be signed off as not fit to carry out any work whatsoever,

he mused – to a jeering chorus of approval from below-the-line comments (and an amplifying echo chamber across the right-wing media, from the *Daily Mail* to *GB News*).

Stride's scrupulously targeted sentiments rolled the pitch for Sunak's 'sick-note culture' speech to come – not to mention a slew of further conservative interventions in the wake of Labour's landslide election victory. Of these, the most knowingly provocative was to come from Fraser Nelson, erstwhile editor of *The Spectator* magazine and long-time critic of the out-of-work benefits system. Nelson used a one-off documentary that autumn in Channel 4's award-winning *Dispatches* strand – headlined 'Britain's Benefits Scandal' – to draw attention to the supposed rise of YouTubers and TikTokers offering their followers tips on how to 'maximize their sick and disability benefits' (*Dispatches* 2024). In spotlighting the emergence of a new form of folk-devil – the 'sickfluencer' – Nelson was playing into (and inflaming) a simmering current of right-wing argument that sought to project into the digital era the concept of 'deviancy amplification' popularized by late moral panic scholar Stanley Cohen. This is the notion that 'the societal reaction' to an identified form of deviance (in this case, a supposed epidemic of work-shy young people faking/exaggerating sickness and disability to avoid work) 'may in fact *increase* rather than decrease or keep in check the amount of deviance' (Cohen 1972: 11).

In Nelson's eyes, the doubling-down of deviance was conceived as a product of inactive people's retreating into social media bubbles in which 'sickfluencers' showed them how to exploit the system – i.e. how to become *more* deviant themselves – whether by using key 'buzzwords' in their PIP application forms or avoiding 'trick questions' during assessments (Howe 2024). There were echoes, too, in his argument of a related (if largely speculative and unevidenced) strand running through right-wing think-tank literature – suggesting that young people might also have been motivated to self-medicalize by 'celebrity self-disclosure about mental health struggles'. In its *Where are the Workers?* report, the Centre for Policy Studies had sought to conflate 'the rise of the smartphone and social networking' with the emergence of a disquieting youth culture that 'glamorised mental health and inspired youths to usurp a diagnostic label as a form of identity, or in some cases to claim benefits' (Williams 2023: 34). In doing so, the CPS set the seal on the latest in a centuries-long tradition of youth moral panics – from nineteenth-century frenzies about 'hooligans' (Pearson 1983) through 1960s panics around student riots to the 1970s mods-versus-rockers furore that inspired Cohen's moral panic concept in the first place, and more recent scares about 'anti-social behaviour' (Squires and Stephen 2005).

Not all conservative commentators were quite so dismissive, however. In a more nuanced intervention by a leading thinker hailing (at least nominally) from the Right, David Willetts – president of the Resolution Foundation and a stalwart of debates about social security and 'the underclass' (Willetts 1992) stretching back nearly as far as the Joseph era – used a blog for *Conservative Home* to give short shrift to suggestions that young people were 'just over-sensitive snowflakes' for whom mental health was 'their latest excuse to skive off' (Willetts 2024). Lamenting the negative impact of social media and 'the effects of COVID lockdowns', he argued that 'the rise of unhappiness and mental health issues amongst young people' could only be arrested by improving support structures in schools and further education, and by rolling out 'youth hubs' offered by the Department for Work and Pensions to *all* youngsters – not just those on benefits.

Nonetheless, the image of a worrying new youth subculture of hypersensitive, 'self-medicalizing' hypochondriacs primed to seek diagnoses for mental health and neurodivergent conditions by a toxic diet of 'sickfluencer' tutorials and misinformation on YouTube, TikTok and Instagram would remain a prominent feature of the unfolding inactivity narrative well into the lifetime of Starmer's administration. Among those entering the debate by early 2025 was a reanimated Sir Tony Blair – until recently a maligned erstwhile prime minister, but now once again an influential figure following his party's re-election on a centrist platform heavily inspired by his 'New Labour' project. In an interview for former Downing Street business adviser Jimmy McLoughlin's *Jimmy's Jobs of the Future* podcast, Blair warned against over-medicalizing 'the normal ups and downs' of life that 'everybody experiences'. He argued that 'you've got to be careful of encouraging people to think they've got some sort of condition other than simply confronting the challenges of life' because 'you really cannot afford to be spending the amount of money we're spending on mental health' (quoted in Lawton and Neal 2025). Blair's remarks were widely criticized – not least by his own former spin-doctor, Alastair Campbell (a long-time mental health campaigner), who used his popular *The Rest is Politics* podcast to comment that he 'didn't actually like what he [Blair] said', at a time when 'we're struggling to keep mental health properly on the NHS agenda' and 'we're going backwards in terms of the media debate around mental health':

> I think there's a danger that he [Blair] doesn't understand that, for a lot of people, depression is *real*, anxiety is *real* – and I think that, particularly now with the numbers of people living in poverty, millions of people that we would say now are living in pretty difficult economic conditions, I think it's just too dismissive to say that these are people who are kind of self-diagnosing.
>
> (*The Rest is Politics* 2025)

As scholars in this field have consistently argued (Cohen 1972; Hall et al. 1978; Goode and Ben-Yehuda 2009), the ultimate test of whether a societal reaction to a perceived moral threat constitutes a panic is how *disproportionate* it is when compared to the demonstrable scale or seriousness of the phenomenon itself. So just how genuine *was* the surge in post-pandemic inactivity – and, by extension, how justified was all the ensuing hysteria? In considering this question, it is telling to note that even some of the more assertive earlier interventions by right-wing think-tanks and other small-c (and big-C) voices had conceded that Britain's overall inactivity picture relative to comparable economies was not quite as severe across all measures as some headlines seemed to suggest. Even in its influential March 2024 paper urging then-Tory Chancellor Hunt to use a mix of nudges and nagging to drive more people back into the workplace, the neoliberal CPS think-tank had awkwardly noted that 'the UK still has a lower inactivity rate than the OECD total (26.8%) or median (22.7%), not to mention G7 countries such as Italy (34.4%), France (26.3%) and the US (25.9%)' (Williams 2023: 9). While it remained the case that the UK was the only G7 economy to be recording higher inactivity rates post-pandemic than those it had experienced beforehand, these were also lower than the first-quarter European Union average of 24.8% (UK Statistics Authority 2025). By the fourth quarter of that year, as the inactivity panic continued to escalate under Labour ministers, Britain's rate still remained lower than those of Italy, France and the US – and had actually fallen back compared to the same period the previous year (dropping by half a percentage point, from 22 to 21.5%) (ONS 2025b).

More damningly inconvenient, however, was the message contained in a Resolution Foundation report published in November 2024 – pointedly entitled *Get Britain's Stats Working*. This found that, contrary to almost all previous analyses (including the foundation's own), in truth the overall rate of economic inactivity was likely to 'be little changed from pre-pandemic' (Corlett 2024: 13). The report did note that there was 'no logical inconsistency between the overall inactivity rate falling and the number of people who are inactive because of ill-health rising' (Corlett 2024: 14) – and that, according to data relating to rising claims for sickness benefits, illness-related inactivity almost certainly *had* risen (albeit to a lesser extent than stated elsewhere). However, it argued that a major methodological weakness in the Labour Force Survey – a plummeting response rate, leading to its understatement of year-on-year employment growth – meant that, while 'the LFS currently says that the 16+ inactivity rate has risen by 1 percentage point from Q4 2019 to Q3 2024', in all likelihood there had been 'zero change' (Corlett 2024: 12). 'A higher employment rate would ... require that the true inactivity rate is now significantly lower than thought and – with much less certainty – it could potentially be no higher than in 2019', wrote the foundation's principal economist Adam Corlett. Indeed, 'a rise in inactivity due to long-term sickness' might, in reality, have been 'offset, among other things, by fewer people out of work because they are looking after their children or home' (Corlett 2024: 3). The latter assumption aligned with findings from the Office for Budget Responsibility (OBR) showing that, while post-pandemic inactivity rates may have appeared inflated, levels of inactivity among 'stay-at-home mothers' had continued on a long-term downward trajectory (but for a brief blip towards the end of the pandemic) (Ring et al. 2024: n.pag.). This decline had been attributed to a melange of factors, ranging from increased conditionality requiring parents with young children to find work in return for continuing benefit eligibility; nominal recent improvements in the availability of free childcare for working parents (up to 30 hours in England); and a 'significant fall in the birth rate over the past decade', with the number of live births plummeting by 98,000 between 2010 and 2021 and a 20.1 per cent fall in the Total Fertility Rate (a measure adjusting for changes in the size and age structure of the female population) (Ring et al. 2024: n.pag.). Although the number of people withdrawing from the labour market to look after family and home had 'started to rise from mid-2021', inactivity for caring purposes later fell back again – 'leaving it 285,000 lower than immediately before the pandemic and at an all-time low of 1.5 million in July 2023' (Ring et al. 2024: n.pag.).

Just as the scale of the recent 'rise' in inactivity had been exaggerated, this was also true of repeated claims that the number of post-pandemic inactives was 'record-breaking' or unprecedented by *historical* standards. So widely accepted had this inaccurate thesis become by early 2025 that it was even repeated in a call for grant applications issued to universities that February by UK Research and Innovation (UKRI), the studiously dispassionate government funding service. In its opening 'Context' section, the call unequivocally stated that a 'record number of people are registered as economically inactive across the UK', before proceeding to outline its appeal for proposals for 'a single innovative, interdisciplinary, and collaborative project' to 'identify ways of supporting good quality, sustainable economic activity in places experiencing high rates of ill-health, disability, and informal care in the UK' (UKRI 2025). This aim might have been lifted wholesale out of any of the major parties' recent election manifestoes.

How inconvenient, then, that Britain's true inactivity record had actually been set more than four decades earlier. According to longitudinal analysis by respected research hubs including the Economic and Social Research Council-funded Economic Observatory, the inactivity rate had been higher in 1971, when one in four working-aged adults (25%) was inactive (Machin and Wadsworth 2023). It hit its 'all time high of 25.90%' in April 1983 (Trading Economics 2025). This was, of course, four years into the mass de-industrialization drive of the Thatcher years, which saw whole industries closed down and many older industrial workers in declining health moved onto a new Invalidity Benefit (in part to hide the true scale of unemployment) (Stone 1986: 11). Moreover, the average inactivity rate for the *entire period* between 1971 and 2025 was 23.15%, suggesting that – far from being exceptional – the number of Britons out of work and not actively seeking it post pandemic was closer to the norm than the exception (Trading

Economics 2025). At the very least, *all* these figures are markedly higher than the 22% inactivity rate in 2022 – a proportion that, in any case, had slipped back to 21.6% by January 2025 (ONS 2025a).

Another inconvenient fact was that recent year-on-year upwards trends in numbers of inactive people could be seen, in part, as a 'natural' reflection of Britain's growing population: between the peak year of 1983 and 2025, the total UK population rose from 56.33 million to 68.18 million (Macrotrends.net 2025). In recent years it has risen at an annual rate of 0.33 to 0.34% (by more than 662,000 between 2023 and 2024 alone) – increases that, in themselves, arguably help explain the growth in activity (ONS 2024b). In addition to all this, inactivity due to illness had, in fact, steadily risen since 2013, increasing by four percentage points between 2013 and 2019 alone – i.e. 'long before the pandemic' (to quote Milburn's 'Pathways to Work' report) (Milburn 2024a: 20). Moreover, amid the flurry of data emphasized in the 2023 report by the CPS nestled the awkward truth that inactivity among the group of gravest moral concern – 16- and 17-year-olds – had actually been *higher* before the pandemic than it was afterwards. Between these years it had fallen back from 68.7 to 67.1% (Williams 2023: 14).

And yet, as Table 0.1 illustrates, none of these awkward facts deterred the news media (and politicians) from relentlessly spotlighting the issue of 'rising' post-pandemic inactivity. According to a high-level keyword search of the LexisNexis newspaper database – the most comprehensive available online archive of full-text press articles, and a resource that today also covers many broadcast news programmes, primarily on radio – the period between 2019 (the year immediately before COVID erupted) and 2024 (the last full year to date at time of writing) saw a significant surge in the appearance of terms relating to economic inactivity. Occurrences of the term 'sick note' or 'sick-note' almost doubled between 2019 and 2020 (rising from 539 to 1016), and then did the same again during the following four years, leaping to 2218 by 2024 – the year Britain's 'sick-note culture' panic erupted in earnest. The number of mentions more than doubled between 2023 and 2024 alone, having risen steadily from a recent low point of just 541 in 2021 – a year when levels of public sympathy for those unable to work owing to the ongoing COVID emergency appears to have peaked. According to the ESRC-funded project 'Welfare at a Social Distance', this was a year that witnessed a significant softening of attitudes towards working-aged benefit recipients who (for one reason or another) had been put out of work by the pandemic (De Vries et al. 2021).

Just as occurrences of the term(s) 'sick-note/sick note' jumped between the start of the pandemic and 2024, so too did those of the officialese 'economic inactivity' and 'economically inactive'. Between 2021 and 2022 the number of times the former term appeared in news coverage more than quadrupled – from

237 to 1153 – and there was a sixfold increase in the latter, which multiplied from 280 to 1687. Thereafter, both figures continued climbing very significantly year on year – more than doubling in each case between 2022 and 2024, from 1153 to 3530 and 1687 to 3646 respectively.

While the terms most closely associated with the inactivity panic rose dramatically over this period, the figures were less conclusive in relation to the word 'workless': a common media and political shorthand for people who are out of work, whether because of inactivity or long-term unemployment (a distinct category, as it covers 'jobseekers' whose benefits are conditional on their efforts to 'actively seek' work). Nonetheless, there was a notable uptick in the use of the word 'workless' between 2020 and 2021, and, after dipping slightly in 2022, it rose again sharply (from 1691 to 1920 mentions) in 2023 – the point when sick-note discourse began to gain serious momentum. Also notable was an increase in occurrences of the favourite go-to tabloid pejoratives for 'undeserving' benefit recipients – 'scrounger' and 'workshy' (or 'work-shy'). After declining slowly but steadily in the years leading up to the pandemic, both of these returned to sharp upwards trajectories from 2021 onwards. It is not much of an imaginative leap to see this as reflecting dwindling levels of sympathy for inactive people as barriers to work directly linked to COVID lockdowns and furlough policies evaporated and opportunities to find or go back to work began returning to something approaching normality. This interpretation aligns with a September 2021 report combining a national survey with analysis of bimonthly YouGov data that concluded that 'the public believes COVID-19 claimants are considerably more deserving of benefits than pre-pandemic claimants' (De Vries et al. 2021).

We are, then, left with a patchwork picture – and one starkly at odds, in many respects, with the sweepingly generalized popular portrayal of soaring inactivity rates across the board. While overall levels of inactivity may indeed be slightly higher than in 2019 (the year immediately before the pandemic), much of this figure can be attributed to people who had already been inactive long term, including those with work-limiting disabilities and chronic health conditions – themselves, of course, a frequent target of media and political opprobrium. In truth, the widely reported 'surge' in inactivity rates since COVID kicked in has been wildly exaggerated. There are certainly now more people classed as inactive owing to early retirement, mental health issues, neurodivergent diagnoses and physical ailments such as musculoskeletal conditions for which they have been forced to wait prolonged periods for NHS treatment (not least owing to backlogs caused by the pandemic itself). However, these numbers are unlikely to be so significant that they would move the dial dramatically enough to constitute a wave of 'new inactivity'.

It is this paradoxical picture – of a comparatively modest *actual* rise in post-pandemic inactivity paired with an irrationally hand-wringing media-political

TABLE 0.1: Occurrence of terms relating to inactivity in news coverage, 2017–24.

	2017	2018	2019	2020	2021	2022	2023	2024
sick note or sick-note	812	760	539	1,016	541	954	1,062	2,218
economic inactivity	234	209	195	256	237	1,153	2,183	3,530
economically inactive	512	470	373	778	280	1,687	3,099	3,646
workless	1,855	1,999	1,579	1,780	2,006	1,691	1,920	1,825
scrounger	1,559	1,261	1,031	952	956	1,137	1,073	1,190
workshy or work-shy	861	448	447	599	532	575	624	886

Source: LexisNexis news database.

overreaction to 'lazy Brits' (Reilly 2022) – that forms the backdrop to the rest of this book. But before we turn to analysing the myths about inactivity circulating through contemporary media-political discourse, it makes sense to start with a longitudinal question. What are the historical precedents for panicky societal responses to perceived (but exaggerated) moral crises about wilfully indolent people who *claim* to be unable to work when, in fact, they are capable of doing so? It is to the task of answering this question that we turn next.

1

'Sturdy Beggars' and 'Swinging the Lead': Images of Inactivity through Time

Of all the odious caricatures populating the historical literature on worklessness and disability none is more pitifully repellent than the 'Clapperdudgeon'. 'These palliards' in 'patched clokes', wrote Thomas Harman in his now-notorious 1566 pamphlet *A Caveat or Warning for Common Cursetors*, would confect the illusion of festering sores by rubbing their skin with caustic substances and 'goe to one house to aske his alms' while 'his wyfe shall go to another, for what they get, as bread, cheese, malte, and woll'. Having sponged off the labours of respectable, God-fearing folk, the disreputable duo would proceed to sell their ill-gotten gains 'for redy money, for so they get more' (Harman 2008: n.pag.).

Here, rolled into one contemptible package, was the distillation of every trope that would come to characterize timeworn representations of that enduring folk-devil: the work-shy or fraudulent scrounger. Not only was the Clapperdudgeon physically repugnant – limping pathetically from house to house with oozing wounds – but the self-inflicted nature of his lesions, and the dishonest methods he deployed to exploit the charity of hardworking subjects for financial gain, made him something worse: a cheat.

The Clapperdudgeon was just one of a litany of semi-mythical chancers and vagabonds defined in the writings of Harman and other authors of a rash of sixteenth-and seventeenth-century 'rogue literature' – antecedents of the Victorian and Edwardian penny dreadfuls that were to prove so popular with audiences predisposed to true-crime horror stories. Other colourful characters in Harman's typology of idle ne'er-do-wells included 'counterfeit cranks', who allegedly faked epileptic seizures, 'Abram men' (pretend lunatics) and 'dummerers' given to feigning inability to speak by doubling-up their tongues so they appeared dismembered. As social historian David M. Turner wrote in his 2012 book *Disability in Eighteenth-Century England*, the 'Elizabethan and Jacobean equivalent of modern "scroungers" were known as "rufflers", "palliards" or "clapperdogeons" – dangerous vagrants who allegedly plastered their bodies with fake sores to dupe the unwary into providing assistance' (Turner 2012: 1). Crucially, while such 'stereotypes' may have been 'largely the invention of sensationalist pamphleteers', they had the potential to exercise a malign influence on public perceptions and dominant discourses – by casting 'the display of all disabilities, real or not, in a suspicious light' (Turner 2012: 1).

Some 460 years later, little seems to have changed: today, the normalization of suspicion and distrust about the motives of people signed off with work-limiting illnesses and disabilities is a consequence of the incessant drip-feed of ministerial briefings about people 'gaming the system' (Starmer 2024b) to the tabloid press and the latter's (at times) daily diet of news stories about 'shirkers' and 'scroungers' (Morrison 2019) – *exceptional* tales of fraud and fakery presented as if they were pervasive, typical, commonplace, even endemic. As political scientist Shanto Iyengar demonstrated so effectively in his classic exploration of framing analysis, *Is Anyone Responsible?*, representing poverty and social welfare issues in such a way is an example of 'episodic framing': a social construction that seeks to ascribe blame for a complex social problem to *individuals*, rather than wider structural factors. Hardly surprising, then, that his own research into the impact of media narratives about benefit dependency on public perceptions concluded that 'support for increased social welfare spending was lowered significantly under conditions of episodic framing of poverty' (Iyengar 1991: 85).

The persistence of these longstanding, centuries-old traditions – the demonization or (at best) episodic framing of people claiming to suffer from disabilities, illnesses and other challenges inhibiting their ability to work – is the focal point of this chapter. Underpinning its analysis is the previously mentioned subject of trust – and, specifically, the suspicion implicit in much of the historical discourse that beggars and those unable to work owing to disease or impairment were (to coin an oft-used nautical idiom) 'swinging the lead'. Defying all such suspicions, as we shall see, is a conspicuous absence of much (or any) hard evidence that widespread exaggeration or hypochondria, let alone industrial-scale fakery and fraudulence, were anything other than figments of the popular imagination or convenient discursive tools enabling powerful interests to displace blame for complex social ills (often caused by their own failings) onto convenient scapegoats: the 'poor' and vulnerable. As English scholar Lindsey Row-Heyveld argues in an incisive recent study, despite the proliferation of stereotypes of 'feigned disability' in early modern literature and contemporaneous cultural debates about poverty and charity, 'there appears to be very little historical evidence of beggars actually faking disability in early modern England'. While historians frequently cite the infamous case of Nicholas Jennings (or Gennings), 'a "counterfeit crank" who faked epilepsy and disfigurement in order to gather undeserved alms', in truth 'few other recorded instances of feigned disability in the early modern era have been discovered' (Row-Heyveld 2018: 3).

Allied to this tension between popular imaginaries and empirical truth are two further important dimensions of the ongoing battle for understanding, tolerance and inclusion faced by people affected by issues restricting their ability to enter the day-to-day workplace. The first of these is the question of socially and culturally accepted ideas about *difference* – and, in particular, aspects of individuals' identities that might limit or prevent them from participating in conventional labour, at least without substantial assistance or adjustments by prospective employers. The second is the recurring historical ambivalence around the desirability and/or legitimacy of *able-bodied* people's opting out of paid work – today's narrowly defined concept of economic activity – in the interests of homemaking, child-rearing and other forms of familial (or non-familial) caregiving.

While this chapter's primary focus is the evolution of discourses around individuals' (asserted and/or diagnosed) *inability* to work – and the socially and culturally acceptable parameters of work-limiting/preventing illness and disability – no overview of historical conceptions of worklessness would be complete without a brief discussion of other drivers and justifications for inactivity. These include the caregiving and child-rearing demands that make it difficult for some *able*-bodied people to take up paid work: unrecognized endeavours common to the lives of many supposedly workless families that are also a central concern of this book. The chapter will therefore conclude with a brief examination of how traditional discourses loudly lauding the moral virtues of the normative nuclear family – a highly gendered ideal that customarily pairs (male) breadwinner with (female) homemaker – has increasingly given way to a more conflicted and hypocritical narrative, particularly on the political Right. The double standard enshrined in this narrative implicitly reserves the privilege of stay-at-home parenting – and wider caregiving – for financially secure single-earner households, while lone-parent families who dare to 'choose' to pursue the same path are framed as workless, and therefore morally deviant.

But to return (for now) to our primary focus – the evolution of historical discourses around work-limiting illness and disability – it is important to note how these have consistently become entangled with a montage of other (mis)conceptions and (mis)understandings about the sick and disabled. Chief among these is the notion that if someone looks, sounds or behaves differently, this alone is sufficient to debar them from work – if only because of the unwanted and/or unsightly distraction they present to others. Today the idea that some people are 'differently abled' (Chhabra 2016), rather than *dis*abled per se, is widely recognized (even if, at times, as a tool for strong-arming them into more – or more onerous – work than they can cope with). By contrast, many of the physical and mental conditions capable of being routinely managed in today's workplace were widely misunderstood in historical times – and often provoked fear, superstition, ridicule or ostracism. Allied to this has been a continuum of secondary discourses, often simmering beneath economistic/militaristic/colonialist narratives about 'defectives' and 'invalids' (or 'in-valids'), that have sought to draw intrinsic and binary distinctions between ability and disability – and, by extension, 'usefulness' and 'uselessness' (Gentes 2011; Mostert 2002; Nielsen 2012).

These and related themes will be revisited in the context of contemporary media and political discourses, and the experiences of disabled people themselves, in the coming chapters. We begin, though, by considering the evolution of portrayals of disability and infirmity – and, more specifically, individuals' *assertions* that they are too sick or disabled to work. In doing so, we confront from the outset a continuum of discourses of distrust that have othered and disparaged people obliged to rely on the social protection of their fellow citizens because of their inability (or limited ability) to provide for themselves. This long and tangled saga of suspicion takes us on a journey from early Christian almshouses through nineteenth century workhouses to today's clinical assessment centres, as we chart the history of how 'work-limiting' disability has been disputed and objectified for 1000 years.

Disability or duplicity? Images of begging and fake infirmity down the ages

In examining how representations of infirmity and impairment have evolved through time, there is no more logical way to start than by exploring the emergence of moral concerns about beggars. As disability studies scholar Rosemarie Garland-Thomson argues in her influential study *Extraordinary Bodies*, 'the history of begging is virtually synonymous with the history of disability' (Garland Thomson 2017: 35) – not least because of how disabled people have persistently been positioned as 'economic' objects: unproductive, poverty-stricken and a burden on respectable, contributing, useful members of society. Indeed, this devaluing economistic narrative – which positions the sick and disabled (and people generally) as *economic*, rather than social and cultural, beings – underpins so much of the contemporary discourse around economic inactivity that is the subject of this book.

If an individual's worth is to be judged solely in terms of their contribution towards measurable man-hours, commercial profit or (in the eyes of today's Treasury) economic growth, it is easy to see how societies with such limited horizons might come to designate people with conditions so serious that they cannot meaningfully participate as worth*less*. Should such individuals then be forced by circumstance to take steps further away from society's conception of value – by abasing themselves as beggars and parading their incapacities to invite pity and charity – they then consign themselves to an even lowlier economic status.

Given the despair and destitution faced by sick and disabled people cast aside so callously, it is easy to understand why they had no choice but to beg – bereft of any means to earn a living and in eras long predating the introduction of welfare states. And yet, historically as now, societies have had a habit of applying a very different moral logic when constructing representations of beggars: lacing their portrayals with an innate suspicion that the ailments and injuries displayed cannot be genuine and must therefore be *fake*. The story of work-limiting infirmity is that of the ongoing consignment of beggars (and, by association, the 'workless' disabled) to an impossible catch-22: paradoxically positioned as both unproductive invalids excluded from the workplace for fear their presence would impede society's economic progress *and* antecedents of today's sick-note scammers, faking incapacity to skive off work and scrounge scraps off everyone else.

Though tales of fake disability allied to performative public displays of agony and abjection date back to classical times, every timeline has to commence somewhere. Given our particular focus here on the origins and evolution of latter-day UK discourses around economic inactivity, it is to a disreputable duo from the Middle Ages that contemporary caricatures arguably owe the most debt: the 'sturdy beggar' and the 'false mendicant'. The first of these concepts was immortalized in the 1388 Statute of Cambridge, which pointedly distinguished between beggars who were 'sturdy' – a term encapsulating the imaginary of a blatantly fit and able person *feigning* infirmity to live off the backs of other people's efforts – and those judged 'impotent', and therefore exempted from work on grounds of *genuine* disability or old age (Bodleian Libraries n.d.). That a category of individuals judged genuinely incapable of work (and not subject to suspicions that they were faking incapacity just to avoid it) existed *at all* might initially seem enlightened – until, that is, one considers the fact that it would be a further 150 years (or thereabouts) before the first Poor Law was introduced (under Henry VIII) requiring town and parish councils to provide some protection for their 'aged, poor and impotent' (Bodleian Libraries n.d.). The clue as to the ruthlessness of the Statute of Cambridge lay in the terms it used to denote genuine from fraudulent cases: the fact that the blamelessly 'impotent' were still classed as 'beggars' spoke volumes for the limits of society's charity in the unforgiving reign of Richard II. Even in an era when some people *were* recognized as genuinely incapacitated, this wasn't a cue to offer them support or charity – but merely an acceptance that they were authentically worthless and should be exempted (or, rather, discarded) from the workforce.

The key to the potency of the sturdy beggar motif lay in the ingenious duality of its semantic construction. The adjective 'sturdy' carried connotations of physical fitness, whether hidden or openly displayed (and contradicting the beggar's pretence of frailty). Conversely, it also connoted threat and intimidation – conjuring up mental images of fit, well-built individuals who might be inclined to meet a refusal to hand over alms with violence. Although they were originally a construct of the high medieval period, they would gain their greatest lease of life many years later, during the reign of Elizabeth I. After a centuries-long odyssey through the annals of popular folklore, these subhuman anti-citizens provided an ideal locus for elite constructions of both indolence and criminality. On one hand, they fitted the mould of archetypal criminal deviants: grotesque predators from whom loyal subjects could expect the Crown's protection in return for paying their dues and doing as they were told (with the implied threat that failing to do so might invite the same punishments as those meted out to sturdy beggars). As Row-Heyveld puts it in a useful summary of recent scholarly arguments to this effect, 'trumped up fears of sturdy beggars helped to legitimate the intense social control already being marshalled by the Tudor government in its project to consolidate state power' (Row-Heyveld 2018: 2). On the other hand (and of more direct relevance here), sturdy beggars represented a shameful example of wilful idleness: of individuals faking incapacity to exploit other people's generosity and undermine national efforts to build and strengthen an emerging imperial project centred around England's colonies and the ideology of mercantilism. As this author and others have argued elsewhere, this global drive led to 'finely honed distinctions (weaponized by statute) between [...] the orphaned, chronically sick or elderly "impotent" – and the "rioters, vagabonds and the idle" lumped together as "thriftless"' (Golding and Middleton 1982: 10) (Morrison 2019: 255–56).

The prevalence of begging and the *scale* of the threat it posed was therefore undoubtedly overstated, and deliberately so at times – with historian William C Carroll noting the disjunction between 'contemporary estimates' putting the total number of beggars in London alone at 1000 and 12,000 respectively in 1517 and 1594, and latter-day analysis suggesting the number of 'wandering homeless' *nationally* rose from 15,000 to 25,000 between 1572 and the 1630s (Carroll 1996: 31). But for all this clear exaggeration, as in all moral panics, there was an element of genuine concern – with plentiful documents showing that 'contemporary observers', including the Privy Council, '*felt* that the problem of beggars was real, acute, and rapidly growing'. Writing in the 1530s, political theorist Thomas Starkey observed that '"...in no cuntrey of Christundome, for the nombur of pepul, you schal find so many beggaris as be here in Englond, and mo[re] now then have bin before time"' (quoted in Carroll 1996: 31–32). Yet rather than being recognized as an indictment of the scale of destitution caused by obscene wealth inequalities, the lack of a safety net and widespread work-limiting illness and injury, these numbers were instead presented as evidence of an infestation of feckless, immoral marauders.

Here, then, in the excited scribblings of pamphleteers (not to say the recorded rulings of local justices of the peace), lurk the ancestral roots of contemporary discourses scapegoating Britain's economically inactive as undermining Britain's *current* national mission: the relentless pursuit of economic growth. As sociologist Bill Hughes recently observed, in an analysis of recurring 'sturdy beggar' tropes through time, from the outset this morally corrupt figure was ripe for repeated resurrection and repurposing by successive regimes intent on cementing their authority, maintaining order and promoting their pet hegemonic projects. Thus, in early medieval England the sturdy beggar was framed as 'a usurper of the sacred system of charity' – one who 'corrupted the munificence of the squire; turned the generous gift of the nobleman into an empty gesture; squandered the good will of bishop or priest; and converted decency, propriety and piety into empty gestures'. But over ensuing eras, they came to 'cast a long shadow of suspicion over *every* disabled person [author's italics], not just those who were forced by necessity to go "cap in hand"' (Hughes 2015: 998). By Tudor times, moreover, those seen as faking disability (and not pulling their weight) were subjected to brutal punishments at the hands of 'state functionaries' of the day – including torture at 'the pillory, the ducking stool, incarceration in local "Bridewells", expulsion from the locality, branding and ear-boring' (the latter two indelibly branding them with a 'criminal record').

Then, as now, the concept of 'sturdiness' was – as Hughes further argues – 'a matter of interpretation' (Hughes 2015: 998). We can see here a clear antecedent of the oft-disputed rulings of clinically bureaucratic Work Capability Assessments (WCAs) to which out-of-work disability benefit applicants are subjected today. Moreover, as Hughes stresses, by stoking a discourse of distrust around the question of whether *anyone* was genuinely disabled – or disabled *enough* to avoid work – the 'criminalisation of the "sturdy beggar" in mediaeval and early modern Europe...drew a veil of suspicion over the legitimate mendicancy of the "impotent poor"'. In doing so, Hughes adds, it 'exacerbated wariness and resentment of disabled people who were forced to survive in the same social space as their rogue counterparts' (Hughes 2015: 998).

What, then, of that other fabular folk-devil – the 'false mendicant'? Like the term 'sturdy beggar', this label was popularized in medieval Europe, but if it could lay claim to making a particular contribution to the mythology of scroungers this was through its personification of a more *generalized* (and generalizable) imaginary of fake disability. Through the discourse of false mendicancy, the deviancy ascribed to begging was seen to plumb new, more sinister depths of fiendish dishonesty – with almost *all* beggars framed as fraudulent, not just those whose 'sturdiness' betrayed their obvious (or thinly disguised) fitness. Indeed, the spectre of the mythical mendicant seems to have grabbed, and held, the popular imagination for quite some time – and right across the continent. By way of example, in thirteenth-century France a particular association appears to have been drawn between false mendicancy and performative displays of blindness.

Medievalist Edward Wheatley identifies instances of plays in which 'blind beggars' were normatively portrayed as 'stingy and greedy' (Wheatley 2010: 92) and blindness itself as something that could be 'persuasively feigned' (Wheatley 2010: 94). And, three centuries later, Italian tribunals setting out conditions for the licensing of 'charlatans' (street hawkers and performers) explicitly referred to the term '*ciarlatano*' – denoting 'the gift of the gab' attributed to 'a false mendicant' or 'someone begging for alms under false pretences' (Gentilcore 2006: 253–54).

Pictured together, these baleful phantoms cast a veil of suspicion over the authenticity of *anyone* claiming to be too sick or disabled to work. In one corner lurked the sturdy beggar: a bogus invalid defined *in opposition to* others deemed to be genuinely 'impotent' (even if not always deserving of society's charity). In the other crouched the false mendicant: an imaginary so disreputable that its fabled misdeeds led good citizens to doubt the genuineness of *any* public displays of work-limiting disease or disability. Hobbling in lockstep, the duo would set the seal on an enduring historical association between claims of work-limiting illness or disability and rapacious duplicity. Once established, this linkage rapidly became the premise for emerging and ongoing approaches to policy – from those that merely exempted (or excluded) genuine cases from their labour obligations to later, more charitable, interventions deigning to provide a modicum of financial or material support to people incapable of earning their own living. With this premise embedded, all that remained was for society to devise sufficiently rigorous and degrading mechanisms to *distinguish* between deserving and undeserving cases. But for a handful of enlightened future intervals, as we shall see, this stark binary would go on to define the trajectory of British social welfare policy up to the present day.

Teasing out the tricksters: Evolution of the 'validation device'

Even as society began to grudgingly acknowledge the *existence* of work-limiting illnesses and disabilities, assumptions continued to prevail that many of those claiming to have them were frauds. Not only that: society's slow awakening to the limitations imposed by disease and disability opened up the question of what balance it should strike between compassion and callousness when confronting the 'genuine cases'. If someone was unable to provide for themselves by contributing to the common weal (or rather, the elite's latest pet economic project), to what extent did society owe them a duty of care? Put differently, if someone was deemed infirm enough to legitimately remain *work*less, did this not also mean they were *worth*less – of no material use to anyone else, and therefore expendable? As successive regimes tussled with such conundrums, they came to symbolize a persistent feature of the experiences of sick and disabled people through time: the sense that they were caught between a rock and a hard place. What was the value of being recognized as a 'deserving case' if Church and state turned their backs on you and the only route to a dignified existence was to submit yourself to the rigours of the mill-house or factory floor – in so doing, worsening your symptoms and hastening your death?

While this tension between compassion and callousness has repeatedly resurfaced through time, other than during a handful of periods (including the aforementioned reign of Richard II) there has been just enough charity to go around to encourage 'genuine cases' to seek what Deborah Stone conceptualizes as the 'political privilege' of disability recognition (Stone 1986: 4). In Stone's words, 'disability functions as a privileged category', in that 'the state accords special treatment to people who are disabled' – chiefly, 'permission to enter the need-based system' (in today's terms, eligibility for 'unconditional' social protection) and exemption from 'the work-based system', under which the fit and able-bodied are expected to fund *their own* welfare entitlement by working and paying taxes (Stone 1986: 28). Of course, the caveat is that the 'reverse side of the "privilege" of being disabled' is 'the harshness of social treatment' meted out to 'those who are not officially categorized as disabled but are nonetheless unable to achieve a decent standard of living' (Stone 1986: 4).

We return to this latter thought – repeatedly – in coming chapters, as it forms the basis for one of the most febrile debates of our time, and an enduring issue underpinning many of this book's concerns. This is the question of which health conditions and/or disabilities can be considered so severe that they genuinely inhibit or prevent people from undertaking conventional day-to-day paid work – and which complaints should instead be viewed as manageable, even routine, enough to permit work. In the context of mental health in particular, these might include the day-to-day 'ups and downs' and 'challenges of life' that (we are repeatedly told) everyone faces (Lawton and Neal 2025). As Stone puts it, the 'very act of defining a disability category determines what is expected of the nondisabled': i.e. 'what injuries, diseases, incapacities, and problems they will be expected to tolerate in their normal working lives' (Stone 1986: 4).

As to the question of how societies have historically controlled/limited disability claims, a key constant has been the quest for reliable, easily bureaucratized mechanisms to sift out undeserving cases. 'The problem of distinguishing those who *cannot* work from those who *will not* work has plagued society for centuries', argues Stone, in outlining a colourful overview of the various 'validating devices' developed by successive regimes to weed out wastrels – from medieval anti-vagrancy laws focusing on individuals' 'ability to serve' to the infamous nineteenth-century 'workhouse test' to 'fitness for work tests' (WCAs) to which working-aged disabled people are subjected today (Stone 1986: 99–108).

Perhaps unsurprisingly, the most detailed historical accounts of such 'validating devices' (and the rationales behind them) are concentrated around periods when efforts to strong-arm people into the labour force or military appear to have been pursued most vigorously. Aided and abetted (as they invariably were) by rhetorical turns clearly designed to shame and stigmatize people claiming disability, these policy pushes were primarily launched at times of acute labour shortage or economic crisis. Thus it was that the 1349 Statute of Laborers, which Stone describes as 'the first law for the control of vagrancy' (idle people travelling from town to town in search of alms, rather than joining the workforce in their own parish), 'was clearly a response to the labor shortage' caused by the 1347–49 'Black Plague' (Stone 1986: 34). But this was nothing compared to Richard II's swingeing 1388 anti-vagrancy law, which introduced the first explicit crackdown on begging itself, in an effort to martial many more people into the workforce (including those previously rejected as unfit). This coincided with a period when labour shortages had become an issue for a different reason – this time because workers were starting to organize, reject poverty wages, and demand better pay and conditions.

It is in the discursive framing of the 1388 statute, however, that we glimpse the earliest antecedent of the scrounger narratives that have been used to legitimize validating devices deployed today. Under the act, local officials were ordered to 'distinguish between beggars "impotent to serve and those able to serve or labor"' – in so doing, closing 'a loophole in earlier laws that had enabled vagrants to leave their towns by *pretending* to be crippled or sick' (Stone 1986: 35). Most strikingly, the small number of individuals exceptionally permitted to leave their parish (and, by extension, to beg) were henceforward issued with permission to do so in the form of official letters. In bureaucratizing begging (and disability) for perhaps the very first time – and specifying in these letters both 'a diagnosis (a cause for the inability to work) and an estimated duration (the expected time of return to work)' – England's fourteenth-century rulers had ushered in a system that bore 'a striking resemblance to the "sick leave certificates" required of people in most current systems of temporary disability insurance' (Stone 1986: 35–36).

The language and effects of anti-begging laws would only become more hostile over the centuries, taking a notably dehumanizing turn by the time they crossed the desks of first Henry VIII and then his daughter, Elizabeth II. Tudor authorities wasted little time stamping their mark (quite literally) on the evolution of that reliable measure of deservingness: the validating device. Under Henry, a 1531 statute ordered convicted beggars and vagabonds to be 'stripped naked, from the privey partes of their bodies upwarde' and 'being so naked, to be bounden, and sharply beaten and skourged' (Carroll 1996: 43). A 1536 statute defined a range of unsavoury characters spanning the spectrum from least to most deserving – from 'vagabonds' who needed to be sent 'on their way' to 'lepers and bed-ridden creatures'. And, with effect from 1547, 'legitimate beggars' were issued with 'identifying badges to be worn "the shoulder or on the breast" ', while vagabonds were branded with hot irons in the breast inscribing the letter V – or, upon further conviction, the letter S, declaring them slaves (Stone 1986: 36–37). In such literal and public displays of stigma, we glimpse a chilling foretaste of the public shaming of disabled people forced to wear black triangles – and Jews the yellow Star of David – in Nazi Germany. Yet Elizabeth went still further. As of the 1572 statute, her ministers confected (in Carroll's words) 'an ingenious alternative to branding', designed to leave what Kentish JP William Lambarde approvingly described as a permanent 'token' of shame on their body (Carroll 1996: 44). This was the ordeal of being 'burned through the gristle of the right ear, with an hot iron of the compass of an inch about, as a manifestation of his wicked life, and due punishment received for the same', in the evocative words of contemporary English chronicler Raphael Holinshed (Carroll 1996: 44).

But if there was a single validating device that could lay claim to matching the clinical brutality of the 1388 statute and the succession of grisly tribute acts that followed it was the invidious dilemma enshrined in the 1834 Poor Law Amendment Act (aka 'New Poor Law'): the infamous 'workhouse test'. It was this innovation that introduced a convention that Stone has conceptualized as the 'revelatory sign'. This is a confected 'situation', constructed in this case by Georgian law-makers and administered with Kafkaesque coldness at parish level by Poor Law Boards of Guardians, 'in which the applicant is required to perform, and the person's behavior reveals, according to some predetermined rule, whether he or she is truly incapable of working or merely feigning inability' (Stone 1986: 101–02). The statutory principle accompanying demands that applicants for poor relief perform a 'revelatory sign' was that of 'least eligibility': the idea that they should be forced to make the impossible choice between submitting themselves, in exchange for assistance, to the rigours of the workhouse or continuing to scavenge a living on the outside. All the while, officials sought to keep levels of social support to the barest minimum by ensuring that 'conditions inside the workhouse' were 'absolutely minimal and even abhorrent' (Stone 1986: 101–02). In essence, the 'framers of the law had faith that when confronted with such a decision, applicants would reveal the true state of their needs'. Yet, while fakers might indeed be rooted out in this way, the underlying logic was that those who were both genuinely poor *and* incapable of work would be left facing the worst of all catch-22s: consigned either to a life of near-incarceration and slavery 'on the inside' or a reliance on enforced begging (and likely criminalization) or starvation 'on the outside' (Stone 1986: 101–02).

E.P. Thompson would later characterize the Act as history's most 'sustained attempt to impose an ideological dogma' legitimized by 'the comforting thesis' (consistently articulated in political propaganda of the time) 'that poverty was both inevitable and morally culpable': in other words, that the poor were to blame for their own poverty and no-one else should feel any guilt or responsibility at the thought that others went without (Thompson 1968: 295). But in the context of a book about discourses around economic inactivity – and conditions that do (or do not) inhibit people from lifting themselves *out of* poverty through their own labour – it represents more than that. In the foundational document presaging the Act itself, the Poor Law Report 1834, questions around the 'relief of the able-bodied' were described as 'the most pressing of the evils' it sought to address (Checkland and Checkland 1974: 334). Moreover, throughout its pages – and in denial of the widespread poverty endured by legions of factory and farm workers – the report reiterated its near-magical belief that it was work (and work alone) that offered the 'cure' to poverty. In a passage laced with unswerving certainty about the material benefits of work – foreshadowing the fervour with which today's ministers extol its virtues over 'welfare' – the report's authors wrote:

> We can state, as the result of the extensive inquiries made under this Commission into the circumstances of the labouring classes, the agricultural labourers when in employment, in common with the other classes of labourer throughout the country, have greatly advanced in condition; that their wages will now produce to them more of the necessaries and comforts of life than at any other period.
>
> (Checkland and Checkland: 336)

Here, then, could be glimpsed an antecedent of the quasi-religious 'worship of work' we witness today in the rhetorics of politicians both Left and Right. In the workhouse test, and the regime of institutionalized drudgery it accompanied, we also glimpse a brutal antecedent of the 'Workfare' policies and 'mandatory work activities' imposed on unemployed people by recent US and UK governments – and the 'revelatory signs' sick and disabled people seeking support are forced to perform today. We see its echoes in the Work Capability Assessments to which people applying for working-aged disability benefits have been subjected since the

2000s and the often similarly gruelling tests faced by those applying for Personal Independence Payment (PIP) to support their day-to-day living costs.

The policy DNA linking the 'workhouse test', via various other experiments with revelatory signs, to today's fitness-for-work tests can be traced through the emergence of a singular concept developed to distinguish between those genuinely too disabled to work and the fakers and exaggerators: that of 'malingering'. As with the numerous morally loaded labels preceding it, this owed its gestation to a period of peculiar national (if not international) 'crisis', during which the needs of individuals and families were rendered subservient to those of nations, as they battled to rebuild themselves and restore their economic fortunes after long periods of warfare. The introduction of the workhouse test came towards the end of a prolonged post-Napoleonic depression – the age of Regency decadence, the Peterloo massacre and years of poor harvests. The next major stage in the evolution of revelatory signs to categorize and chastise the disabled into work followed a century or more later, in post-Second World War America. In what now looks like a chilling foretaste of the medicalized bureaucracies used to divide disability claimants into 'deserving' and 'undeserving' cases today, in 1948 the United States would establish an Advisory Council tasked with administering a 'strict test' and 'strict eligibility requirements' designed to limit 'compensable disabilities' to 'those which can be *objectively determined by medical examination or tests*' – with common or routine complaints such as lumbago, rheumatism and 'various nervous disorders' falling outside the scope of this definition (Stone 1986: 79). The acid test of an individual's inability to work would henceforth be 'a permanent and total disability' that could be 'medically demonstrable by objective tests' and prevented workers from doing 'any substantially gainful activity, and which is likely to be of long and continued duration'. Significantly, claims would be disallowed for those refusing to submit to medical examination, and 'periodic re-examinations' thereafter – an eligibility condition likely to produce shivers of recognition among those obliged to undergo reassessments today (Stone 1986: 79).

Complicating (but supposedly simplifying) the evolution of the US approach to teasing out malingerers was a concept that began to evolve in parallel: that of 'impairment'. Tracing the origins and logic of this term, Stone notes how almost 'every medical article or text on the subject of disability evaluation begins with liturgical cant distinguishing between "impairment" and "disability"', with the medical profession viewing the former as 'a purely medical phenomenon', but disability itself as 'a medical-administrative-legal phenomenon' – the existence of which (in terms sufficient to merit the award of benefits) can only be determined by 'administrative agencies' (Stone 1986: 107–08). Nonetheless, the 'critical element in public decision-making about access to disability benefits' remains the question of whether someone suffers from 'medical impairment' in the first place, making this classification a precondition for acceptance into the 'needs-based' welfare system (and exemption from the work-based one).

America's moralistic obsession with the 'malingerer' – a singular folk devil defined as 'a person who pretends to be ill in order to avoid having to work' (malingerer, *Cambridge Dictionary* 2025: n.pag.) – continues to the present day, most recently seeping into much of the policy and public discourse around disability in Britain. A key revelatory sign to smoke out malingerers traceable in US medical literature is the assessment of expressions of 'pain', which seem to have provoked as much (metaphorical) agony for those doing the assessing as they did (literally) for claimants examined. 'The clinical literature frequently discusses the problem of distinguishing genuine from faked pain and thus repeats, in its own language, the larger social problem of distinguishing genuine from feigned inability to work', with 'numerous texts' relaying 'specific indications of "real" pain' (Stone 1986: 135). As one text observes, the 'facial expression of *true* pain [author's italics] – the pinched features, the pallor, the clammy skin, the dilated pupils, the knotted brow – cannot be imitated by the MALINGERER', as it produces' an 'intermittent involuntary cry or groan' and 'characteristic writhing or bodily contortions' – 'an unmistakable picture of suffering' (Stone 1986: 135).

The durability of the 'malingerer' trope, and its longer-term impact on disability benefit and assessment policies in the UK and elsewhere, was explored by neuroscientist Peter Halligan and psychologists Christopher Bass and David A. Oakley in their 2003 book *Malingering and Illness Deception*, which – among other things – drew attention to a largely unpublicized 2001 conference of the same name. As extensively chronicled elsewhere by disability rights activist and scholar Mo Stewart, the Malingering and Illness Deception Conference, held at Woodstock near Oxford, offered a platform for representatives of (largely US-based) private healthcare companies to recommend the adoption by Britain's Department of Work and Pensions (DWP) of a 'BPS [biopsychosocial] assessment model' designed to identify 'malingering' disability benefit claimants (see, for example, Stewart 2020). These and other recommendations would go on to inform the discourse of distrust underpinning 'welfare reforms' introduced by, first, Gordon Brown's Labour government (which initiated the WCA regime under its right-leaning work and pensions secretary, James Purnell) and, in turn, the more ideologically 'small (welfare) state' 2010–15 Conservative-led coalition government, in which Purnell's successor, Iain Duncan Smith, pursued a 'moral mission' to drive down benefit dependency (Hardman 2014).

One of the principal architects of these reforms (under both governments) had been the former City financier Lord (David) Freud, who published a report in 2007 (shortly after Brown replaced Tony Blair as prime minister) recommending the introduction of a drastically more intrusive system for monitoring and (re)assessing people claiming disability-related benefits framed almost entirely through a discourse of 'work'. In his report, normatively entitled 'Reducing dependency, increasing opportunity: options for the future of welfare to work', Freud recommended the privatization and outsourcing of 'tailored support' for economically inactive disabled people (not to mention the long-term unemployed), backed by the introduction of 'a detailed database' on 'each client' (a term infused with neoliberal logic repositioning benefit recipients as market consumers). Crucially, it also introduced the concept of sanctions for those considered capable of work but refusing to engage with it (Freud 2007: 107). Elsewhere in the report, claimants were explicitly reframed as 'customers', while lessons on how to reintegrate sick and disabled people into the workforce were conspicuously drawn from overseas systems that, Freud suggested, offered useful lessons on how to impose tougher 'mutual obligations' and remove 'disincentives to work' – notably those of the US and Australia (Freud 2007: 107).

The Freudian approach was incorporated ever more comprehensively into government with its originator's appointment as minister for welfare reform under Tory premier David Cameron. It went on to cast a long shadow over Coalition welfare policies, legitimized by the moralizing certainties condemning the 'evil' of 'benefit dependency' that infused the rhetorics of Duncan Smith (Duncan Smith 2014) and his right-wing media cheerleaders (Glover 2014). In weaving together work, disability and benefit dependency as a discursively constructed nexus of interlinked strands, these rhetorics drew on (and repurposed) a long continuum of moralizing 'welfare' discourses stretching back to the conditional charity dispensed by medieval Christian almshouses and the sermons of, among others, the fourteenth-century Archbishop of Armagh, who advised that beggars and others reliant on poor relief should be 'hated by their neighbours' for eschewing God's teachings about the 'merits of labour' (quoted in McIntosh 2011: 17).

In the late modern age, these moralizing tropes had already been channelled by successive ministerial 'moral missionaries' (Morrison 2019: 84–85) – from Sir Keith Joseph, the father of Thatcherism, through Margaret Thatcher herself (daughter of a self-made businessman and Methodist preacher) and the Church of England traditions observed by Labour's Frank Field and Blair, to Brown (a Presbyterian 'son of the manse'). Brown's reign, first as chancellor, then as PM, was pockmarked with speeches invoking the deservingness of 'hardworking families' (Brown 1999) – and juxtaposing people who 'play by the rules' (Brown 1999) with those who 'play the system (Purnell 2008). Indeed, in time they would pave the way not only for Rishi Sunak's 'moral mission' against 'sick-note culture' (Sunak 2024) but for suggestions by his own party's future welfare secretary, Liz Kendall, that some inactive claimants were 'taking the mickey' (Nevett 2025).

Degrees of 'deservingness': From wounded warriors to weak (and 'woke') worriers

As the above discussion suggests, the task of distinguishing between disability and illness *per se* and conditions that are sufficiently serious to cause work-limiting (or work-preventing) 'impairment' has led to considerable rhetorical and policy hair-splitting over time, not to mention increasingly pedantic and onerous assessment regimes. Perhaps unsurprisingly, the perilously fine judgments assessors have had to make about individuals' (in)eligibility for support and/or exemption from the work-based system can be particularly challenging when they declare conditions whose signs and symptoms fluctuate or are invisible to the eye. Of these, many (though not all) belong to a collection of illnesses and disorders that today are bracketed under the umbrella of mental ill health.

Interlaced with these distinctions – between the fakers and the genuine, the serious and the mild cases – is a discursively implied hierarchy not only between *levels* of (legitimate) sickness/disability but between more- and less-deserving *conditions*. With one or two notable episodic exceptions, if there is any consensus to be discerned from history about disabled categories that have consistently (if not universally) been treated as deserving, they would include the war-wounded and those crippled through industrial accidents: i.e. people injured in the defence or economic 'service' of their nation. 'During a century of frequent warfare, the disabled soldier emerged as a figure of patriotic sympathy', notes historian David M Turner, with reference to the discursive currents of the 1700s, and the 'term disabled was often used specifically to refer to injured ex-servicemen, to emphasise their heroic sacrifice in the national cause' (Turner 2012: n.pag.). To illustrate, in his *Explanatory Dictionary of the Living Great Russian Language*, published in 1863, the Tsarist lexicographer Vladimir Dal defined the term 'invalid' (later to be appropriated in the context of wider policies relating to the disabled) as a 'revered warrior' or 'worn out one', who had 'served' but was now 'unable to serve because of wounds or physical damage' (quoted in Phillips 2009: n.pag.).

In late nineteenth-century Germany, meanwhile, the otherwise conservative regime of Kaiser Wilhelm I and Otto von Bismarck would introduce one of the first prototype (if partial) welfare states. This was to specifically prioritize the protection of people suffering industrial injuries through, among other measures, an Invalidity and Pension Law – funded by a compulsory national insurance scheme. While these particular interventions might be viewed through the prism of cynical *realpolitik* – as moves calculated (in Wilhelm's own words) to quell rising support among 'the working classes' for 'Social Democratic movements' – by enshrining them in statute he nonetheless telegraphed a bold message explicitly recognizing the legitimacy of claims for industrial accidents (Stone 1986: 58). Moreover, this early initiative would presage a wave of similar approaches across Europe in coming decades – including the widespread recognition (by the 1930s) of the debilitating, at times fatal, impact on industrial workers of asbestosis and related lung conditions (Hourihane and McCaughey 1966).

Meanwhile, hard-wired associations between valour in battle and industrial ardour with the automatic deservingness of any resulting injuries have persisted to this day, with a 2011 study of newspaper articles focusing on work-limiting disability noting that only a 'small number of articles mentioning the "deserving" claimant' appeared in the UK press across the two years 2004–05 and 2010–11. Of these, however, several mentioned 'physical injuries, particularly those inflicted through events such as war, or accidents' (Briant et al. 2011: 50). Significantly, when ministers decided to limit the eligibility of some individuals with war pensions for Pension Credit (a 'minimum income' entitlement targeted at the poorest pensioners), 'the case of these disabled "war heroes" was taken up by [right-wing tabloid] *The Express*, as a "deserving" case, in their strong attack of New Labour [the then government]' (Briant et al. 2011: 50).

In contrast to acceptance of the manifest deservingness of the (provably) war wounded and industrially injured, however, attitudes have long been considerably less compassionate towards two other recurring categories. These are, on the one hand, people claiming incapacity due to conditions or symptoms that others manage without complaint and, on the other, those judged to have brought illness or disability on *themselves*, invariably through deviant behaviours. To begin (briefly) with the latter, as history has evolved, there have developed a series of broad societal consensuses around the extent and limits of civilized, normative 'moral' standards of conduct – or, as they tend to be discursively framed in contemporary discussions around illness and incapacity, 'lifestyle choices'. For the economist and cleric Thomas Malthus, writing in 1798, it was overpopulation that should be held to blame for spreading illness and disease – making *procreation* itself (particularly among 'the poor') a primary form of immoral behaviour that needed to be checked. It was 'not improbable', he wrote, in characteristically hedged prose, that among the 'secondary causes' contributing to 'sickly seasons and epidemics' should be 'ranked a crowded population and unwholesome and insufficient food' (Malthus 1967: 36).

Even during the modern scientific era – with a plethora of illnesses recognized as both existing and contributing to widespread sickness and infirmity, especially among 'the poor' – societal elites invariably found ways of blaming the virulence and rapidity of their transmission on individuals' (immoral) lifestyles and habits. To take one example, symptoms attributed to the 'continuous malaria' prevalent in the American South during the early twentieth century included 'dirt-eating and lethargy' (Stone 1986: 94). But rather than identifying these as evidence of the unbearable suffering of socially deprived people deserving sympathy, charity and/or publicly funded remedial treatment, state authorities instead mounted a circular argument that these demeaning *symptoms* were somehow the (behavioural) *causes* of their poverty. This narrative was able to take root, argues Stone, because, unlike cholera, 'hookworm stayed within the confines of a single social class' and 'affected the rural poor in the South but, for some reason, not blacks' (Stone 1986: 94). It was only when eminent parasitologist Dr Charles Wardell Stiles eventually found a '50 cent cure' for hookworm that 'the successful and well-to-do southern elite not only had to stop blaming the "poor white trash" for their laziness but could no longer take quite so much credit for their own socioeconomic positions'. Prior to this, the situation was as set out below, with hookworm discursively mobilized to keep the rural poor in their place – and (through public health advice) effectively segregated from the wider populace:

> The disease made people listless, tired, disinclined to work, and apparently also mentally less alert, if not slow-witted. But what Stiles saw as symptoms, the popular conception saw as the malady itself. 'Poor white trash', it was held, were dirty and lazy. That was enough of an explanation for the socioeconomic position of the white rural poor, but should anyone feel compelled to explain their apparent sickness, then the 'anemia' or 'malaria' was alleged to be the consequence of bad moral habits.
> (Stone 1986: 94)

Over ensuing decades, ongoing developments in germ theory would come to mirror emerging policy approaches to ameliorating the physical, social and economic suffering of workers blamelessly incapacitated by industry. As Stone stresses, the 'movement towards insurance compensation...had an effect similar to that of germ theory in medicine', by reducing 'the importance of individual behavior as a causal factor'. Just as controversies around industrial accidents 'decreased individual responsibility by attributing job injuries to the anonymous, collective forces of industrialization', germ theory also reduced the focus on personal culpability and shifted it towards systemic factors – 'by attributing disease to specific, non-human, external agents'. Evolving in tandem, these parallel progressive turns had the effect – for a time – of 'enlarging the sphere of conditions under which a person would not be held responsible for his inability to work' (Stone 1986: 99).

Wind forward another century, though, and today levels of tolerance towards even genuine and chronic illnesses associated with deviant behaviours are still consistently distinguished through policy – and media-political exhortations defining accepted standards of public morality – from those whose sufferers are considered 'blameless', such as inherited illnesses, genetic defects or accidental injuries. In an important 2014 paper focusing on the 'pathologizing' of poverty, anthropologists Helena Hansen and Philippe Bourgeois, together with late public health scholar Ernest Drucker, drew attention to the fact that 'alcoholism and addiction were eliminated as a qualifying diagnosis' for US Social Security Insurance eligibility in 1996 (Hansen et al. 2014: n.pag.). Today, growing numbers of people classified as economically inactive in Britain and elsewhere are managing multiple health conditions (or comorbidities), with those such as type 2 diabetes, obesity, lung and liver disease, and particular types of cancer, often linked with smoking, heavy alcohol consumption, lack of exercise and overreliance on junk food. Moreover, a growing body of evidence suggests that such diagnoses are most heavily concentrated in areas with the highest rates of socioeconomic deprivation (Cancer Research UK 2025). These 'behaviours' are consistently framed as anything from unwise to deviant across the spectrum of dominant discourses, from the medical to the political to those of news media and wider popular culture (e.g. LeBesco 2010). In both the UK and US iterations of long-running television comedy-drama *Shameless*, lead protagonist Frank Gallagher – who is unemployed and 'earns' a living through a mix of untaxed cash-in-hand work, dodgy deals and criminality – is depicted as an alcoholic with a personality disorder. In America's version his son, Ian, is diagnosed with bipolar disorder and, ultimately, liver failure.

As for charges of hypochondria and feebleness, these too have deep historical roots – and, at times, have become heavily intertwined with those castigating sick and disabled people for over-egging genuine incapacities. In a useful overview in *The Disabled State*, Stone conceives of this view as the *economistic* framing of disabled people (or those 'identifying' as such), which positions them as 'rational', instrumentalist social actors inclined to exploit their labels as passports to maintain access to alms or welfare – and escape the (often punishing) work-based systems into which others are corralled. 'Economic theory takes the perspective of the welfare-maximizing rational man and suggests that people will define themselves as disabled when the material benefits of that role are greater than those derived from work', she writes, adding, 'in this model, the individual implicitly compares his potential income from unearned sources, including disability benefits, with his potential income from work, which is a product of the wage he could earn and his likelihood of employment' (Stone 1986: 142–43). Implicit in this framing is a suggestion that, even when someone *is* genuinely impaired, it is often in their rational economic interests to both publicly emphasize and internally cling to their diagnosis, and to present it as sufficiently debilitating to prevent them from labour participation. Here, then, is an antecedent of the inference by everyone from the Resolution Foundation to the 'Pathways to Work' Commission that those professing to be sick or disabled have a vested interest in self-diagnosing/labelling in this way, because of 'perverse incentives' to claim (more generous) disability, rather than unemployment, benefits (Milburn 2024a: 22).

Winding back, so ingrained had the ideology of work become by the early modern period that all but those cursed with the most extreme disabilities were expected to put their hands to the wheel (often literally). The sixteenth-century Spanish educationalist Juan Luis Vives – widely seen as the father of modern psychology – was among thinkers who envisaged workhouses in which blind people could be set to work, crafting 'little boxes and chests, fruit baskets, and cages', performing music, or even 'working the treadmills and treading the wine presses, all according to their particular talents' (Stone 1986: 55). Britain's own Jeremy Bentham had similar ideas, proposing that the sightless be set to work knitting, and that children be tied to seesaws that would be used to pump water 'as a by-product of their play' (Stone 1986: 55). By the time of the Industrial Revolution, this ideological obsession with the virtues of work and the duty of all but the most decrepit and incapable to contribute to oiling the cogs of industry had passed into 'the regulations of Poor Law administration' to such an extent that only five categories of person were any longer seen to exist within 'the internal universe of paupers'. These were children, the sick, the insane, 'defectives' and the 'aged and infirm' – all of whom (bar juveniles) remain 'part of today's concept of disability' (Stone 1986: 55). By using this bureaucratically defined typology to identify who was (and was not) 'able-bodied', the law (and commissioners) effectively pronounced anyone and everyone who failed to fall into a neat category as 'able-bodied by default'. In constructing this binary, economistic distinction between disability and ability (to work), Georgian government was setting the seal on a definitional framework that 'remains at the core of current disability programs' – both in centralized command economies and in deregulated, marketized welfare systems promoted by neoliberalism. The concept of being 'able to work' has, in turn, become 'a residual category whose meaning can be known only after all the "unable to work" categories have been precisely defined' (Stone 1986: 40–41).

To cite some more modern-day examples of particular groups accused of systematically deploying their infirmities for financial gain and/or to avoid the call to work, historian K Walter Hickel relates how US First World War veterans were often accused of exaggerating injury and illness by doctors assessing them for compensation (Hickel 2001). Decades later, similar charges would initially be levelled at British service personnel seeking recompense for suffering post-traumatic stress disorder (PTSD) and conditions such as 'Gulf War Syndrome' (Kilshaw 2005). More generally, the term 'shirker' owes its origins to the context of efforts to swell the draft in the Great War, when it was levelled both at conscientious objectors and those seen as avoiding the call to enlist by presenting themselves as too incapacitated to serve (Gullace 2015). By this time, a mythology of widespread 'malingering and feigning disability for the purpose of avoiding the draft or combat' had long since passed into 'the folklore of military medicine' (Stone 1986: 145).

Set against the impossibly severe demonstrations of disablement required of those seeking leave to legitimately 'dodge' the draft, there is (to quote Stone) 'a certain irony' that it was *mental* illness – the 'type of disease we now consider hardest to define' – that 'should have been separated conceptually and practically in welfare policy before *physical* illness' (Stone 1986: 44). There is insufficient space here to discuss the historical evolution of conceptualizations of mental health/illness in any detail (that way lies an extensive, and rapidly growing, literature in its own right). However, it is notable that, as far back as the Middle Ages, the dominant discursive positioning of people 'of unsound mind' was more inclined towards a discourse of *care* than one of *work* – with the duty to provide for such unfortunates placed firmly on the state and their own community, rather than the individuals themselves. In an illuminating 1995 article for the *British Medical Journal*, historians David and Christine Roffe describe how 'a semi-official tract known as the Praerogativa regis', published in the reign of the English king Edward I (1272–1307), 'distinguished for the first time between the natural born idiot and the lunatic' (Roffe and Roffe 1995: n.pag.). The former was designated 'incompetent from birth' and therefore eligible (based on a presumption of blamelessness) for 'the wardship' and material protection of the King – albeit at the sacrifice of 'the profits of his estates' to the Crown, at least 'until they passed to the idiot's heir on his death'. As for the lunatic, he was someone who 'became incompetent in the course of his life', rendering the king duty bound 'to provide for his maintenance and that of his family' and (in this case) 'without taking profit for himself' (Roffe and Roffe 1995: n.pag.).

All the more curious, perhaps, that some of the most hotly contested recent debates about legal and moral conceptions of 'ability to work' have revolved around the extent to which workforce participation should be demanded of people with 'invisible' conditions – especially those relating to mental health and/or neurodiversity. While wounded warriors have long been viewed as deserving of unconditional public sympathy and social protection, the same cannot be said for those who might crudely be termed *worriers*. In a mix of surveys, focus groups and textual analysis of newspaper articles conducted for their compendious 2011 analysis *Bad News for Disabled People*, the Strathclyde Centre for Disability Research and Glasgow Media Group found that, even prior to the full onslaught of the then-coalition government's swingeing 'welfare reform' and benefit cuts programme, attitudes towards people with disabling mental health conditions were highly sceptical. According to the researchers, mental health was referred to in only 8 out of 25 press articles mentioning a disability they categorized as 'deserving' between October 2004 and January 2005, but this figure plummeted to just 2 out of 30 articles by the three-month period October–January 2010–11. 'Mental illnesses and conditions which are otherwise "hidden" (such as chronic pain), or socially "unsympathetic" (such as HIV/AIDS, addiction or obesity), are of particular interest regarding their representation by tabloid newspaper articles in which attacks on the "undeserving" are prominent', the researchers added – drawing attention to a suite of other conditions that had historically (if erroneously) been associated with moral deviancy (Briant et al. 2011: 49–50).

This 2011 report was also notable for insights it offered into what appeared to be steadily hardening public opinion towards invisible and/or (by inference) more easily 'fakable' conditions entitling individuals to claim inability to work and, by extension, support from the welfare state. Coming as it did shortly after the 2007–08 global financial crash – a period during which wages stagnated and household budgets tightened – this qualitative snapshot strongly echoed the findings of numerous earlier studies demonstrating that levels of distrust and disapproval of working-aged people who are *out of* work intensify at times when those *in* work are struggling. When asked what proportion of individuals claiming disability-related benefits were fraudulent, focus-group participants' responses ranged from 10–70 per cent – with these wild figures often justified by references to newspaper articles, as well as their own asserted (direct or vicarious) experiences. Moreover, 'almost all' those citing personal knowledge said they 'knew people who were fraudulently claiming one form of disability benefit or another'. One respondent invoked the time-worn trope of deviant familiar strangers they claimed to see or encounter in passing in their daily life, by asserting that they 'know people who do it' and had 'a neighbour who does it' (Briant et al. 2011: 62–63).

At a time when the then newly installed government was toughening the regime for determining whether disabled people were 'fit for work', participants also seemed acutely sensitized to images of just how those feigning sickness or disability might do so. One suggested that it was 'really easy to fake symptoms', including 'bad backs'. Even during a more nuanced discussion around the question of why the number of people claiming out-of-work disability benefits had jumped from 700,000 to nearly 2.6 million over the preceding 40 years, the well of sympathy seemed noticeably dry. While some participants blamed an increasing population or rises in the cost of living (itself implying that certain people had taken rational economistic decisions to feign or exaggerate disability in order to make themselves eligible for more generous working-aged support), others suggested that the growth in claims had more to do with 'more people "knowing the system; knowing how to do it" '. 'Makes you angry for people who work full time and there are loads of people who are scamming it', remarked one, while another argued that 'they [disabled claimants] get the best of everything ... Because they're getting their rent paid ... They've learned the system'. Yet another added that they had to juggle 'three jobs, two cleaning jobs, one in the morning and one at night', while there was evidence of distrust even among some respondents who were disabled themselves or had close relatives with disabilities. One emphasized how their father had so internalized the discourse of shirkers and scroungers that he was embarrassed to admit he himself received disability-related benefits. They described how 'he's disabled and like there are people who are scamming it, but he isn't and he is embarrassed to tell people he's on benefits' or 'that he is going on holiday', for fear that they might 'think he is taking the piss'. Significantly, this respondent also positioned their father in one of history's manifestly deserving categories, by revealing that he had only qualified for help with his housing costs 'because he was in an accident and he got compensation' (Briant et al. 2011: 62–63).

Fifteen years on, and, amid ongoing tabloid headlines deriding those accused of faking 'bad backs' and other disabilities (visible and invisible), the present moral panic around 'sick-note culture' has seen the mantle of prime exploiter of Britain's benefits system pass to those diagnosed (or self-diagnosing) with autism, ADHD and other neurodiverse disorders. A useful 2023 scoping review of the international research literature focusing on media portrayals of autism found that, in general, print and online newspapers 'still seem to endorse stigmatising portrayals', including 'the use of negative language' and 'a focus on negative aspects'. Crucially, in more than half of the studies examined, 'a missing representation of autistic individuals in the news stories was mentioned' – meaning that articles invariably talked *about* autism (and those with the condition), rather than balancing clinical and statistical (elite) portrayals with quotes and opinions conveying *their own* voices and lived experiences (Mittman et al. 2023: 8010).

This marginalization and objectification of people with neurodivergent disorders (especially those who are economically inactive) has become ever more entrenched in today's UK, as we shall see in the next chapter. All the more reason that listening to (and amplifying) the personal stories of individuals living with these and other misunderstood conditions is so important – a task to which we turn in Chapters 3 to 5. But before we consider such matters, our discussion of the historical evolution of discursive positionings (and treatment) of people with mental ill health – many of whom might also have suffered from neurodivergent conditions, in eras when the existence of such disorders was unknown – leads neatly into two wider discussions. One of these is the evolving conceptualization of 'normality' versus 'abnormality' – or difference. The other is that of 'usefulness' (and validity) versus 'uselessness'/invalidity.

Fear of difference: From deformity to diversity

In the context of evolving conceptualizations of work-limiting impediments, historical ideas about the tolerable limits of physical and mental 'difference' have tended to coalesce around society's collective aversion to two distinct but similarly aberrant states: mania and deformity (or 'ugliness'). Indeed, at times both these qualities have become so heavily stigmatized that they have acted to erode or erase the 'rights' of individuals to contribute their labour who might otherwise have been perfectly capable of doing so – purely because their appearance and conduct offended or frightened 'sane' and 'normal' folk who, in turn, did not wish to encounter or in any way associate with them.

While there is insufficient room here to embark on a detailed history of either of these two sources of stigma, both are worthy of note as dimensions of human experience that, at times (and often for long periods), have led to individuals being wholly discarded by their fellow citizens: segregated, excluded from the workplace and, *in extremis*, abandoned to their fates and left to scavenge just in order to survive. Moreover, as each of these outward conditions tends to signify and accompany underlying comorbidities – notably severe mental illness (or insanity) on the one hand and physical disability and/or disease on the other – the effect of such abandonment is to double down on the acute inequalities and disadvantages invariably already faced by the individuals affected.

To take a handful of specific historical illustrations of how (supposedly) 'mad' and/or deformed people have repeatedly been rejected and ostracized from wider society – both practically and symbolically – medieval depictions of both commonly characterized them as 'monsters'. Among other things, they were the source of many societal myths about lycanthropes, witches and monstrous interspecies births (Godden and Mittman 2019). But some of the most vivid examples of the routine discursive dehumanization of people we would today recognize as mentally ill or physically disabled can be found in Renaissance literature – which offers perhaps the earliest collection of rich fictional portrayals of 'difference', at a time when classical ideals of anatomical and intellectual beauty were being revived and reappraised. Reflecting on how the 'medical meaning of *disability* as in "having a disability" emerged only in 1633, and *disabled* as a category of people only in the mid-seventeenth century', linguist Alice Equestri observes that 'the vast majority of occurrences of the terms in the Middle Ages and the Renaissance pointed at either someone excluded or barred from something' and/or 'someone/something "rendered incapable of action or use"'. Concurrently, the forms of 'human variation' that would today see people defined as mentally unwell, disabled, differently abled or, indeed, neurodiverse were 'indicated through other words' such as '*deformity, monstrosity, lameness*, or *foolishness*' – all of which pointedly distinguished them from 'what the Renaissance called the *ideal*, rather than *norm*' (Equestri 2022: n.pag.). This strand of argument is echoed in English scholar Elizabeth B. Bearden's authoritative monograph *Monstrous Kinds* (also focusing on the Renaissance), which offers the first book-length investigation into 'how people with disabilities defined and were defined by early modern representations of bodies, space, and narratives' (Bearden 2019: 4).

Writing a century or two later, in 1797, Bentham 'concocted' what Stone describes as 'an amazing plan', under which the 'unpleasantness of living with the disabled would be minimized by another type of matching'. 'Lunatics', he suggested, could 'be housed next to the deaf, and the physically deformed next to the blind' – thereby sparing all able-bodied people the discomfort of being subjected to the ravings of 'the mad' and the ugliness of the disfigured (Stone 1986: 55). Subsequently, the decades following the introduction of the 'workhouse test' would only add further layers of categorization to define (and discursively distinguish) individuals with illnesses and disabilities that were seen to render them especially alarming and unsavoury – and, by extension, even more worthless than the sick and disabled generally. Stone notes how the term 'defectives' was introduced into English Poor Law administration initially to denote people who were blind, deaf and dumb, with 'terms like "lame" and "deformed"...later added to list', and 'epileptics included for first time' as of 1899. The term 'mental defectives' was introduced (notably for children with what we might now recognize as learning disabilities) in 1903 (Stone 1986: 44).

Another example of how *physical* 'defectives' have at times been routinely, and pointedly, separated from the rest of society was through the proliferation in late nineteenth-century America of a wave of statutes outlawing displays of suffering by any 'unsightly beggar': legal instruments collectively conceptualized as 'the ugly laws' (Schweik 2009: 2). In her recent book of the same name, English and disability studies scholar Susan M. Schweik traces the spread of these prohibitions from as far west as San Francisco (where the first one came into effect in 1867) and Portland, Oregon, via Chicago over to Pennsylvania in the east. The sheer brutality with which 'miserable' beggars – a latter-day iteration of medieval 'sturdy beggars' – were normatively objectified as 'ugly' and aberrant can be glimpsed through a contemporary characterization of one such ordinance in the popular press. According to the *San Francisco Call*, the city's Board of Supervisors had passed an 'order to prohibit street begging, and to prohibit certain persons from appearing in streets and public places' – the 'certain persons' in question being people who could be described as 'perfect wrecks' or those observably 'diseased, maimed, mutilated, or in any way deformed' (Schweik 2009: 2).

In unpacking the ancestral roots of these dehumanizing discourses eliding disability with ugliness (both of the outer and, by inference, inner kind), Schweik identifies a litany of earlier records documenting the revulsion with which 'miserable beggars' and 'perfect wrecks' were consistently regarded. Among other choice extracts, she cites a letter penned by a London merchant in 1729 in which he 'suggested whippings, workhouses and the establishment of a national institution for "receiving and strictly confining ... People ... who wander about to extort Money by exposing ... dismal sights" ' – including 'creatures that go about the Streets to show their maim'd Limbs' (Schweik 2009: 2).

Wasted humans: Towards eliminating 'uselessness'?

In light of the (by then) longstanding framing of people with severe physical and mental impediments as objects of, at best, pity and, at worst, fear and menace, by the early twentieth century the question had begun to arise as to whether the kindest action would to put such unfortunates out of their misery. This would also have the wider societal fringe benefit of preventing them from breeding and passing on congenital, even infectious, defects (and behaviours) to their offspring. The emergence and popularization of the pseudoscience of eugenics would lead to even supposedly 'liberal' thinkers, such as H.G. Wells, William Beveridge and future Labour Party parliamentary candidate David Caradog Jones, expending endless energy identifying a typology of (often overlapping and ill-defined) groups of 'abnormal people'. These ranged from 'those who are born blind, the very deaf, the epileptic, the mentally deficient' to 'those who are persistently addicted to drink, crime or vice' (quoted in Welshman 2013: 72). Moreover, a measure of how freely and uncritically such 'worthless' individuals were conflated with those consigned to other subcategories of the overarching 'social problem group' – and 'the poor' generally – could be glimpsed in Caradog Jones's dismissal of 'problem families' and others who were the subject of (limited) social support at the time as 'utterly useless human material' (quoted in Welshman 2013: 72).

The logical extension of such sentiments was, of course, to find ways of both removing such 'material' from society in the *present* and preventing it from returning in the *future*: eliminating such elements by banishing them so far away that they would wither and die without issue and/or forcibly 'breeding them out' of the gene pool. Taken to its extreme, such social-Darwinian ideas would ultimately inform the horrific 'Aktion T4' programme of mass extermination by involuntary euthanasia of institutionalized disabled people in Nazi Germany (and, of course, Hitler's Final Solution against the Jews). But its logic can also be traced through the systematic, state-directed discourse of dehumanization to which the war-wounded were subjected in Stalin's Soviet Union. Citing the Russian sociologist Lev Gudkov, anthropologist Sarah D. Phillips recounts how, in a perverse inversion of the reverence with which injured veterans had widely been regarded in Tsarist times, amputees in wheelchairs were colloquially othered there as 'samovars' (a term likening them to a traditional Russian metal container used to boil tea) and framed as 'a grim and "superfluous" reminder to the populace of the inhumane traumas of war'. The implication was that this was a history it was healthier for society to collectively deny than repeatedly relive (Phillips 2009: n.pag.). Moreover, in emphasizing the sense of public distaste at the sight of combat survivors reduced to the status of 'human stumps on little wheels', Gudkov himself reflects how society was 'ashamed of them, turned away from them' and (as far as it could) 'hid them'. It rationalized this approach through ambivalent feelings combining 'guilt' with 'a sense of the ugliness of life', and doing 'everything' it could 'to keep them [in-valids] out of the official gala picture of peacetime life' (Gudkov 2005: 4).

This matter-of-fact dismissal as 'useless material' of the most severely (or *visibly*) sick and disabled people – not to mention wider groups experiencing poverty and exclusion – might be viewed as one of history's most brazen and callous expressions of sociologist Zygmunt Bauman's concept of 'wasted humans' or 'wasted lives' (Bauman 2013). Updating and building on Bauman's ideas in a recent article for the journal *Disability and Society*, social policy scholars Eva Duda-Mikulin, Lisa Scullion and Richard Currie argued that, 'in a time of austerity, populism and disablism that sweep across Europe', contemporary media-political representations of disabled people are often so belittling and stigmatizing as to cast them as 'wasted humans' (Duda-Mikulin et al. 2020: 1375). In a passage eloquently crystallizing the argument that moral panics about difference act as discursive tools allowing governing elites to distract attention from their own failings and displace blame for complex problems onto (vulnerable) scapegoats, they added:

> In a time of cuts to public services, there have been sustained attempts by successive governments to cast some members of the population as undesirable (them), in contrast with the hard working, independent, rational and economically active individuals who contribute to the neoliberal dream (us). This context is becoming increasingly universal.
>
> (Duda-Mikulin et al. 2020: 1375)

It is *this* antimony – the endless, repeatedly rebooted, binary drawn between the deserving and undeserving, the 'useful' and the 'useless' – that forms the focus for the coming chapters, as we unpack the tensions and contradictions between dominant discourses about economic (in)activity and the lived experiences of those it affects.

But before we turn to exploring these real-world experiences and perspectives, it is necessary to make one last detour on our historical journey through Britain's evolving oppositions between worklessness and worthlessness, usefulness and uselessness. This is to examine the growing emergence, particularly in recent decades, of a disingenuous discursive distinction between two supposedly antithetical forms of family organization. On the one hand nestles the financially secure two-parent family – a unit which, even with only one wage earner, slots into the hallowed political imaginary of the 'working family'. On the other slumps the 'broken' (Mann and Roseneil 1994: 317) or lone-parent household, which (when encumbered by lack of wider support networks and unaffordable childcare) is positioned as its equal and opposite: the 'workless family'. In keeping with this chapter's focus on hegemonic societal norms and deviations, these antithetical imaginaries are here conceptualized as deserving versus undeserving parents/carers.

The undeserving parent: From (worthy) stay-at-home to (worthless) single mums

For the past two or more decades, the story of Britain's ongoing obsession with the scourge of worklessness has been that of a stop-start state-directed pursuit of unemployed 'shirkers', inactive 'malingerers', and disability benefit fraudsters. Given this backdrop, it is easy to forget that the last great panic over economic inactivity prior to this took the form of an, at times, hysterical furore about the moral failings of a rather more distinct and specific folk-devil held up as a symbol of pathological worklessness: single mothers.

The context for the great 1990s maternal panic (Morrison 2019: 100) was a perfect storm of interlocking social, economic and political crises that, after brewing quietly for some years, bubbled to a frothing head in 1993 – a period sociologists Kirk Mann and Sasha Roseneil aptly dubbed at the time 'the year of the single mother' (1994: 317). First came a crisis of the *economy*, in the form of a biting recession that left millions of families fearful for their jobs and living standards, and ideally primed for media and political discourses stoking resentment towards anyone who might be perceived as being (undeservedly) insulated from all the turbulence, such as (already workless) benefit recipients. This sense of indignant disdain at Britain's supposed 'something-for-nothing society' was most memorably symbolized by the contemptuous relish with which then newly appointed Social Security Secretary Peter Lilley used his 1992 Conservative Party Conference speech to promise a crackdown on 'young ladies who get pregnant just to jump the housing queue' and 'dads who won't support' their 'kids' (Lilley 1992). Lilley's sometimes hysterical speech channelled a long historical tradition of governments (and, in earlier eras, monarchs and ecclesiasts) pitting the working against the workless poor at times of economic malaise – often as a tool for displacing blame for the incumbent regime's own fiscal mismanagement (see Golding and Middleton 1982: 9; Morrison 2019: 47–51).

Next came the first stirrings of a *fin de siècle* crisis of *government*, itself partially rooted in tensions over how best to fix the economy but most clearly manifest in a protracted period of infighting over Britain's ongoing membership of the European Union Exchange Rate Mechanism (and, by proxy, the EU itself), and a succession of simmering, at times explosive challenges to Prime Minister John Major's authority. Added to this toxic mix – and heavily interlaced with the third crisis to come – was the beginning of a slow-burn drip-drip of salacious revelations about ministers' private lives that stood starkly at odds with their public proclamations of performative morality – particularly when sermonizing about the supposed deviancy of broken families and feckless single parents.

But finally, and most decisively, came the apotheosis of a long-smouldering crisis of *society*. Tapping into years of tabloid-fuelled scares about teenage football hooligans and joyriders, this crystallized through the chorus of collective moral outrage surrounding a singular appalling crime – weaponized by some on the political Right as the culmination of the UK's long, slow slide into moral degeneracy. This was the February 1993 murder of toddler James Bulger by two 10-year-old boys – both portrayed in the media as the products of dysfunctional families with histories of drunkenness, drug addiction, violence and (on-and-off) worklessness. As *The Guardian* recalled in a 'special report' revisiting the case seven years later, the back stories of Jon Venables and Robert Thompson read like a distillation of all the tropes most often reeled out by a press and political class who, by this time, had become morbidly obsessed with the moral failings of 'broken families' (Mann and Roseneil 1994: 317) and jobless single parents. Theirs was a 'world of social and economic deprivation, of trashy television and cultural poverty, inadequate social services, failed schooling and general confusion' (*The Guardian* 2000: n.pag.). Never mind the fact that both boys' mothers had very understandable reasons for struggling to cope, and for not working – the first managing two children (besides Venables) with learning difficulties; the second having been long since abandoned by Thompson's father to raise her seven children on her own. For those already signed up to the single-parent panic (and many hitherto not yet persuaded), the Bulger case was all that was needed to cement the framing of 'lone mothers' and their 'fatherless, supposedly criminally inclined children' as 'the core of the underclass' and the cause of numerous 'social problems' (Mann and Roseneil 1994: 317).

Fanning the flames of this omni-crisis, meanwhile, were various other actors, including those on the New Right who had long been ideologically fixated on the idea that Britain's welfare state had bred a culture of intergenerational benefit dependency – most notably the American social explorer Charles Murray. In *Underclass*, his baleful essay reviving the most Orientalizing tropes of *In Darkest England*, he constructed a nexus of evils that (he argued) both exemplified and explained the dysfunction of welfare-dependant households, and the threat they posed to Britain's overall moral order: out-of-wedlock births; violent crime; and (perhaps above all else) worklessness (Murray 1990). For Murray and others like him, the benefits system was less a patchy, inadequate solution to poverty than one of its primary causes – and the principal driver of a culture of moral decay in Britain's dark underbelly; a netherworld from which the respectable classes deserved protection.

Given that the overall life-cycle of Britain's prolonged 1990s maternal panic is chronicled in depth elsewhere – including by this author (Morrison 2019: 97–104) – there is little need to revisit every detail here. However, what *is* worth examining is the way in which single parenthood *per se* came to be repeatedly and powerfully (re)constructed as a signifier of supposed dysfunction and 'moral vacuum' (*The Guardian* 2000), not least through its persistent association with economic inactivity and/or unemployment (invariably framed as fecklessness and moral deviancy). The conflation of broken – and, increasingly, 'problem' or 'troubled' – families with imaginaries of worklessness and (at times) lawlessness was to become a trademark of both the later years of the Major government and at least the first term of the 'New Labour' administration that succeeded it. In the tradition of earlier law-and-order panics (e.g. Hall et al. 1978), this narrative would weave its way through a continuum of news articles, op-ed pieces, ministerial speeches, court judgments and sermons from the pulpit throughout the 1990s and into the early years of the new millennium. But the discursive framework underpinning it was undoubtedly set by a handful of carefully choreographed rhetorical interventions from successive moral missionaries in government. These ranged from the more 'common-sense' secular morality espoused by Major's ill-fated paean to family values, 'Back to Basics' (Chidwick 2023), to the more orthodox Christian values inspiring Labour's Tony Blair and Frank Field and the near-biblical epiphany on Glasgow's Easterhouse estate that moved Iain Duncan Smith (a devout Roman Catholic) to launch the Centre for Social Justice and, through it, his mission to heal Britain's 'broken society' (Slater 2014). Moreover, while many important interventions took place at the height of the panic itself, others dated back decades and had roots in the emergence of the new, more individualistic, order that had supplanted a more communitarian post-war consensus from the mid-1970s onwards.

Similarly, while the immediate causes of the 1990s single mother panic can be put down to the maelstrom of social, economic and political factors leading up to the state-of-the-nation debate sparked by the Bulger murder, their discursive taproots went back much further. Decades before Murray, they had formed the nexus of a succession of moralizing policy prospectuses flowing from the pen of Britain's own Keith Joseph – another doyen of the New Right. As social services secretary in Ted Heath's Tory government, Joseph was responsible for popularizing two notions that would become recurring tropes of inactivity discourse over the coming decades: the imagery of supposed cultures of intergenerational worklessness and welfare dependency (a negative spiral he infamously conceptualized as the 'cycle' of 'transmitted deprivation'), and that of 'problem families' (see Welshman 2007: 25). Joseph's chosen moral mission was to arrest what he saw as the most pernicious symptoms of this 'cycle': under-age pregnancy, marital breakdown, domestic violence and other intergenerationally transmitted deviant behaviours. His prospectus for doing so? A proposed – but never fully realized – 1973 initiative by his Department for Health and Social Security, entitled 'Preparation for Parenthood', in which he planned to target children from poorer families (particularly girls) with an understanding of the moral responsibilities attached to parenting.

Wind forward two decades, and, in the months and years encompassing Britain's latest crises of youth and family – the Bulger-era maternal panic – the baton would pass to a succession of other moral missionaries, many of whom (like Joseph, a devout Jew), were individuals with strong religious convictions. While Joseph himself would make a fresh intervention, in a pamphlet lamenting the plight of children reared by jobless single mothers and fathers with 'dangerous masculinities' (quoted in Haylett 2001: 358), by far the biggest agenda-setting was the then shadow home secretary and soon-to-be PM-in-waiting. In a prescient article published less than a month before the Bulger killing, Blair set out what would become one of his defining moral missions in government – his war against crime and antisocial behaviour – by painting a dystopian picture of waves of 'arson or hoaxes' he attributed to 'young teenagers' in the Tyne-and-Wear area, and evoking images of 'our old people' on 'inner-city estates' living 'in a state of fear' (Blair [1993] 2015). More significant was his article's denunciation of the blight of 'poor education and housing, inadequate or cruel family backgrounds, low employment prospects and drug abuse' – a montage of social evils that risked leaving 'young people' exiled from 'mainstream culture' and increasing their chances of 'going wrong' (Blair [1993] 2015).

Four and a half years on, a similar maelstrom of evils would provide the discursive template for Blair's earliest (and perhaps most often quoted) intervention in the worklessness debate in government: the (now infamous) 'single mothers speech' he delivered on 2 June 1997 against the Brutalist backdrop of London's Aylesbury estate. In his heavily intertextual address – which drew positive write-ups across the spectrum of the press – Blair shamelessly repurposed Lilley's slavering condemnation of Britain's 'something-for-nothing society' (Lilley 1992) by re-framing it through the more progressive discourse of the common good and reciprocal social relations that political scientist Robert Putnam famously conceptualized as 'social capital'. These are 'features of social organization, such as networks, norms, and trust, that facilitate cooperation for mutual benefit' (Putnam 1994: 6–7). As Blair put it, a new 'ethic of mutual responsibility or duty' should be paired with a 'something for something' culture (Blair 1997). Yet, in drawing on these progressive ideals, Blair also used a turn of phrase that would itself echo down the years – and repeatedly be appropriated and repackaged by politicians of Left and Right (notably his successor, Gordon Brown, and Coalition premier David Cameron) – by warning that new rights and protections would be contingent on families agreeing to 'play by the rules' and 'only take out' if they 'put in' (Blair 1997).

Here, and in ensuing passages lamenting 'a generation of young women' for whom 'early pregnancies and the absence of a reliable father almost guarantee a life of poverty' and pledging to 'get tough' on 'the workshy young' and 'single parents', Blair called back to both Joseph and Lilley's images of queue-jumping, under-aged single mums and the inter-generationally 'workless' (Deans and Hopkins 1997). Most significantly, he warned – in language that could have been lifted from any of a number of recent speeches and policy announcements about Britain's current 'inactivity crisis' – 'there will and should be' no 'option for an inactive life on benefit' (Blair 1997). Within months he followed through on this threat to those he cast (in the same breath) as Britain's 'forgotten people', by cutting Child Benefit for lone parents, ostensibly to incentivize them 'off welfare into work' (Hansard 1997). It was this policy that would lead to his first major Commons rebellion – and foreshadow the deeper divisions to come, decades later, under Starmer.

The privileged invisibles? Deserving versus undeserving 'homemakers'

The discursive position to which we are led by all this sermonizing about 'broken families' trapped in cycles of intergenerational worklessness is a curious one. Although it is consistent with the more general stigma – if not demonization – directed against people defined as economically inactive (and, indeed, the long-term unemployed), it stands starkly *at odds with* another popular moral discourse that, until recently, sought to position the role of stay-at-home parents (typically married mothers) as sacrosanct. While there is insufficient space here to explore in any detail the evolution of ideals and conceptions of the nuclear family, and patriarchal (male) breadwinner/(female) homemaker traditions, a growing body of critical and more popular histories testifies to a longstanding public veneration of the idea of the 'non-working' housewife and mother as a bedrock of household, even societal, stability (see, for example, Matthews 1989; Draznin 2000;

Robertson 1997, 2000). None of this is to dispute the fact that, in contrast with gendered popular stereotypes, throughout much of history the 'private' realities of many women involved a great deal of hard work outside their households – particularly at times of rapid industrial expansion and/or warfare. In Britain alone, they included 'scurriers' forced to toil for twelve-hour days, alongside their husbands and children, in nineteenth-century coal mines across the industrial North and the legions of female workers who manned Dundee's jute mills in place of their 'kettle-boiler' husbands (Cox 2013). This is to say nothing of the legions of 'land girls', code breakers and munitions factory workers who powered the war effort. In other words (to quote the anthropologist Michel-Rolph Trouillot), there is always 'history 1' and 'history 2': 'what happened' versus 'what was *said* to have happened [author's italics] in the past' (Trouillot 2015: 4).

Nevertheless, the popular imaginary of the virtuous homemaker/housewife was, until recently, an enduring one, particularly in socially (and politically) conservative circles: ironically, those who have tended to invest the most energy in disparaging 'workless' single mothers and driving them into the labour force. Set against this backdrop, even today it may just about be tenable for families fortunate enough to be economically self-supporting – or, indeed, independently wealthy – to continue bucking the growing societal push towards multi-earner households (if they so choose). But this, in itself, creates a clear disparity between the positions of the 'haves' and 'have-nots', through a curious inversion of the symbolic annihilation most often experienced by those in the latter category. In essence, stay-at-home mothers and carers in families fortunate enough to be able to survive as single-earner units are effectively rendered invisible in the dominant discourse. This is because of its single-minded preoccupation with the moral burden of *out-of-work* (lone) parents – rather than any meaningful discussion about the intrinsic merits of parenting itself (full time or otherwise).

So what has changed over time to transform the idea of a worthy (if, in the narrowest sense of the term, 'workless') stay-at-home mother into such a heavily qualified concept – one that potentially still applies in certain (self-supporting and/or two-parent) contexts but much less so in single-parent households, and certainly not in those without a wage-earner, and reliant for their incomes on the state? It is an argument of this book that the only clear explanation for this disjuncture is the onset of a form of socioeconomic order that has come to conceptualize households less as a network of interrelated and interdependent *social and/or community* units (in all their varied forms and configurations) than as hermetically sealed, self-determining *economic* units whose primary societal value lies in their mobilization as agents of material productivity, exchange and consumption. In essence, this is the ideology of neoliberalism: one that values self-reliance and individualism over any pursuit of virtuous circles based on a more communitarian ethos of reciprocity, social capital and collective pursuit of the common good. In (re)adopting this model, contemporary capitalism is, then, throwing us back to earlier historical eras in which individuals and households were similarly socially constructed as economistic subjects – for example, under the proto-capitalism of the mercantilist era and through the 'workhouse tests' of the Industrial Revolution. Then, as now, women and families living in poverty – like sick and disabled people – were ridiculed, hectored, punished and even enslaved if they failed to submit themselves, for however meagre a wage, to the economic mission of the day. Sturdy beggars, Clapperdudgeons and all iterations of the mobile, 'voluntary' and workless poor, able-bodied and disabled alike: all were units of production to be conscripted into the workforce, or they were nothing.

As we shall see, it is the neoliberal version of this value system and its obsession with functionalist, transactional notions of the role of individuals and families in society – in today's terms, the interdependent pursuit of (national) economic growth and (personal) aspiration – that underpins the discourses and personal stories we explore throughout the rest of this book.

2

From Scroungers to Snowflakes: Economic Inactivity in UK Public Discourse

There can be no clearer sign that escalating concern about a social issue has reached the point of moral panic than when it comes to dominate everything from a live peak-time national radio debate to the normally staid pages of an industry bible for HR professionals. 'Is there a moral case for cutting welfare?' began the blurb for the 12 March 2025 episode of BBC Radio 4's provocative topical discussion show *The Moral Maze*, after reeling out a succession of questions laced with straw-man tropes positioning economically inactive benefit recipients as dependent non-contributors. Opening with a normative, taken-for-granted description of 'welfare' as 'morally complex', it asked:

> While it is an important safety net, at what point does it disempower people to pursue a better life, encourage passivity rather than self-reliance, and foster self-entitlement over personal responsibility? Even if we could discern these things, we live in an imperfect world. Life is a lottery. What some perceive as 'lifestyle' choices, others argue are often made from few options, due to entrenched structural inequalities. How much is this really a matter of nurturing individual moral character and virtue?
>
> ('Is there a moral case for cutting welfare?' 2025)

This single paragraph ran like an intertextual greatest-hits collection – harking back to the mantras of successive chancellors and work and pensions secretaries who had venerated 'personal responsibility' over 'dependency' (Osborne 2013) and promoted the implausible imaginary of legions of out-of-work claimants voluntarily opting for lives bedevilled by stigma, symbolic annihilation and poverty as a 'lifestyle choice' (Osborne 2013).

That very same day the human resources trade magazine *Personnel Today* ran a more restrained but equally concerned-sounding story under the hand-wringing headline 'UK is only advanced economy where economic inactivity is increasing' (McCulloch 2025). Unlike most other articles published that week on the same topic, however, this one was noteworthy for focusing on an angle largely neglected in the popular press: the fact that culpability for rising health-related inactivity partly rested with recent governments, for presiding over some of the lowest rates of statutory sick pay in the OECD. Citing early findings from a 'Keep Britain Working Review' overseen by Sir Charles Mayfield, ex-chairman of the John Lewis Partnership, it noted that 'confused financial incentives for employers and employees were one reason economic inactivity had worsened in the UK in comparison with other countries'. So meagre was the compensation paid to bosses to help them retain workers by paying them fairly while they were off recovering from sickness, the article noted, that it had become 'cheaper to replace workers who fell sick than to invest in their retention' (McCulloch 2025).

Yet this refreshing emphasis on some of the 'push-factors' driving young adults out of the job market – inadequate statutory sick pay, impatient/disloyal employers and declining investment in apprenticeships – made the story a remarkable outlier, rather than a harbinger of any more enlightened public conversation around inactivity. This was the week, after all, in which then Work and Pensions Secretary Liz Kendall was putting the finishing touches to her long-awaited (and ultimately ill-fated) 'Pathways to Work' green paper, emboldened by loyalist Labour outriders proclaiming it their party's 'moral duty' to tackle the 'crisis of economic inactivity'. It was also the week of a headmasterly sermon from Keir Starmer warning left-wing backbenchers that taxpayers felt 'in their bones' that it was 'unsustainable', 'indefensible' and 'unfair' to be expected to foot a 'spiralling' welfare bill (Nevett and Catt 2025).

Indeed, news of the impending government crackdown was welcomed by a cacophonous chorus of approval resounding right across the spectrum of the mainstream media – from customary klaxons of the tabloid Right to usually measured news magazines like *The Economist*, which carried a 13 March headline despairing at 'Britain's worklessness disaster' (*The Economist* 2025). Among the loudest propagandists for the scale of the UK's inactivity crisis was right-wing tabloid news-site *www.express.co.uk*, which framed the situation, divisively, as an intergenerational battle – with a provocative intro paragraph emphasizing the 'shocking new figures' that showed Chancellor Rachel Reeves was now 'more reliant on pensioners for income tax than Gen Z workers'. While '5.45m Brits aged over 70 paid income tax in the 2022–23 financial year', the report claimed, a commensurate 'rise in economically inactive youths contributes to the contrast', with 'many young adults not even looking for a job' (O'Brien 2025: n.pag.). Meanwhile, an editorial in conservative broadsheet *The Daily Telegraph* – headlined 'Cut welfare to size' – foregrounded the dubious assertion that 'many people' were 'claiming benefits under no obligation to look for work' (*Daily Telegraph* 2025: 15). The story was disingenuous in multiple ways, not least in failing to acknowledge that benefit recipiency was no indicator that someone was out of the labour market. As the government's own data showed, nearly one in four Universal Credit claimants were *in* work (Department for Work and Pensions 2025d). However, its central assertion seemed to be based, in part, on comments in Alan Milburn's then-recent 'Pathways to Work' report (the basis for Kendall's reforms) in which its author had criticized the disproportionate benefit sanctions placed on unemployed people who failed to engage in job-search activities compared to the less conditional entitlements enjoyed by those receiving out-of-work health and disability benefits. Not to be outdone, the red-top *Sun* ran a splashy story unhesitatingly blaming 'under-25s' for 'damning figures' showing they were 'driving up "worklessness" levels', under the screamingly capitalized headline 'GEN Z JOB SLUMP' (Armstrong 2025).

In more liberal corners of the press, the tone was noticeably more sober, but journalists were no less engaged with the issues driving the hysteria – even if more inclined to couch their reports and commentaries in sceptical terms. Most indignant was disabled *Guardian* columnist Frances Ryan, who discerned in Labour's blizzard of moralistic kite-flying something more sinister than Reeves's literal-minded, pounds-and-pence obsession with cutting the 'welfare budget'. Its apparent ideological 'belief', argued Ryan, was implicit in the reverence for 'working people' that Starmer had already made 'a central tenet' of his government: a misty-eyed conviction that 'paid work' was 'a virtue' and that 'people who don't perform it deserve a worse life than everyone else' (Ryan 2025). Elsewhere in the same issue, cartoonist Ben Jennings offered a scabrous take on the prime minister's alarm at Britain's mounting benefits bill. His image depicted a weary-looking Starmer, dressed as a parking enforcement officer, preparing to post a penalty charge notice on a car bearing a disability sticker, neatly installed in a bay reserved for 'blue badge holders only', beside a carelessly parked (but un-ticketed) sports car (Jennings 2025). Meanwhile, *The New Statesman* carried the knowingly loaded headline 'Why Britain isn't working' – an intertextual allusion to the notorious Saatchi and Saatchi-designed 'Labour isn't working' poster campaign that had helped seal the party's defeat to Margaret Thatcher in the 1979 general election (Dunn 2025). Belying its clickbait-friendly top line, the article offered a refreshingly well-evidenced sense of proportion by pointing out that – 'despite the many headlines warning about "millions of Britons not working" ' – the 'national statistics around economic activity' make for 'an unusually boring graph'. In truth, 'the line of economic inactivity' had been 'mostly flat since 1971' (Dunn 2025: n.pag.).

But while this was undoubtedly a week for right-wing commentators to bare their fangs – emboldened by a nominally Centre-Left premier's tough-love pep-talk to Britain's 'wasted generation' (Nevett and Catt 2025) of NEETS – it was just the latest convulsion in a narrative arc that had slowly unfolded since the late stages of the pandemic. It had been visible in Tory Chancellor Jeremy Hunt's threat to 'toughen up' sanctions for 'those on benefits who can work but refuse to' ahead of his 2023 'Back to Work' Budget (Hunt 2023: 16); his DWP colleague Mel Stride's sweeping statement a year later that 'mental health culture' had 'gone too far' (Gutteridge 2024a); and, most strikingly, the Downing Street speech in which soon-to-be-defenestrated premier Rishi Sunak set out his 'moral mission' to rid Britain of 'sick-note culture' (Sunak 2024).

Fanning the frames: Tracking the media-political agenda-setting loop

How, then, did this moral panic about Britain's latest crisis of worklessness first come about, gain momentum, and accelerate in its reach and ferocity? What were the shape and trajectory of its overall discursive life-cycle, and the key triggers that most contributed to crystallizing and escalating it? And how did audiences – that is voters, taxpayers, the general public – respond (and contribute) to the unfolding narrative?

This chapter addresses these questions through a multi-level qualitative textual analysis of three primary sites of media and political discourse around the problem of rising (or at least stubbornly high) levels of UK economic inactivity in the years following the pandemic. The first of these is the print and online news sphere – here represented by coverage of individual stories, policy initiatives and debates around inactivity and worklessness in the legacy national and regional press. The second is the political sphere, primarily as manifested through Hansard: the official record of speeches, debates and other interventions in the UK Parliament. The third arena is that of published reactions – and contributions – to the debate from audience members themselves, in this case considered through the prism of comments posted beneath online newspaper articles.

Analysed texts were obtained from three key sources: the LexisNexis digital database of full-text UK newspaper articles; the online Hansard record of parliamentary proceedings; and successive pages of comment posts published on newspapers' own websites. Three principal analytical approaches were used. In the case of the extensive corpus collected of print and online press articles, framing analysis was initially used to identify the range and nature of primary discursive frames used to portray inactivity/worklessness and those it affects, and to map this overall 'discursive field' (Ullrich and Keller 2014) – by assigning individual articles to categories and enumerating the overall balance of frames across the whole sample. The theoretical approach used drew on sociologist Todd Gitlin's concern with understanding the organizing 'principles of selection, emphasis and presentation' intrinsic to a text (Gitlin 1980: 6) and Robert Entman's conceptualization of frames as narrative structures that propose a particular 'definition, causal interpretation, moral evaluation and/or treatment' for an identified 'problem' (Entman 1993: 53). As politicians and media commentators have consistently portrayed Britain's current rate of inactivity – and the groups it affects – as problematic, Entman's concern with the importance of 'problem frames' seemed singularly appropriate to this task.

Following initial categorization and counting of overarching frames, critical discourse analysis (CDA) was used to unpack the historical and contextual associations – and underlying power relations – underpinning both the press representations and the much smaller sample of texts obtained from Hansard. In Hansard's case, initial high-level framing analysis was not undertaken, as the number of individual contributions was so limited – though the extensive length of many of these rendered them rich sources of discourse for CDA purposes. The CDA framework used was based on Ruth Wodak's discourse-historical approach, which extracts meaning from texts by situating and interpreting them through the lens of 'available knowledge about the historical sources and the background of the political fields in which discursive "events" are embedded' (Wodak 2001: 65).

Finally, a similar 'two-tier' approach was deployed for analysis of online comments posted by readers beneath newspaper articles. First, the samples were categorized (coded) through manual sentiment analysis, which employs a similar high-level approach to framing analysis in order to identify and enumerate the occurrence of audience sentiments. Secondly, a smaller subsample of the extensive initial corpus of comments was subjected to in-depth analysis through CDA. A more detailed explanation of the overall framework(s) and approaches to textual analysis is given in Appendix 1.

The focus of this book is on deconstructing how the twin concepts of economic inactivity and worklessness have been discursively (re)constructed in media, political and wider public debate in the years succeeding the COVID-19 pandemic – a period during which (by almost any measure) both have been consistently high. Reflecting this focus, sampling and analysis of press articles, audience comments and parliamentary interventions were clustered around ten key discursive events (Wodak 2001: 48), or extended moments, spanning the two-and-a-half-year period between December 2022 and March 2025. The selected events were all significant fiscal and/or policy interventions that acted as discursive 'pinch-points' in the (still ongoing) public conversation around Britain's inactivity 'problem'. The list of discursive events was as follows:

1. 13–19 December 2022 – the week when the UK was ranked as one of seven OECD countries to have a higher economic inactivity rate than prior to COVID-19;
2. 5–11 February 2023 – the week during which new figures were published exposing chronic labour shortages across major sectors of the UK economy;
3. 12–18 March 2023 – the week of Conservative Chancellor Jeremy Hunt's 'Back to Work Budget' announcing 'boot-camps' for older workers returning to the workplace and tax breaks to discourage people from retiring early;
4. 19–25 November 2023 – the week when Work and Pensions Secretary Mel Stride launched a 'Back to Work' scheme to implement the Budget's measures;
5. 13–19 February 2024 – the week that new data from the Office for National Statistics (ONS) revealed the extent of the impact of rising long-term sickness on inactivity rates;
6. 19–25 April 2024 – the week during which Prime Minister Rishi Sunak launched his 'moral mission' to end Britain's 'sick note culture';
7. 7–13 May 2024 – the week when new 'WorkWell' pilots were launched by the Department for Work and Pensions to road-test government 'back to work' plans amid new data showing rising rates of women on sickness-related benefits;
8. 21–27 July 2024 – the week ex-Labour Health Secretary Alan Milburn launched his 'deep-dive' 'Pathways to Work' Report focusing on inactivity in Barnsley to an audience including incoming Labour Work and Pensions Secretary Liz Kendall;
9. 24–30 November 2024 – the week when Kendall published Labour's 'Get Britain Working' white paper, focusing on boosting activity among young people;
10. 16–22 March 2025 – the week during which Kendall published Labour's 'Pathways to Work' green paper outlining £6 billion in disability benefit cuts.

Before we turn to the question of how *audiences* responded (and contributed) to elite-level media-political framing of economic inactivity, it is necessary to map the discourse(s) across our primary discursive fields: the national and regional press and deliberations in the UK Parliament. As previously mentioned, Hansard sampling generated only a small dataset of parliamentary interventions, so coding in this case was limited to in-depth qualitative analysis (CDA). By contrast, the press sample produced a final dataset of 1110 relevant articles spread over the ten discursive events. Articles were initially coded, quantitatively, into six broad categories identified during a process of immersion in the dataset:

- 'hard negative' – articles positioning inactive people as non-contributors exploiting the benefits system, often using overtly discriminatory language;
- 'soft negative' – articles portraying inactive people as non-contributors in more subtle ways and/or stopping short of more overtly stigmatizing language;
- 'neutral' – articles adopting a broadly neutral and/or descriptive approach (e.g. to report on the latest policy initiative or official data on inactivity);
- 'soft positive' – articles defending inactive people from criticism, but often in a qualified way and/or focusing on specific subgroups (e.g. unpaid carers);
- 'hard positive' – articles mounting stronger defences of inactive people, including those adopting overtly counter-discursive approaches;
- 'incidental' – articles in which economic inactivity and/or worklessness are mentioned but only in passing (e.g. in reports about overall state of economy).

As illustrated in Table 2.1, articles that could broadly be described as 'neutral' constituted by far the biggest category – amounting to more than half of the total number (562 out of 1110). Though uncontroversial on the face of it, the dominance of neutral texts in an overall discursive field can be problematic, as it indicates the prevalence of normative societal conceptions of an issue that tend to privilege elite narratives and deny or downplay those that are counter-discursive or counter-hegemonic. For example, the high occurrence of straightforward news stories that uncritically reported the latest figures from the ONS recording levels of economic inactivity acted to emphasize both taken-for-granted, normative *definitions* of inactivity and *assumptions* about its scale and importance – i.e. that the number of inactive people was rising and that this was, axiomatically, a 'problem'.

Disregarding the articles coded 'incidental' – which, numbering 259, comprised nearly a quarter of the sample – the next biggest categories were those adopting 'soft positive' and 'soft negative' framings of inactive people respectively. But while the overall number of articles *speaking up for* inactive people outnumbered those criticizing them (157 compared to 133) noticeably more pieces adopted 'hard negative' than 'hard positive' frames (15 to 11). The former included tabloid news stories and comment pieces incorporating overtly stigmatizing language such as 'scrounger' and 'shirker', as well as some that edged perilously close to hate speech (a concept to which we return later) by – for example – likening out-of-work benefit recipients to lower life forms, such as 'parasites'. Taken in sum, then, the combined tally of articles that applied either neutral or negative discursive frames in portraying economic inactivity, thereby endorsing and amplifying dominant elite problem frames, was 694 – approaching two-thirds of the overall

TABLE 2.1: Balance of high-level frames across newspaper sample.

	E1	E2	E3	E4	E5	E6	E7	E8	E9	E10	Total
Hard negative	0	0	3	1	2	2	0	3	2	2	**15**
Soft negative	0	3	7	3	13	24	5	11	29	23	**118**
Neutral	30	12	83	13	28	78	47	43	120	107	**561**
Soft positive	3	3	22	5	13	22	20	22	14	22	**146**
Hard positive	0	4	1	1	0	2	0	2	0	1	**11**
Incidental	37	32	76	20	14	3	22	23	3	29	**259**
Total	70	54	**192**	43	70	**131**	94	104	**168**	**184**	1,110

sample. In other words, the vast majority of newspaper articles adopted hegemonic representations of economically inactive people (or those *defined* as inactive – even if inaccurately – such as full-time carers): i.e. by constructing inactivity as a problem. Of these, a small but significant minority – nearly one in five (133 out of 694) – went further, by portraying inactive people in stigmatizing or even demonizing terms.

Mapping the life-cycle of the inactivity panic

While the overall bias of framing across the newspaper *field* was significant, equally important was the shifting trajectory press discourse took over *time*. As Figure 2.1 shows, the proportion of articles adopting 'neutral' framing oscillated repeatedly throughout the sample period but remained consistently high from the time of the eighth discursive event onwards. This near-year-long time-frame encompassed the heightened political climate commencing with Sunak's 'sick-note culture' speech, followed by the 2024 general election campaign and the subsequent nine-month period of policy announcements initiated by the then new Labour government. In terms of the overall sample sizes generated by each discursive event, there were consistently high levels of press attention in events 8–10 – the first three to occur on Labour's watch (amid expectations that any policy measures proposed to tackle inactivity might actually reach fruition, given its hefty Commons majority). However, there were also earlier spikes in coverage around events 3 and 6. Both of these were sparked by high-profile declarations of intent to tackle the scourge of inactivity from the preceding Tory government: Chancellor Hunt's March 2023 'Back to Work Budget' (the single biggest discursive event) and Sunak's aforementioned 'sick-note culture' speech respectively.

Of equal note was the fact that the proportion of articles adopting clearly delineated ideological positions – whether to *condemn* or to *defend* inactive people – was a consistent feature of the discourse between events 5 and 10. At times, the overall balance of framing tipped one way or the other: in event 7 (the week during which 'WorkWell' pilots were launched to get more inactive people back to work), four times as many articles adopted positive (counter-hegemonic) frames as those condemning inactive people (20 to 4), whereas in event 9 (the week of Labour's 'Get Britain Working' white paper) more than twice as many articles adopted negative as positive frames (31 to 14). In general, however, as the UK's unfolding economic inactivity debate gained ever-greater traction, the discursive positionality of newspapers increased – and polarized – to the extent that, by March 2025, almost exactly the same number of articles were portraying inactive people negatively as positively (23 to 22). This means that the point at which polarization became most marked was during the week encompassing the unveiling of the long-anticipated (and, in many quarters, long-dreaded) 'Pathways to Work' green paper. Of singular note, then, is the fact that it took until the first truly significant intervention by the Labour government – an event whose salience was heightened by its proximity to a heavily trailed (and welfare-focused) Spring Statement – for this polarized climate to crystallize. By this point, the voice(s) of journalists willing to question or criticize the relentless political problematization of inactivity had grown conspicuously louder – even if the majority of overtly condemnatory and counter-discursive articles were of the 'softer' (more compromised) variety, and pieces problematizing inactives continued to slightly outnumber those defending them.

As might be expected, the most overtly critical articles – whether castigating or defending inactive people – were largely confined to comment and op-ed pages and columns, rather than news pages (with some notable exceptions). They also primarily appeared in conservative newspapers and their accompanying websites, notably the *Daily Mail*, *MailOnline*, the *Daily Telegraph* and www.telegraph.co.uk. But while this was the case throughout the sample period, it took until the proposed introduction of tough new benefit conditions (and cuts) by Labour – the party that founded the UK's welfare state and had long been associated with relatively generous social security policies – for commentaries and editorials to become truly combative. As might be expected, the dominant right-wing press used the occasion of the green paper to pile scorn on Labour ministers for not going far enough to slash Britain's burgeoning welfare bill – with a combination of Tory grandees and tabloid controversialists lining up to condemn them. Conversely, the comparative

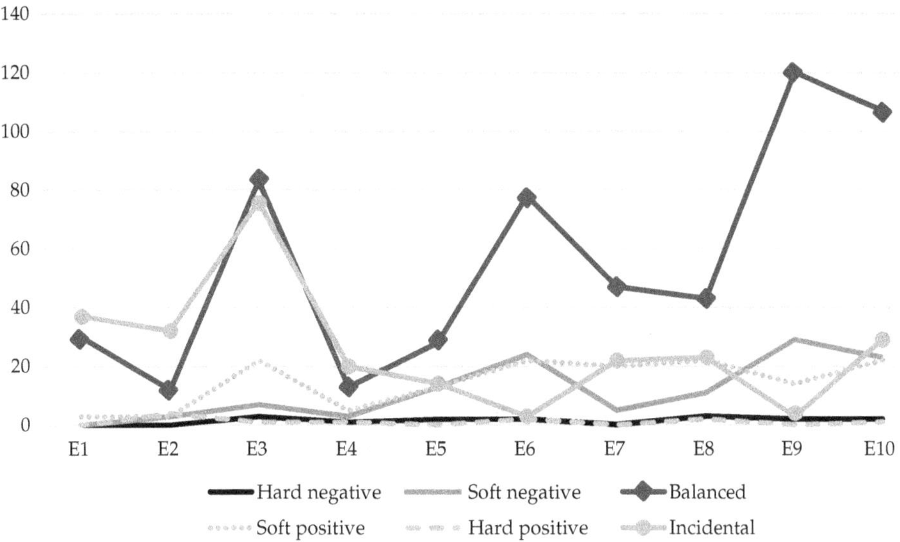

FIGURE 2.1: Trajectory of inactivity discourse over time. *Source*: Author's own.

harshness of some measures that were unveiled – notably stricter needs-based eligibility requirements for disabled people needing help with personal care – drew sharp critical barbs from commentators in liberal-Left papers (including long-time champions of the party, such as *The Guardian's* Polly Toynbee).

This, then, was the 'big picture': a slow-burn rise in heat and intensity across the (physical and virtual) pages of the UK press as the inactivity panic spiralled into its third post-pandemic year. But precisely how were *inactive people* – and inactivity itself – discursively constructed by journalists and commentators, individually and collectively? How similar or dissimilar were the negative portrayals of inactives to the 'scrounger' narratives that had been endlessly recycled and repurposed through history – most recently during the tenure of Britain's 2010–15 coalition government? On what tropes and allusions did commentators draw in shaping their representations of inactivity, and how might we discern their intertextual and interdiscursive roots? It is to these questions that we now turn.

Chronicling inactivity: 'Neutral' news coverage and normative discourse

If a single factor contributed to fuelling the escalating panic about the UK's simmering inactivity crisis, it was the creeping normalization of this narrative in the country's media and political fields. A classic example of a nominally neutral newspaper report using an unquestioning problem frame to characterize the economic inactivity issue was published on 19 December 2022 beneath the lengthy, clickbait-friendly headline 'Rise in Brits dropping out of the workforce puts UK behind only Colombia, Chile and Switzerland in global league table of economic inactivity' (Heffer 2022). The 555-word piece appeared on Britain's most visited news-site, *MailOnline*, during a week when OECD figures were published exposing the country's post-pandemic inactivity challenge.

Of note from the article's outset was its disingenuous framing of the actual scale of the 'problem'. While the headline ranked Britain fourth in an ignominious global 'league table', more detailed data relayed in the main body of the report showed it to be one of four countries whose inactivity rate had risen since COVID but one of *seven* (including Germany, Italy and Canada) that still had higher rates than before the pandemic. But, as in numerous other news stories of this kind, more mundane but important indicators of credibility were used to convey the gravity of the inactivity problem. First, the story deployed a toolkit of performative narrative devices to signify objectivity that sociologist Gaye Tuchman memorably conceptualized as a 'strategic ritual' (Tuchman 1972). Its introduction doubled down on the headline assertion that Britain had 'experienced the fourth-highest increase in economic inactivity since the start of the COVID pandemic' of the world's 'top economies' by citing 'data' – an oft-used journalistic synonym for 'hard facts'. These 'data' were subsequently attributed to the Office for National Statistics: normatively presented as an authoritative, non-partisan, expert custodian and interpreter of these facts. As in Tuchman's taxonomy, the story went on to support its factual claims with this robust quote from the ONS emphatically affirming the UK's *prima facie* inactivity problem and forcefully insinuating that it had become peculiarly acute compared to those of other countries: 'The UK is one of the few advanced economies that is still experiencing this "participation puzzle", which might be indicative of health concerns of workers having more of an impact on labour force participation in the UK' (Heffer 2022: n.pag.).

As we shall see, data and quotes from nominally neutral state authorities like the ONS – or 'respected' independent think-tanks such as the Institute for Fiscal Studies – were tactics frequently deployed by journalists as signifiers of the accuracy of their truth-claims and insulate them from charges of bias. As other researchers have argued (e.g. Berry 2016), this practice is problematic, as such bodies are institutionally inclined to perpetuate normative neoliberal conceptions of economic problems and solutions – including definitions of what counts as inactivity, what drives it, and how to reduce it.

Another typical example of a news story repeating a dominant (but largely inaccurate) framing of economic inactivity appeared on www.telegraph.co.uk during the week in February 2023 when data were published exposing the extent of post-COVID labour shortages (event 2). The story, headlined 'Lockdown "added to work crisis by making people scared to leave homes" ', focused on evidence presented by employment experts to the House of Commons Work and Pensions Committee, outlining how 'an increase in health problems including anxiety linked to COVID restrictions' was the 'biggest driver of rising joblessness'. In keeping with the *Telegraph's* well-documented criticisms of 'work-from-home' policies introduced in the pandemic, the story included a number of quotes insinuating that ministers, rather than individuals, were primarily to blame for rising health-related inactivity rates. These included a lengthy quote from Rhodri Thomas, an executive at the recruitment firm Reed Group, in which he claimed to have met 'a lot' of people 'reluctant to work in environments where they have to deal with retail customer service' and those with 'worsening mental health conditions' – due, in part, to 'the impact of the lockdowns' that left them 'concerned about going back into work' (Gutteridge 2023: n.pag.).

For all its measured, non-judgmental approach to portraying Britain's rising number of inactives, however, the story contained several misleading (but well-worn) tropes conflating issues that were, in truth, distinct or more nuanced. In a paragraph introducing Thomas's remarks, the reporter framed his focus as 'the unemployed' (people out of work but required to actively seek it in return for benefits), whereas the following passage clarified that the committee's focus was on reducing the number of *inactive* people (working-aged adults not in work and *not* seeking it). Moreover, the quotes from Thomas reproduced here contained misleading conflations, by eliding those 'reluctant' to return to 'busy work environments' – a phrase suggesting this was a matter of individual *choice*, rather than illness-related inactivity – with those experiencing 'worsening mental health conditions' caused by the isolating/antisocial effects of lockdowns.

Elsewhere, the article repeated what were rapidly becoming received truths about Britain's growing levels of inactivity – despite being, at least partly, inaccurate. In an intertextual echoing of a crude statistic often cited in ministerial speeches, opinion columns and the pages of right-wing think-tank reports, it casually stated that 'nine million' people were inactive. This blunt analysis failed to acknowledge that nearly three million of these 'inactives' were full-time students (a group that, at least prior to recent cost-of-living pressures, no-one *expected* to work) and that more than two million were 'looking after home or family' (Garlick 2022) – including the very stay-at-home mothers and housewives that formed the bedrock of the 'nuclear family' ideals *The Telegraph* and its conservative allies had hitherto persisted in championing (see, most recently, *The Telegraph* 2023;

Cates 2023). The article also included the sweeping assertion that the UK was 'the only major country to have experienced a sustained rise in joblessness since the start of COVID, fuelled by long-term illness and over-50s retiring early' – a reference to the short-lived phenomenon known as the 'Great Resignation'. Again, this normative statement belied a much more nuanced reality. While some forms of inactivity *were* taking longer to fall back to pre-pandemic levels than in other developed economies, this applied (as the Resolution Foundation and others had demonstrated) to *health-related* inactivity, not inactivity as a whole – let alone wider 'joblessness' (Corlett 2024).

While many neutral articles were guilty of repeating normative statements framing inactivity as a problem, and exaggerating its scale/rate of increase, the sheer number in this category gave rise to some intriguing subgroupings. One particular approach, adopted at times when new data was published documenting the inactivity 'problem', itemized the size of this challenge using bar charts, line graphs or other forms of infographic. At the national level, such figures were often presented as 'rogues' galleries' of the worst inactivity blackspots, while areas identified as having the highest numbers of inactive people provided their local papers with sources of easy (and somewhat lazy) news copy. Examples of local coverage of this kind appeared across several titles published by major regional newspaper groups JPI Media and Reach Plc on 13 February 2024 (during event 5). JPI's *Sunderland Echo* carried the bleak headline, 'More than one-in-four North East workers is "economically inactive"' (Clark 2024). Reach's *chroniclelive.co.uk* (website of the *Newcastle Chronicle*) bore a variant of the same: 'More than a quarter of North East workforce classed as "economically inactive"' (Whitfield 2024).

Another significant subtype was the news story that presented its readers with a handy how-to guide to navigating proposed changes to the benefits system, which tended to appear at times when the discursive focus switched towards corrective policy actions by government. But even these (largely informational) articles were not averse to recycling normative, ideologically loaded, representations infused with an underlying scrounger discourse. A notable example appeared in April 2024, during a week when then Work and Pensions Secretary Mel Stride and prime minister Sunak had unveiled details of their 'WorkWell' policies to drive down inactivity rates (event 7). The article took the form of an exhaustive 1309-word explainer on birmingmail.co.uk headlined 'Five new DWP benefit changes announced by Rishi Sunak and what they mean for you' (Bentley 2024a). Its pointed use of the second person implicitly acknowledged that many of its own readers were likely to be affected by at least some of the proposed changes. Nevertheless, in setting out its compendious coverage of measures announced by the prime minister, it fell into a trap familiar from many other nominally neutral pieces: that of echoing (and implicitly endorsing) normative truisms about the nature and extent of Britain's inactivity problem. By quoting Sunak so frequently and at such length – if only to lay out the detail of his announcement – it amplified statements that were intrinsically ideological, notably his warnings about the supposed dangers of 'over-medicalising the everyday challenges and worries of life'. But its most uncritical reproduction of Sunak's (unsubstantiated) assertions came in a passage of unabashed 'churnalism' (Davies 2008), in which it reproduced a verbatim three-paragraph-long quote from his speech. In the extract, he stated – among other dubious claims – that 'fully half' of economically inactive people '*say* [author's italics] they have depression or anxiety' (Bentley 2024a: n.pag.). His use of the hedged term 'say' was a lexical cue that nudged his (and, indirectly, the *Mail*'s and other papers') audience to question the honesty of individuals' claims to suffer from work-limiting health conditions.

Despite its (superficially) informational overall approach, then, this article repeated the normative errors of many other neutral pieces across the sample. By unquestioningly repeating Sunak's lexical cues – themselves intertextual allusions to historical imaginaries of untrustworthy benefit recipients and soaring welfare bills – it implicitly bought into the discourse that out-of-work benefits (and working-aged welfare generally) were a costly, increasingly unaffordable burden. Moreover, in itemizing a list of Tory proposals to address the latest (alleged) 'spiralling increase' in Britain's 'welfare bill', it extended the sweep of this (mis)characterization by including in this list of measures a 'tougher benefit fraud crackdown'. Once again, this was relayed through a direct quote from Sunak, this time vowing to deploy 'all the developments in modern technology, including Artificial Intelligence, to crack down on exploitation in the welfare system that's taking advantage of the hardworking taxpayers who fund it' (Bentley 2024a: n.pag.).

Moreover, the article's conflation of inactivity with fraud was problematic on several counts. By prefiguring Sunak's quote with a sentence normatively relaying his determination 'to stamp out fraud', it portrayed as axiomatic the fact that this wide-scale problem existed – as conveyed in a line describing ministers' plans to 'align DWP with HMRC so benefit fraud is treated like tax fraud with new powers to make seizures and arrests'. Yet, according to Full Fact and other respected independent sources, there is no parity between the scale of benefit and tax fraud – with falsely claimed (or over-claimed) benefits amounting to around one-fifth of the value of unpaid tax in any year (Full Fact 2024). The other problem with the framing was its matter-of-fact conflation of anti-fraud measures with the wider suite of policies for reducing levels of inactivity. Juxtaposed with repeatedly quoted insinuations from Sunak that many work-limiting health complaints were faked – or, at least, wildly exaggerated – this conflation had the discursive effect of portraying out-of-work benefit recipients not only as hypochondriacs but (in some cases at least) as out-and-out cheats.

From 'neutral' normativity to 'soft scrounger' narratives

As we have seen, balanced news reports generally bolstered hegemonic representations of inactivity through the simple act of reproducing normative problem frame(s) – often backed by high-level official data that was insufficiently digested or interrogated. By definition, this meant they also tended to adopt the form of broad-brush stories focusing on 'big-picture' portrayals and diagnoses of Britain's inactivity problem: articles that presented the issue in dry statistical terms, and disproportionately relied on formal interventions from government and other official sources, rather than the voices, experiences and human stories of inactive individuals themselves. The journalists responsible could be held culpable for reproducing dominant narratives (and their underlying discourses) for any of a number of reasons – from laziness and incuriousness to simply lacking the time and resources needed to unpack and/or humanize a complex issue amid the maelstrom of today's relentless, commercially pressurized 24/7 newsrooms (Harro-Loit and Josephi 2020). It is also highly probable that many (non-specialist, often regionally based) reporters assigned the task of chronicling the latest developments in Britain's unfolding inactivity 'crisis' were simply out of their depth: lacking knowledge of the finer details and definitions required to fully understand a subject as complex as economic inactivity, much as previous studies have identified deficiencies in the expertise of (among others) general reporters required to contribute to covering the 2007–08 global financial crash (see Schifferes and Roberts 2015).

More overtly stigmatizing (if still subtly so) were articles adopting what might best be termed 'soft' negative frames. As might be expected for pieces projecting a more explicit discursive position – e.g. portraying inactive people as drains on (rather than contributors to) the public purse – many of these took the form of op-eds authored by high-profile commentators or expressing the 'voices' of their newspapers, rather than news stories or background features written by either generalist or specialist reporters. As previously detailed, the prevalence of frames portraying inactive people in expressly critical or stigmatizing terms grew steadily across the sample – from a low of two articles in event 2 to highs of 24, 27 and 23 in events 6, 9 and 10, as the level and tenor of media and political coverage of Britain's rising inactivity rates reached fever pitch.

Early signs of what was to come were visible in a handful of articles (seven in total) that appeared during event 3 – the week of Jeremy Hunt's 'back-to-work Budget'. Perhaps fittingly, these kicked off with an editorial in the *Sun* penned by the chancellor himself. This carefully sculpted rhetorical flourish, framed stoutly around the twin problems of the 'cost-of-living crisis' and rising economic inactivity, began with a Churchillian rallying cry declaring that 'Britain has proved our doubters wrong time and time again', before going on to itemize the plethora of challenges facing 'struggling Brits' thanks to a succession of 'huge global challenges' – from 'the pandemic' to 'Putin's war' in Ukraine (Hunt 2023: 16). Hunt's use of the first-person plural 'our' was carefully crafted to project a sense of unity in the face of adversity – casting those 'struggling Brits' and 'families...cutting back to make ends meet' as its virtuous in-group while pointedly excluding from its embrace those failing to pull their weight and contribute to the country's economic recovery. Given the government's plummeting poll ratings at the time, there was a strong political emphasis on measures successive Conservative governments had introduced to protect the country's strivers – including 'a decade of reforms' to the tax system allowing 'Brits' to 'earn £1,000 a month without paying a penny in income tax and National Insurance' and pledges to 'step in' to help the 'millions of people who are boxed out of work', through a mix of increased childcare support; protected entitlements allowing disabled people to enter 'work' without 'fear of losing those benefits'; and 'returnships' to coax back to the workplace those who 'had previous careers' (Hunt 2023: 16). But all this was juxtaposed with a stark warning to 'those on benefits who can work' but 'refuse to' that 'we are going to toughen up our enforcement of sanctions'. Of still greater significance was a notable symbolic annihilation throughout the article: the omission of any acknowledgement whatsoever that some people of working age were genuinely *unable* to work. On the contrary, the 'fix' for Britain's inactivity problem was put down solely to a need to 'break down barriers', implying that the only issues stopping anyone from putting in an honest day's graft were external obstacles that a few judicious policy tweaks could remove.

Elsewhere, Hunt's piece repeated a number of widely accepted (but misleading) tropes. There was a typical retread of a mantra beloved of British politicians of Left and Right: deification of the dignity of labour. Work wasn't 'just about paying the bills', sermonized the public school-educated multimillionaire with one of the biggest personal fortunes in British politics (Sommerlad and Gregory 2023). Rather, 'when you are in the right job, work is a point of pride, friends and purpose'. More disingenuous was the chancellor's sweeping claim that 'what holds us back' is the fact that 'nearly nine million people are economically inactive' – an inflated figure again belying the inconvenient reality that at least a third of these were full-time students (Hunt 2023: 16).

The piece also exposed one of the biggest myths of inactivity discourse – by juxtaposing the bogus nine million figure with an assertion that, by getting these people back to work, 'we can also fill the 1.1 million vacancies in this country, rather than importing workers from abroad'. Hunt's suggestion that there were nine million working-aged adults either choosing not to work or blocked from doing so only by easily removed external barriers (not disability, long-term illness or long waits for NHS treatment) was one thing. But the admission – in almost his next breath – that jobs only actually existed for *one in nine* of these people was illustrative of a nonsensical, contradictory thread that would continue to run through successive ministerial pronouncements on inactivity, including under the ensuing Labour government. A further inconvenient fact absent from his call to arms was any reference to the specific nature of the workforce vacancies to which he referred. Many of these (as widely reported elsewhere – including by no less a bastion of normative neoliberal thinking than the International Monetary Fund/IMF) were in sectors of the economy that had struggled to fill specialist roles since an exodus of skilled migrants following the UK's withdrawal from the European Union (Deb and Li 2024).

Of the remaining 'soft negative' articles published during budget week, most took the form of appreciative commentaries welcoming the chancellor's inactivity crackdown. In the mid-market tabloid the *Express*, redoubtable conservative columnist Leo McKinstry despaired of the 'huge drain on the welfare system' caused by rising inactivity. McKinstry mobilized an even more bafflingly inconsistent set of figures, by decrying the 'prodigious waste of human talent' represented by 'no fewer than seven million people of working age' who were inactive – '5.3 million of them on benefits' (a tacit admission, perhaps, that this was not an option for the several million full-time students in their ranks) (McKinstry 2023: 12–13). While qualifying his criticisms of inactives with praise for proposals to expand free childcare and abolish Work Capability Assessments for disabled people, he followed this with a regurgitation of Hunt's image of people 'who can work but refuse to do so', and a lengthy, trope-riddled broadside against 'benefits dependency' and 'welfare' as an 'easy choice' (McKinstry 2023: 12–13). This called back, interdiscursively, to playbooks of the past – notably the 'scroungerphobia' (Deacon 1978) and 'shirkerphobia' (Morrison 2019) panics of the late 1970s and early 2010s respectively.

By April 2024, with a general election looming, media representations of inactivity had begun to noticeably harden, resulting in a spike in the number of negatively framed articles around the time of Sunak's widely publicized 'sick-note culture' speech (event 6) – more than doubling the tally for event 5. Of the 24 'soft negative' articles to appear during event 6, several were opinion pieces vocally praising the PM's diagnosis. Writing on red-top news-site www.thesun.co.uk, Ross Clark, a long-time associate of right-wing think-tank Policy Exchange, lamented a 'change in attitude toward work' since COVID, which had 'made some more inclined to seek excuses not to do it' (Clark 2024: n.pag.). In an extraordinary feat of rhetorical gymnastics, he encompassed a litany of libertarian shibboleths in the causes he held responsible for 'medicalising the ordinary challenges of life' (terms directly echoing Sunak, Stride, Blair and others). These ranged from the folly of 'months of lockdown' to normalizing work-from-home employment practices – blamed here on (among others) 'civil service unions threatening to strike because they have been asked to go into the office just two days a week' (Clark 2024: n.pag.). Taking full advantage of the multimodal affordances of online publication, Clark's words were visually framed by an extended video extract of Sunak's 'sick-note culture' speech and a (presumably posed) photograph of a man in pyjamas sitting at the end of his bed, head in hands.

Though, at first sight, this image might have appeared to signify sympathy with people suffering from such severe mental ill health that they were incapable of work, this impression was somewhat undermined by the dismissive accompanying caption, which read: 'PM Rishi Sunak has blasted a culture of sick notes and has urged Brits to get back to work'. Elsewhere in the conservative press, Sunak's speech received a similarly warm welcome, with an opinion piece on (lockdown-sceptic) news-site www.telegraph.co.uk once more conflating Britain's inactivity problem with the rise of WFH culture by remarking on the 'irony' of the 'Prime Minister making a speech on worklessness on a Friday when swathes of Whitehall are empty due to the rise in home-working'. Invoking what would become a recurring trope in coverage of the inactivity debate in ensuing months, it added that, while it was 'clearly right' that those who 'genuinely need it' received support, the 'safety net must not become a hammock' (*The Telegraph* 2024a).

By the point when this debate had begun maturing into a full-blown moral panic (event 9 – the week of Liz Kendall's November 2024 'Get Britain Working' white paper), nearly a quarter of all articles (27 out of 112) were adopting 'soft negative' frames. Among the standout commentaries was a leader column on the website of centre-Right quality title *The Times*, whose headline emphasized the 'mountain to climb' for a newly elected Labour government that had been 'talking a good game on tackling Britain's spiralling welfare bill' (*The Times* 2024b). Although notably more sober and measured in tone than fellow conservative titles such as the *Telegraph* and *Mail*, this went on to ventriloquize a divide-and-rule trope familiar through years of repetition by right-leaning politicians and papers, by pitting the 'workless' against the 'working poor' - here imagined, in a nod to then-ongoing debates about the struggles of 'left behind' post-industrial communities, as 'working classes' (see Morrison 2022):

> Yet many people, many of them working class, feel a sense of division from swelling numbers of sickness benefit claimants. They ask, with good reason, why they must work hard simply for their living standards to stand still while more and more of

> their taxes are taken up subsidising a relentlessly expanding cohort of working-age but economically inactive people.
>
> (*The Times* 2024b: n.pag.)

Besides invoking this discourse of 'division' (explicitly using this word – an unusual gesture), the passage was notable for once more uncritically amplifying the repeated claims of ministers, commentators and economists – particularly those on the political Right – that Britain was in the grip of an unprecedented inactivity spiral, here symbolized by the image of a 'relentlessly expanding cohort' of inactive people 'of working-age' (*The Times* 2024b).

A day later, similar images were deployed in a *Telegraph* editorial, which condemned ministers for failing to grasp the 'gargantuan task' of curbing Britain's 'unsustainable welfare bill' (*The Telegraph* 2024b). This deeply misleading (if oft-repeated) claim failed to acknowledge the fact that (according to the European Commission) in 2023 the UK spent less on social protection than all but three other European countries (Ireland, Malta and Iceland) and less than half as much as the highest-spending countries (Finland, Austria and Italy), when measured as a proportion of its GDP (10.9% compared to 25.7, 21.4 and 21.1% respectively). As for sickness and disability benefits – the main focus of its concern with what it variously labelled Britain's 'disease' or 'malady' of 'worklessness' – their unsustainability was wildly exaggerated, given that the same data showed they amounted to no more than 3.2 per cent of GDP. However many people might be receiving benefits at a given moment, the levels of payment received by *individual* claimants and households were much less generous than in other countries (Hagopian and Maddox 2025).

The editorial also contained a string of other hysterical claims, including the description of rising inactivity as a 'tide' (a form of water metaphor often used in moral panic discourses around benefit recipients, migrants and other supposedly deviant groups – Mujagić 2018; Taylor 2022). It asserted that 'Britain will soon have almost as many people on long-term sickness benefits as Panama does citizens' – imposing 'a crushing burden on the state and a terrible waste of human potential' (*The Telegraph* 2024b: n.pag.). This was also one of many articles (and numerous political interventions) to assert that 'the story since the pandemic has been one of rising economic inactivity' – a claim that, though widely accepted, the Resolution Foundation and others had by then largely debunked, while accepting that the number of people inactive for *health-related* reasons had indeed risen (Corlett 2024). To top off all the hysteria, the article bore the richly intertextual headline 'Labour isn't working' – another allusion to the political 'attack ad' of the same name which had contributed to the downfall of James Callaghan's late 1970s Labour government (and the rise of Thatcherism) amid rising unemployment and the wave of industrial disputes that characterized the 1978–79 'winter of discontent'.

While 'soft scrounger' frames often appeared in overtly opinionated articles, as the inactivity panic ground on, they cut through more frequently to news stories, features and other types of nominally objective output. A classic example of a *news* story incorporating strong inferences conflating inactivity (and unemployment) with idleness appeared in the conservative-leaning *Times* in event 2. This front-page splash was headlined 'Learn work skills or face benefits cut, jobless told'. It opened with the following misleading intro: 'Benefit claimants will be required to spend a fortnight on an intensive programme designed to get them back into work or risk losing universal credit payments under government plans to reduce unemployment' (Swinford 2023: 1–2).

This opening sentence was inaccurate on two fronts. First, it conflated 'benefit claimants' with unemployed people. This was a wholly misleading association, given that more than 35 per cent of recipients of the main working-aged benefit, Universal Credit, were employed (Department for Work and Pensions 2025d). But it also contained a secondary inaccurate conflation, by (as in numerous other articles) eliding unemployment with inactivity. Whether the journalist was unaware of this important distinction or knowingly conflated the two conditions – lumping together everyone defined as 'jobless' as similarly dependent non-contributors – was unclear. However, while his report adhered to many structural and stylistic norms of journalistic objectivity (inverted pyramid structure, supporting quotes, contextual background outlining the scale of Britain's post-COVID inactivity challenge), it did contain telltale lexical choices that had the effect of framing worklessness as a personal choice. After briefly outlining the 'carrot' part of the government's back-to-work strategy – its offer of a two-week intensive programme of 'daily face-to-face appointments' to 'help' long-term workless people to 'return to work' – it went on to emphasize the proposed 'stick' for those who 'repeatedly refuse to attend meetings' (Swinford 2023: 1–2). The phrase 'repeatedly refuse' called back intertextually to numerous ministerial speeches and opinion columns over recent decades, framing *non*-engagement with the workplace as active *dis*engagement: a 'refusal' to make efforts to find work and contribute, and (through the disingenuous conflation of 'jobless' people with benefit recipients as a whole) to lift oneself off the taxpayer-funded welfare state.

Leading the charge for 'soft negative' news stories in event 6, meanwhile, was an excitedly written *MailOnline* report piggybacking on Sunak's imaginary of 'sick-note culture' to castigate 'online firms selling same-day sick-notes for as little as £25' that (allegedly) allowed 'customers' to be 'signed off work by UK-regulated medics' (presumably moonlighting GPs) (Stearn 2024). As ever in such stories, sources quoted – either as originators of or responders to truth-claims – were heavily biased towards go-to welfare-sceptics and/or fiscal conservatives. They included Jonathan Eida, from the right-wing campaign group the Taxpayers'

Alliance – who blithely described the task of 'getting signed off sick' as 'little more than a box-ticking exercise for many' – and 'labour market expert' Professor Len Shackleton, from the Thatcherite think-tank the Institute of Economic Affairs. As usual, no quotes were included from anyone representing the voice(s) of people inactive for health-related reasons themselves, such as disability charities. The only minor corrective to the story's one-sided framing was its inclusion of a short quote (in the last of its 22 paragraphs) from the ex-president of the Royal College of General Practitioners. But far from contesting the idea that many or most sickness benefit recipients were faking illness, they merely defended GPs for failing to notice such scams, by arguing that they 'simply may not have time to see every person who is off sick'.

Perhaps the clearest measure of the creeping pervasiveness of 'soft negative' discursive frames – ones at least *insinuating* that many inactive people were scroungers – was their increasing appearance, over time, not only in more obvious places (the pages of avowedly right-wing nationals) but in local and regional papers. A case in point was a lengthy 848-word story on the website of the *Birmingham Mail*, angled around criticisms of the Labour government's 'Get Britain Working' white paper from the Centre for Social Justice (CSJ) – the right-wing think-tank set up by former Tory Work and Pensions Secretary Iain Duncan Smith that, barely six months earlier, had provided the launch pad for Sunak's 'sick-note culture' speech. In one sense, the report – its headline directly quoting the CSJ's charge that Labour's plan 'fails to tackle soaring claims for DWP disability benefits' (Bentley 2024b) – did strive to balance its coverage, by including quotes from the target of these criticisms (ministers) by way of a right of reply. However, as a supposedly impartial or objective account of the true picture of inactivity, the story fell well short. Not only did it privilege a diagnosis of the scale of Britain's supposed inactivity crisis put forward by a highly partisan small-state think-tank, but even the 'counterweight' it presented (actions being taken by then Work and Pensions Secretary Kendall) shared with the CSJ a normative representation of levels of inactivity as being unacceptable. This was especially true of the problem group that was the main target of Kendall's 'crackdown': NEETS (young adults not in employment, education or training). While the CSJ dismissed her initiative as 'slow or insufficiently ambitious', she was (we were told) determined to 'not allow' youngsters to 'not to be in education, employment or training' (Bentley 2024b).

Speaking up for the inactives: The emergence of counter-discourse

Not all newspaper coverage accepted the dominant portrayal of Britain's inactivity issue – i.e. as a growing problem steadily escalating towards crisis. Although the overarching discursive trajectory was towards this increasingly dominant hegemonic narrative, from event 3 onwards (and especially after event 7) the doubling down of normative problem/crisis frames and the creeping emergence of overtly negative depictions of inactive people was partially countered – and occasionally eclipsed – by articles *rejecting* these despairing portraits, and the language of blame and stigma accompanying them.

Perhaps the earliest point in the discursive arc at which 'soft positive' (and occasionally outright counter-hegemonic) articles encountered a spike was during event 3: the week of the 'back-to-work Budget'. An example of the reflexive way in which the substance of Hunt's statement was presented in some papers appeared in a lengthy explainer article in the liberal-Left *Independent*, which began with the following line:

> Welfare reforms promising to help people into work without the worry of losing their benefits have been welcomed but the Government has been warned it must win back trust from disabled people who have faced "cruel sanctions" in the past.
>
> (Fox 2023: n.pag.)

This introduction was notable on several counts. First was its stark emphasis on the central role 'welfare reforms' would play in the strategy outlined in the Budget – a term likely to have carried familiar associations for many readers after its mobilization as a euphemism for benefit cuts and sanctions by successive governments, from New Labour through the Coalition to those of Boris Johnson and, latterly, Sunak. That *these* welfare reforms were set to involve 'helping' people into work 'without the worry of losing their benefits' offered an intriguing counterpoint to previous initiatives – an interdiscursive call-back that was further emphasized by the accompanying warning (from unattributed sources) that ministers 'must win back trust from disabled people'. Most striking of all, though, was the decision to include in this opening line a direct quote (again, as yet unsourced) reminding readers of 'cruel sanctions' imposed on inactive people in the past.

By the time 'soft positive' portrayals had become more firmly established – around the release of Alan Milburn's July 2024 'Pathways to Work' report (event 8) – these early strands of sympathy towards historically hard-done-by inactives, especially people unable to work owing to disability or chronic health conditions, had noticeably strengthened.

An interesting variant of 'soft positive' articles during this snapshot period could be found in pieces focusing on specific subgroupings perceived as relatively more virtuous (or less deserving of opprobrium) than inactives *generally* – and therefore meriting coaxing, rather than coercing, back to work. Chief among these subgroups were the middle-aged and older workers who had been spurred to opt out of the labour market early since the late stages of the pandemic – a phenomenon that had (periodically) been reported as the 'Great Resignation' or 'Great Retirement'. A key measure outlined in Chancellor Hunt's budget with this group in mind was his announcement of a new tax break allowing employees to save more for their retirements without being penalized, while those in need of upskilling or reskilling to help fill gaps in particular sectors of the economy would be welcomed back with 'mid-life MOTs' and 'returnships' (late-career apprenticeships). These and other initiatives were greeted in overwhelmingly positive terms across the right-wing press, with an editorial in the Scottish edition of the *Express* framing them as moves to recognize older workers' 'unique talents' and enable them to 'boost their incomes and help companies and public services thrive' – a phrase channelling normative neoliberal conceptions of work as self-evidently financially rewarding, both to individuals and UK Plc (*Scottish Express* 2023: 12). There was also some sympathy for 'the mix of sticks and carrots for benefit claimants' (Smith 2023: 37), with *Sunday Times* economics editor David Smith praising Hunt for offering up-front, rather than 'in arrears', support with childcare costs to entice parents back to work (a break with more conventional Tory measures, such as the benefit cuts used to strong-arm single mothers into employment during the maternal panic of the 1990s).

A robust and colourful defence of the predicament of older workers 'lost' to the workplace since COVID was offered by *MailOnline* columnist Maggie Pagano, during the week of Milburn's report. Though she began by outlining figures documenting the scale of Britain's 'missing workers' crisis – 1.7 million inactives out of work for health-related reasons who would largely 'love to work' – Pagano's commentary was less a hand-wringing lament to their departure than a rallying cry for ministers to unfurl the red carpet to usher them back, in recognition of their (assumed) experience and wisdom. In a playful pop cultural reference, she invoked the fictional example of Ben Whitaker, the septuagenarian intern played by Robert De Niro in the film of the same name, to despair of what was fast becoming a favourite shibboleth of right-wing commentators: creeping ageism and disrespect for older workers. To Pagano's eyes, the loss of employees in their 50s and 60s was less to do with widescale flight for the hills in middle age, as more people decided life was too short to spend it toiling at the coalface, and more a reflection of blinkered workplace cultures in which managers increasingly overlooked older workers' expertise and institutional knowledge in preference for younger, cheaper, more malleable raw recruits. 'What's ironic', she lamented, in a swipe at 'woke culture' that became a recurrent feature of comments posted below online articles by people self-identifying as elective inactives (as we see in Chapter 5), 'is that in an age when everyone is obsessed about diversity, age diversity hardly gets a look-in' (Pagano 2024: n.pag.).

But perhaps the most significant intervention came from 'Pathways to Work' report author Milburn, in a richly intertextual op-ed heralding his findings in the quality newspaper *The Times*. Befitting the patrician-like authority with which he launched the report in Barnsley, clutching it to his breast like a tablet of stone, the article was topped by a headmasterly picture byline depicting the erstwhile health secretary and 'social mobility tsar' in studious black-rimmed spectacles, staring prophetically at the reader. Milburn's choice of platform was symbolic, given that the Rupert Murdoch-owned *Times* had long acted as a barometer for the dominant direction of political travel – its recent history being a twisty tale of oscillating loyalties between Labour and Conservatives, notably at times when (as at the July 2024 election) the tide decisively turned from one to the other. The article's scope was expansive. It invoked baleful images of the 'tide' of anti-immigrant 'populism', in an interdiscursive allusion to everything from the Brexit referendum and ongoing rise of Reform UK to wider currents rippling across Europe, America and beyond (Milburn 2024b). It also called back to the infamous 2007 Labour conference speech in which Milburn's former colleague, Gordon Brown, had himself flirted with populist language by pledging to preserve 'British jobs for British workers' (Parkinson 2007) – by urging 'policymakers and employers' to 'wean themselves off the easy solution of importing more workers from overseas', by 'getting more out-of-work Brits into work' (Milburn 2024b: n.pag.).

Yet amid the predictable flurry of figures from his report and alarmist warnings that the 'growing number of people' not seeking a job made up 'more than one in five working-age people', Milburn strained to articulate a more compassionate tone towards this new iteration of workless Britons than had been the custom under other recent governments (including his own). In truth, he argued – invoking the spectre of stigmatizing discourses portraying inactive people as work-shy – 'many more' of the country's 'pool of unused talent…want to work' than 'has often been assumed'. His closing peroration was also hopeful, portraying the twin tasks of addressing the 'enormous challenge' of 'moving people out of being inactive into employment' and countering anti-immigrant extremism as a win-win opportunity: 'the biggest opportunity both to grow the British economy and deal with the most toxic issue in British politics' (Milburn 2024b: n.pag.).

While the dominant discourse positioned inactive people as a problem, then, it was contested, as time passed, by a steadily building strain of empathy and understanding. But even though the above examples were illustrative of *comparatively* sympathetic characterizations, what marked them out as 'soft' rather than 'hard positive' correctives was the fact that they qualified their positions by singling out for sympathy *particular types* of inactive people – not those outside the labour market *in general*. In other words, far from being counter-hegemonic per se, such articles tended to be as divisive (in their way) as those that openly stigmatized inactive people. Their divisiveness lay not in any explicit castigation of workless people but in the implicit distinctions made between more and less deserving forms of inactivity. While parents struggling to find flexible, affordable childcare and (some) disabled people were cast as relatively deserving (at least in some quarters), the only subgroup treated with unqualified empathy was the older cohort who had been put out to pasture prematurely or had opted for early retirement – and who (in many cases) had no financial need or were too wealthy to claim benefits. In other words, the paradoxical effect of this discourse of deservingness was to award the status of *most* deserving to a group of people who – in the truest sense – had made the conscious 'lifestyle choice' to quit the workplace. Ironically, this is precisely the same accusation that has so often been levelled critically by politicians and the media at unemployed and disabled benefit recipients in narratives demonizing scroungers and shirkers.

Hardening battle lines? From soft-ball barbs to the return of scroungerphobia

As the above sections illustrate, subtle but significant divergences in the framing of inactives began to emerge from early on in the life-cycle of Britain's inactivity panic. The dominant discourse was one that portrayed inactivity as a major social problem – if not a crisis – and, as time wore on, more columnists and 'neutral' reporters directed barbs at inactives themselves, particularly those claiming out-of-work benefits. However, while only a small minority of articles ever adopted 'hard negative' frames, there were slight but noticeable upticks in their number during two key stages in the narrative cycle. These were the periods commencing with the launch of an explicit Tory mission to get inactive Britons 'back to work', using the stick of benefit sanctions if necessary (a phase starting with then-Chancellor Hunt's self-styled 'back-to-work Budget'), and the declaration of Labour's 'moral' crusade to tackle inactivity – ostensibly motivated by a its desire to support people keen to work but currently locked out of the labour market (a quest initiated by the 'Pathways to Work' report). In other words, the hardening of positions grew particularly noticeable during phases when the rhetorics of incumbent governments around the supposed crisis of inactivity themselves hardened. This suggests that commentators felt emboldened to give fuller voice to their prejudices and preconceptions about inactive people at times when counter-hegemonic voices (especially in the political realm) were less audible, with fewer actors willing to speak up for disabled people or unpaid carers, let alone inactives in general.

An early foretaste of 'hard negative' frames to come appeared in a lengthy *Business Telegraph* explainer/comment piece published during event 5 – a week in February 2024 when the Office for National Statistics published alarming new figures emphasizing the full scale of sickness-related inactivity and broke down the most heavily affected age groups. In the article, Jeremy Warner, a stalwart of scrounger-bashing columns stretching back a number of years, demanded a more vigorous carrot-and-stick approach to tackling Britain's burgeoning 'welfare budget' (Warner 2024). His opening salvo was delivered with an intertextual nod to the foundation document for the welfare state, the Beveridge Report. This near-sacred text had long been used as a discursive battleground by both Left and Right, with the former emphasizing its championing of the principle of cradle-to-grave social protection, and the latter appropriating its emphasis on the principle that people should put into the system (not just take out of it) to weaponize it as a manifesto for contributory, conditional approaches to welfare. As Warner (2024: n.pag.) put it:

> In establishing the welfare state after the war, Sir William Beveridge sought to banish what he called the five "giant evils" - want, disease, ignorance, squalor and idleness. Much progress has been made on the first four, but it seems the fifth is making a welfare dependent comeback.

In conflating 'welfare dependency' with 'idleness' – a term primarily intended to address the scourge of involuntary unemployment, not wilful worklessness – Warner channelled the ghosts of a long line of moral missionaries who had invoked this age-old shibboleth, from Keith Joseph, doyen of the New Right, via Labour's Frank Field to latter-day Tory Iain Duncan Smith. 'This may sound harsh' but 'there is also a certain eloquence to the pincer grip on worklessness' combining carrots with sticks, he added, before mounting a full-throated defence of ex-Chancellor George Osborne (co-architect, with IDS, of the Coalition's 'shirkerphobia' panic): a man unfairly 'lacerated' for 'cruel austerity' on taking 'the axe to working-age benefits', despite the fact that 'popular opinion was behind him'. The best remedy for the problem of 'workshy Britain', Warner concluded normatively, was to remove 'incentives not to work' and make 'living on welfare less of a choice'. Here was another interdiscursive homage, this time to the 'lifestyle choice' trope beloved of politicians past and present – not least Osborne himself (Warner 2024).

Elsewhere, 'hard negative' perspectives were most often vocalized by well-known tabloid controversialists, from the *Sun's* Rod Liddle to *MailOnline's* Richard Littlejohn. Never afraid to 'say the unsayable', Littlejohn greeted the news of escalating numbers of young adults claiming sickness benefits (event 5) with a lengthy rant decrying Britain's 'generation of workshy millennial snowflakes, too frightened to leave the security of their bedrooms'. Adopting a knowingly mocking tone to lampoon one of the main health concerns to emerge from the pandemic, he ridiculed the '200,000 18-to-24-year-olds' who 'claim to be too ill to work' due to '"mental health ishoos"' (Littlejohn 2024). Meanwhile, Leo McKinstry's ire on *MailOnline* spotlighted not one but two of his long-time hobbyhorses: the supposed menace of benefit fraud and the 'crippling burden' of non-contributing welfare recipients on that most virtuous of contributors, 'the taxpayer'. Reflecting on the cost of the benefits bill during event 8 (the week of the Milburn report), McKinstry referred to it by the hysterical term 'leviathan' – recycling a £266 million figure oft repeated in his paper to quantify the supposed monthly rise in the cost of disability benefits. Nowhere was there mention that this was the *total* monthly cost of sickness and disability-related benefits – not that of the rise itself – nor the fact that this included Personal Independence Payments (PIP) paid to those *in* work as well as those classed as inactive.

But perhaps the most overtly stigmatizing article of all appeared in the guise not of an honestly labelled op-ed or comment but a nominally objective piece of reportage published on www.telegraph.co.uk during event 10: the week of Kendall's controversial 'Pathways to Work' green paper. This 2479-word colour feature bore all the Orientalizing hallmarks of a piece of Victorian-style social exploration, as two intrepid London-based journalists ventured into the post-industrial wasteland of East Marsh, 'on the edge of Grimsby' – an odious netherworld where 'pavements crunch underfoot with broken glass and the boarded houses and peeling facades stand as testimony to an area blighted by crime, unemployment and deprivation' (Woods and Eijsberg 2025: n.pag.). In this scornful latter-day iteration of William Booth's *In Darkest England* (Booth 2014), the *Telegraph's* overwhelmingly ABC1 readership were introduced to a picaresque array of denizens ranging from 'ex-rocker' Alfred Eckersley, caricatured as 'a jaunty, twinkling character despite his fearsome braided beard', and a woman who had moved to the area to be closer to her terminally ill niece ('a mother of seven'), and was appalled to find 'people living around here who have never done a day's work in their lives – and neither have their kids'. Throughout the article – vividly headlined '"They get benefits for doing nothing": The town that sums up Britain's youth worklessness crisis' – distinct categories (the unemployed, NEETs and other workless groups) were repeatedly conflated. Never mind finer distinctions: all were used as interchangeable terms for an underclass of morally deviant, borderline feral, ne'er-do-wells, in the grand tradition of scrounger discourse.

Though reasonably rare, out-and-out stigmatizing pieces of this kind also occurred periodically at earlier stages in the life cycle of the inactivity panic. Another example was a 1643-word background feature published during the week of then-PM Sunak's 'sick-note culture' speech on *MailOnline*. It opened with this no-holds-barred introduction that read like an unabashed throwback to the most extreme examples of scroungerphobia: 'Benefits scroungers in a seaside town described as one of the "most-deprived" in Britain have boasted how they don't want a job because they can "chill out" and "enjoy life" while not having to work' (Crowson and Christie 2024: n.pag.).

The most overtly stigmatizing signifier was the journalists' decision to begin by explicitly using the term 'benefits scroungers', but the introduction was also notable for its repeated use of inverted commas – pointed punctuation marks that acted as cynical winks to the reader apparently signifying doubt and disdain. Inverted commas around the term 'most-deprived' appeared to signal disapproval of the official status 'a recent survey' had accorded the town – Jaywick in Essex – as if to ridicule the suggestion that we should feel sorry for residents who (as one local admitted) had 'no desire to work' and were 'happy' living on benefits. As in the *Telegraph* article, the feature introduced readers to a colourful cast of reprobates, including one who was quoted as saying he did not 'feel' he could 'work at the moment', as he was too busy being left alone to 'chill out and look at the sea' (Crowson and Christie 2024).

But the feature's ambit did not stop with Jaywick. It also took readers on a voyeuristic road-trip that stopped off in Gainsborough in Lincolnshire and Grangetown near Middlesbrough, adopting an othering lens redolent of the 'circus freak-show' (Morrison 2019: 36) portrayals associated with 'poverty porn' television shows such as Channel 4's *Benefits Street*. Its framing was amplified by a gallery of 21 images, presented as a slideshow, which had clearly been carefully chosen to emphasize the run-down, decrepit nature of 'deprived areas' like these, where there was (to quote one pensioner) 'nothing to do'. The images included various pictures of derelict industrial buildings and boarded-up shops, and a shot of a bare-chested man chatting to a woman in a mobility scooter above the stigmatizing caption: 'The unemployed in Jaywick, Essex are claiming "thousands of pounds" a month of taxpayer's cash – while locals complain there are jobs, people just don't want them'.

Besides its mocking language, the article was notable (like others) for containing a number of significant untruths. Most importantly, it repeatedly conflated unemployment (the specified status of most of those it quoted) with economic inactivity, including in the following brazen, clickbait-friendly headline claim:

> 'Why would I want a job?' Shameless benefit scroungers in a seaside town boast they 'chill out and enjoy life' while claiming 'thousands a month' of YOUR cash as 10m go unemployed and 4,000 a day sign off sick in workshy Britain.
>
> (Crowson and Christie 2024)

The heavily rounded-up figure of 10 million used to denote the scale of UK unemployment was wholly misleading, given that it actually referred to the 9.4 million people classed as economically inactive – not those who were out of work and seeking it (the unemployed). Moreover, even this figure was grossly inflated, given that around a third of that number were students in full-time education – and not expected to be working or job seeking. The article also stoked division, by pitting deserving against undeserving residents, and doing so intergenerationally – quoting 'retired locals' who had 'blasted the "work shy attitude" of the unemployed'. This pointed binary between contributors and non-contributors – takers and givers – was also emphasized through the headline's use of the collective second person, to distinguish between the 'shameless benefit scroungers' (takers) and dutiful tax-payers (givers). The latter in-group was elided with the paper's own (virtuous) readers through the use of the capitalized phrase 'YOUR cash' (Crowson and Christie 2024). In adopting this discourse of division, the article tapped in, intertextually, to a growing public debate about perceived inequalities disadvantaging younger generations in comparison to their parents and grandparents – and the relative merits of investing in housing, education, social security, jobs and training for (questionably deserving) working-aged adults versus funding pensions and social care for the (manifestly deserving) elderly.

While stigmatizing frames became more overt at particular points in the life cycle of the inactivity panic, it would be wrong to suggest they did not meet their match in a similar doubling down by journalists on the other side of the debate. As with 'hard negative' frames, those adopting a 'hard positive' (or outspokenly counter-hegemonic) position were limited to small handfuls during most discursive events. Nevertheless, there was one small but significant spike, around event 6. Chief among these was an editorial in *The Guardian*, laden with statistics from reputable sources, including social inequality think-tank the Joseph Rowntree Foundation. While the paper acknowledged that having 2.8 million working-aged people economically inactive for health reasons (the correct figure) was 'not good or sustainable', it nonetheless disputed the entire premise of Sunak's 'moral mission', by framing its argument with a headline declaring 'there is no sick note culture'. Instead, it argued, growing NHS waiting lists and rising poverty – 'much of it caused by benefit cuts and sanctions' – were to blame for a genuine 'decline in the population's wellbeing' (*The Guardian* 2024a: n.pag.).

There were also one or two notable examples of 'hard positive' frames being projected in straight news articles, including in the regional press. One story published in the *Birmingham Mail* on 19 April 2024 focused on condemnation of the 'demonising' language in Sunak's 'sick-note culture' speech from disability charities and academics (Rodger 2024). An implicit bias of this piece was evident in the absence of a right of reply for Downing Street or the Department for Work and Pensions (the targets of multiple critics it quoted).

As time wore on, then, the coverage of news stories about Britain's inactivity 'problem', and the interpretive lens through which these developments were framed, digested and commented upon, became significantly more polarized across the legacy press. While right-wing papers doubled down on their already stigmatizing, at times despairing, portrayals, those on the liberal-Left increasingly responded in kind. But how was the evolving inactivity crisis represented and responded to in the wider public sphere?

Into the lion's den? Deliberating inactivity in Parliament

As noted previously, debates about economic inactivity in Parliament generated a relatively modest sample of individual interventions – for all the media sound and fury that greeted key political events, such as Hunt's 'back-to-work Budget', Sunak's 'sick-note culture' speech, and Labour's subsequent legislative proposals. While some parliamentary interventions were openly critical of people classed as inactive, on the whole these were exceptional. By contrast, MPs and peers speaking in open debate were generally more circumspect, with most adopting a broadly sympathetic tone towards the economically inactive – even if this attitude was sometimes compromised by rather patronizing suggestions for how to solve their predicaments. There was, though, a widespread consensus across all major political parties about one thing: the normative diagnosis that Britain was experiencing a major, perhaps unprecedented, problem of rising inactivity, even if it was unwise or unfair to 'blame' specific individuals (or types of individual) for *being* inactive.

In common with the newspaper sample, there were notable examples of parliamentarians raising concerns about the struggles and inequities experienced by specific (deserving) inactive groups. One such illustration surfaced in an exchange during event 2 (a week in which new ONS figures demonstrated the extent of labour shortages in the economy) between then Conservative Chief Secretary to the Treasury John Glen and one of his own backbenchers, Chloe Smith. In his remarks, Glen made the normative (but misleading and largely inaccurate) claim that 'labour shortages in the economy' were 'due, in part' to rising 'working-age inactivity' – an assertion widely disputed in economic analyses (including the IMF's) that consistently demonstrated a disconnect between the skills of inactive people and the nature of job vacancies available. While Smith applauded Glen's emphasis on 'the urgent issue' of inactivity, she countered by asking whether he agreed 'that support for disability and poor health must be improved' in order to 'help people to start, to stay and to succeed at work' (Hansard 2023a: n.pag.). An even earlier example of deserving cases being raised occurred in a question to ministers from Liberal Democrat MP Wendy Chamberlain during a December 2022 debate (in event 1) on the West Midlands economy. In it she raised the plight of unpaid carers who were disincentivized from taking jobs because they risked losing their carers' allowance in doing so. 'Can the Prime Minister explain to me', she asked, 'the rationale behind that decision, given that we are trying to get economically inactive people back into work?' (Hansard 2022: n.pag.).

The overwhelmingly hegemonic representation of inactivity, then, was one framing the issue in normative terms – typically through descriptive, taken-for-granted statements about the worrying scale of the ongoing 'crisis'. The only notable variation, for the most part, was when this dominant narrative was moderated by (qualified) displays of empathy towards this or that deserving group of inactive people. Moreover, this often occurred in highly performative contexts: high-profile occasions, such as prime minister's questions or debates on the budget or Labour's white and green papers focusing on welfare and work.

Nonetheless, the sample did include a small handful of more stigmatizing parliamentary interventions. The majority of these occurred in the context of lengthier speeches, notably Chancellor Hunt's budget statements and Kendall's welfare announcements. These tended to veer from one discursive position to another depending on which *aspect* of the inactivity issue they were addressing – in so doing, acting as microcosms of the overarching discourse in the wider political public sphere. Thus, in the course of a single speech – his March 2023 'back-to-work Budget' – Hunt moved from a balanced (if normative) description of Britain's inactivity problem (observing that the country had 'higher economic inactivity than other countries') through sympathetic acknowledgement that some (deserving) inactive people needed help to re-engage with work (a pledge to 'bring forward reforms to remove the barriers that stop people who want to work from doing so'), all the way to explicitly othering undeserving inactives (Hansard 2023b). 'Independence is always better than dependence', he announced in lecture-like terms, before vowing to apply benefit sanctions 'more rigorously to those who fail to meet strict work search requirements or choose not to take up a reasonable job offer'. Significantly, Hunt's words also foreshadowed a mantra later intertextually appropriated by Starmer's Labour government: the maxim that 'those who can work, should'.

But perhaps the lengthiest single instance of (implied) scrounger-bashing came in the guise of Shadow Work and Pensions Secretary Helen Whateley's response to Labour's 'Pathways to Work' green paper announcement in March 2025 (event 10). In a speech reprising a long-time Conservative narrative portraying young inactive people, in particular, as 'snowflakes' incapable of coping with 'life's normal ups and downs', she rounded off with a lengthy peroration incorporating a quick-fire, over-lexicalized list of questions laced with oft-repeated tropes of anti-welfare discourse:

> This is a now-or-never chance to seize the moment—a now or never for millions of people who will otherwise be signed off for what could end up being a lifetime on

> benefits—but today's announcement leaves me with more questions than answers. How many people will be helped back into work and by when? Surely we have not been waiting eight months for just another Green Paper. Where is the fit note reform crucial to stem the flow of people on to benefits? Where is the action on people being signed off sick for the everyday ups and downs of life?
>
> (Hansard 2025a: n.pag.)

By now the inactivity problem frame had morphed wholesale into a crisis frame, as symbolized by Whateley's apocalyptic and cliché-ridden warning that this was a 'now-or-never chance to seize the moment'. The only alternative, she warned, was the despairing spectacle of 'millions of people' being 'signed off' to spend 'a lifetime on benefits' – a phrase intertextually reviving one of the most notorious rhetorical imaginaries of the Coalition years. This was then-Chancellor George Osborne's divisive juxtaposition, in his address to the 2012 Conservative Conference, of a 'shift worker, leaving home in the dark hours of the early morning' beneath the 'closed blinds' of a slumbering neighbour 'sleeping off a life on benefits' (Osborne 2012).

Giving the punters what they want? Amplification and stigma on comment threads

This, then, was the measure of elite-level representations of economic inactivity. But what did the great British *public* make of the issue? Specifically, how did news audiences respond or contribute to the normative 'national conversation' around inactivity – or (to put it more academically) its overall representation in the political public sphere?

This final section of the chapter combines manual sentiment analysis with CDA to offer an indicative exploration of how the subject of inactivity was deliberated among individuals who posted their views and reactions as online comments beneath articles published at key stages during the sample period. Owing to the sheer number of articles – and comments posted – during the two-and-a-half years (and counting) over which Britain's great inactivity debate had unfolded at time of writing, the scope of this analysis is unavoidably limited and can be viewed only as an indicative snapshot (or *series* of snapshots) of the overall picture. Moreover, the volume of coverage and amount of space devoted to reader discussion were both disproportionately extensive on certain news sites, particularly *MailOnline* and www.telegraph.co.uk. Both of these are right-wing national titles with long histories of amplifying welfare-sceptic/anti-benefit narratives and, for this reason, ascribing high degrees of normative newsworthiness to issues like worklessness.

As the majority of comments examined here are drawn from these two titles, the sample is inevitably rendered biased towards a particular (right-wing) worldview. As previous research has established, comment threads are just as much self-selecting fora as wider social media, such as X or TikTok, and they also appeal to particular demographics – often to the (self-)exclusion of others. It is therefore impossible to ever treat them as proxies for wider social attitudes – and this is especially true here, as the threads examined are almost exclusively drawn from conservative-leaning news-sites, rather than a broader cross-section encompassing liberal titles such as www.theguardian.com. Where this analysis *does* offer a useful barometer, however, is in giving a flavour of the overall balance and tone of sentiments expressed by audience-members engaged with the inactivity debate on the news sites that devoted most attention to the subject. To this extent, it can be regarded as broadly 'representative' of reader sentiments published across the national online press between discursive events 1 and 10 – even if those threads in themselves can in no way be seen as indicative of wider public opinion.

Despite the fact that comment threads were typically published on only a handful of news sites during the course of the inactivity debate, when they did appear, they could be extensive – running to hundreds, if not thousands, of posts. For this reason, samples of comments were limited to the first ten pages of posts (for articles publishing more than that), as this volume was considered to generate a substantial enough sample to reach analytical saturation: 'the point at which no new data or themes are emerging from the data set' (Rowlands et al. 2016). In order to ensure the multi-page samples painted as representative as possible a picture of reader sentiments on the individual threads, posts were initially ordered by 'best rated', 'most popular' or 'most liked' (depending on each site's favoured term). A more detailed explanation of the methodology is offered in Appendix 1.

Even after this process of repeated fine tuning, the *overall* sample numbered many thousands of posts across the ten discursive events – an impossibly high volume to subject to granular analysis. As a result, the final subsample examined here represents only a small fraction of the tens of thousands of comments posted in total, and is drawn from just three discursive moments. In order to give a broad (if imperfect) impression of how audience sentiments evolved during the life cycle of the inactivity debate, the decision was taken to focus analysis around moments positioned at the start, in the middle and towards the end of the overall sample period. These were moment 1 (the week in December 2022 when data revealed Britain had one of the highest inactivity rates in the world); moment 5 (the week in February 2024 when new figures exposed the scale of rising sickness benefit claims, especially among young adults); and moment 9 (the week in November that year when Labour published its 'Get Britain Working' green paper).

As the object of analysis in this case was not so much to identify discursive frames (the ways in which inactivity was constructed by readers) as to discern the sentiments they expressed towards *inactive people*, comments were coded using a different set of categories to those deployed in analysing newspaper articles and Hansard records. The initial working assumption was that individuals' reactions and contributions to the news discourse on which they commented were likely to fall into broadly 'negative', 'positive' and 'balanced' (or neutral) categories: i.e. posts criticizing inactive people, those defending them, and a perhaps larger number that expressed alarm or concern at statistics emphasizing the rising inactivity rate but without making any explicit judgments about those affected. However, as the coding process began, it rapidly became clear that the nature and tenor of many comments was much more openly stigmatizing (and, at times, ferocious) than those of news narratives themselves, with posts expressing critical/hostile sentiments representing the overwhelmingly dominant discourse – and vastly outnumbering those that were counter-discursive. Moreover, very few posts that indicated any kind of discursive position in relation to the inactivity debate could be described as 'non-aligned' or neutral, with the result that the decision was taken to remove from the sample all comments that did not express a clear viewpoint towards the subject.

Overall, 1181 out of a total of 1378 coded comments – nearly 86% – endorsed and/or amplified the dominant discourse constructing inactive people in more-or-less negative terms. Of these, a small number (60, or just over 8%) mobilized language and/or tropes that were so overtly stigmatizing they would be considered hate speech if existing statutory and regulatory safeguards protecting people on grounds of gender, age and other aspects of their identities extended to discrimination based on socioeconomic status. Only 14% of posts (197) defended and/or expressed empathy towards people classed as inactive. But of these, nearly one in five (36 posts) were compromised by an implicit acceptance that many inactives did play the system (even if they could not be blamed for doing so) – often articulated as a shoulder-shrugging attitude of 'what do you expect?' In the end, the following seven categories emerged from coding:

- negative – posts normatively critical of inactive people (especially benefit recipients) but conceding that not all are work-shy and some genuinely can't work;
- 'soft' negative – posts condemning benefit cheats and undeserving recipients but conceding that not all claimants are scroungers;
- second-order hatred – comments so negative that they meet basic definitions of hate speech (e.g. by expressing "hostility or prejudice" – see CPS n.d.);
- first-order hatred – posts expressing extreme hostility (e.g. moving beyond 'scroungerphobia' to liken inactive people/benefit recipients to lower forms of life);

- empathetic – posts acknowledging that some inactive people exploit the benefits system but expressing empathy about their reasons or motives for doing so;
- 'soft' counter-discursive – posts defending inactive benefit recipients but typically focusing on one or more 'deserving' groups (e.g. early retirees, disabled people);
- 'hard' counter-discursive – comments unequivocally critical of stigmatizing posts.

An indicative breakdown of sentiments across the coded sub-sample is given in Table 2.2.

Baiting the inactives: From stigma to hate speech in the media's new 'wild west'

Two decades after publicly visible comment threads first began appearing on news sites, one abiding question remains to be settled: that of how much (or how little) interference by moderators is desirable in the free flow of honestly held opinions and intra-audience dialogue around published articles. While news publishers invariably couch their reluctance to proactively moderate (or delete) offensive posts in high-minded terms – invoking liberal democratic traditions of free speech and an aversion to censorship – critics tend to attribute their inaction more to the resource limitations imposed by commercially driven news operations (though this excuse is itself likely to become harder to justify as editorial processes become increasingly AI-automated). Nonetheless, a combination of libertarian ideology and more or less *laissez-faire* regulatory policies – with the Office of Communications (2024) imposing somewhat stricter rules on legacy broadcast media than the Independent Press Standards Organization (Editors' Code Committee n.d.) does on the legacy press – have allowed editorial conventions to coalesce around one form or other of *reactive* moderation. This is the practice of publishers relying on audience members themselves (increasingly styled as 'community members') to report offensive or discriminatory language, with a particular focus on insults and hate speech directed at people with legally 'protected characteristics', as enshrined in the Equality Act 2010 (gov.uk n.d.).

Herein lies the problem. If members of online communities – self-selecting bubbles of confirmation bias – see no problem with the tenor of their peers' comments, who will raise the red flags when discourse gets out of hand? Our analysis of intra-audience inactivity debates suggests that this light-touch approach to policing news sites' internal comment threads is fostering a 'wild west' of shoot-from-the-hip opinions every bit as divisive and toxic as the more febrile debates

TABLE 2.2: Balance of audience sentiments across events 1, 5 and 9.

	News site	First-order hatred	Second-order hatred	Hard negative	Soft negative	Empathy	Soft counter	Hard counter	Total
event 1	*MailOnline*	1	4	59	0	6	25	4	**99**
	Telegraph.co.uk	2	4	143	0	4	0	0	**153**
event 5	*MailOnline*	1	10	129	1	4	19	3	**167**
	Telegraph 1	0	2	58	2	7	30	0	**99**
	Telegraph 2	2	0	38	0	4	9	8	**61**
event 9	*MailOnline* 1	0	1	87	5	2	4	0	**99**
	MailOnline 2	1	8	259	14	6	30	0	**318**
	Telegraph 1	3	8	150	3	2	7	0	**173**
	Telegraph 2	6	7	168	5	1	22	0	**209**
Totals		**16**	**44**	**1,091**	**30**	**36**	**146**	**15**	**1,378**

oft-condemned on external social media platforms, such as X. If our selective snapshots are anything to go by, a great deal more needs to be done to mitigate discrimination and hatred towards *protected* groups – let alone those who are not yet afforded the same (notional) statutory safeguards (e.g. people abused because of their poverty, social class or wider socioeconomic status). 'Scroungers', 'shirkers', 'snowflakes', 'layabouts' and 'malingerers' were some of the milder terms of ridicule observed in comments criticizing inactive people – including those unable to work owing to disability or domestic/caregiving roles often related to gender (both nominally protected groups). And these were as nothing compared to some of the harsher invectives – 'parasites', 'leeches', 'scum' and 'dregs of the world' – that dragged the already normatively stigmatizing lexicon of this discursive field into full-on hate speech.

Though only representing a small minority of the overall sample of posts coded, when overtly stigmatizing – even hate-filled – comments appeared, they tended to manifest in a handful of regular forms. Of these, perhaps the most commonplace were individual comments, or exchanges between two or more posters, in which readers sought to contrast their own positions (normally presented as materially and financially struggling – often despite the fact that they had always worked hard) with the privilege enjoyed by nameless others who declined to work and lived at taxpayers' expense. In other words, invective emerged through a discourse of *self-identified deservingness* among posters whose own lifestyles (however modest) were 'earned', as opposed to the undeservingness of familiar strangers or archetypes whose (supposedly greater) comfort was 'unearned'.

An example of one such comment was published on *MailOnline* in response to the aforementioned 19 December 2022 article proclaiming that the 'rise in Brits dropping out of the workforce' had put the country 'behind only Colombia, Chile and Switzerland in global league table of economic inactivity'. In it, the poster painted an evocative picture of hardworking taxpayers working themselves 'to death, chasing a pension you will never likely see' to 'keep paying taxes and NI [National Insurance] for scroungers and illegals who will never pay in, but always take out'. The post owed its impact to a number of interdiscursive references. The image of working people 'chasing a pension' they would 'likely never see' was an allusion to the incremental raising of the state retirement age in Britain under successive recent chancellors – the latest stage of which was due to take effect on 6 May 2026, when it would rise from 66 to 67 for adults born on or after April 1960 (Age UK n.d.). Equally notable was the pointed conflation of 'scroungers' with 'illegals'. This widened the scope of the poster's discriminatory lens to encompass another group besides benefit recipients that is frequently targeted in negative media-political discourses: undocumented migrants (including asylum seekers and refugees). But most significant of all was the binary distinction drawn between this fanciful montage of undeserving exploiters and people who were *deservingly* inactive. These were envisioned as '50 plus aged people' who had 'worked all their adult lives, paid taxes, NI etc' and 'taken nothing from the state' – an unlikely assertion, in view of historical analyses demonstrating that middle-aged and older adults, especially those in the 'baby boomer' generation(s), have been disproportionate beneficiaries of the welfare state (Bangham et al. 2018). If such virtuous career contributors could 'manage', added the poster, 'then good luck to them I say – enjoy life, leave the rat race to the younger gens' and (in a phrase evoking images of armies of scroungers) 'let the inept Govt worry about the benefits brigades'.

In other cases, posters deployed 'us-versus-them' framing less to construct a 'worker-versus-workless' dichotomy than to distinguish between the relative worthiness of *their own* claims for social security support (benefits) – again casting themselves as deserving and others (by inference, some or all of those referred to in the accompanying article) as undeserving. In this vein, one poster commenting on the above story despaired at the 'huge struggle' they faced because they were only permitted to work 'a maximum of 12 hours a week' because their partner's had multiple sclerosis – presumably a reference to DWP rules limiting individuals' entitlements to sickness-related benefits if other members of their households were in paid employment. Cue a resentful tirade casting out-of-work benefit recipients as not only lazy but fraudulent (signalled by the use of the term 'pretenders') and deploying the (partially self-censored) invective 'scum': 'How come all these layabouts and "pretenders" can get everything? I am so sick of paying tax all my life just to for others...m to get what i [sic] should be able to'.

By event 5 – the point at which the inactivity debate began morphing into a full-blown moral panic – the depth of disdain displayed in some comments had grown noticeably greater, in some cases edging further into the realms of hate speech. While social media platforms like X and Facebook are often rightly called out for their *laissez-faire* approaches to moderation, in fact their official lines on forms of discourse seen to constitute hatred are stricter than those of most news sites. Even under Elon Musk, at time of writing X barred all 'hateful conduct' involving attacks on 'other people on the basis of race, ethnicity, national origin, caste, sexual orientation, gender, gender identity, religious affiliation, age, disability, or serious disease' – a more expansive range of characteristics than those protected under UK law (with terms like 'caste' potentially dragging into the net tropes such as 'scrounger') (X n.d.). Facebook's rules, meanwhile, explicitly instruct users to 'not post' a raft of dehumanizing terms, among them those likening people to 'insects (including, but not limited to, cockroaches, locusts)'; animals 'in general or specific types of animal that are culturally perceived as inferior (including, but not limited to, Black people and apes or ape-like creatures; Jewish people and rats; Muslim people and pigs; Mexican people and worms)'; 'bacteria, viruses or microbes'; and 'subhumanity (including, but not limited to: savages, devils, monsters)' (Meta 2025). Yet if anyone has ever told the editors of www.telegraph.co.uk and *MailOnline* that such pernicious terminology constitutes hate speech, there was little evidence of this, judging by some of the posts observable on unmoderated threads.

One of the nastier examples of dehumanizing discourse surfaced in the course of a lengthy exchange between a number of posters on *MailOnline* (several of whom, intriguingly, identified as coming from eastern European countries). This increasingly demonizing dialogic interplay appeared beneath the earlier-mentioned 19 February 2024 opinion column by Richard Littlejohn lamenting the need to import cleaners from other countries because British people were too lazy to do such work. 'Cleaning is for people who are willing to work', remarked a poster from Poland towards the end of this exchange, adding sweepingly that 'people on benefits are not interested in work because if they were they would not be on benefits', and this was why cleaners were being hired from 'far away' – where people were 'willing to work'. In an example of asserted direct personal observation – a form of 'evidence-based' posting that was a common device used by posters to validate their truth-claims – they claimed to 'know kiwi gardeners who travelled 12 000 miles' to 'get a job in UK'. But, though heavily laced with scrounging familiar stranger tropes, this comment at least steered clear of using explicitly stigmatizing terms – unlike the uncompromising post that immediately followed. This read: 'they have no hygiene, same sponge for everything, yuk, next wife get mate'.

Given the focus of Littlejohn's article – the UK's over-reliance on foreign workers – deciphering the precise focus of the poster's invective was far from straightforward. The us-versus-them discourse implicit in their derogatory pairing of the dehumanizing term 'they' with phrases like 'next wife get mate' could easily be interpreted as a racist and/or Islamophobic trope, othering people from cultures that (supposedly) allow polygamy while caricaturing them as having 'no hygiene'. Conversely, the reference to those without 'hygiene' in the context of an article opening with an anecdote about Brits being too idle to take cleaning jobs might also be viewed as a dig at British scroungers.

Elsewhere in the samples for both events 5 and 9, several posters described inactive people (and benefit recipients in general) as parasites. Beneath a 2024 Valentine's Day article hopelessly headlined 'Workless Britain', a poster ridiculed the Tories for having had '14 years to deal with these malingerers and parasites", while doing "****** all about them'. Another used a *MailOnline* story from that November confirming that 'if people refuse to work they WILL lose their benefits' (Tapsfield 2024) as an opportunity to revive the conflation of benefit 'scroungers' with (illegal) migrants. The poster (who, perhaps ironically, was based in the

United States) did this by castigating 'cap in hand parasites arriving on boats' – an interdiscursive cross-reference to another dominant news narrative of the moment (the perceived ongoing 'small boats crisis' affecting Britain's porous southern sea border). It was also not unusual to see posters remark that people unwilling to work should be left to 'starve', with one or two even proposing this as a deliberate policy solution.

A flavour of relatively 'milder' posts likening inactive people to wildlife, meanwhile, was contained in a comment beneath an article published a few weeks *after* event 5 (i.e. outside our main periods of analysis): a 7 March post-budget analysis headlined, 'The looming crisis that Hunt's budget failed to address' (Ping Chan et al. 2024). In it, the poster invoked social-Darwinian discourse to reflect that, if 'you are drone and not a worker bee', then 'nature takes care of the problem' – before steering close to advocating the use of eugenics to remove such non-productive 'drones' from society. 'There should be more of that in real life', they added, before training their fire (like an earlier mentioned poster) on a conflated imaginary of homegrown and migrant inactives with the dismissive declaration that, 'if you havent [sic]contributed to society with taxes and you werent [sic] born in the UK and earned your keep', society 'cannot afford you'. There were also a handful of instances in which posters suggested even more brutal forms of corrective action – in comments that (in some cases) bordered on inciting violence. One post on a *Telegraph* thread appeared to relate the issue of inactivity to the then-current debate about whether MPs should approve a new law allowing 'assisted dying' (euthanasia) in cases of extreme end-of-life suffering for terminally ill patients. In it, the reader warned (with gallows humour) that 'the "suicidal thoughts" tactic could back fire these days and before you can say "two doctors and a high court judge" you'll be getting a lethal injection instead of your giro'. Others vocalized similar sentiments in less dissembling terms. One suggested that 'maybe they [inactive people] should be offered assisted dying instead of benefits', as this could encourage them to 'make a remarkable recovery', while another took a step closer towards advocating enforced euthanasia: 'Just remove the benefits. With the new assisted dying bill, if they want to slip off then it's simple enough to do so without bothering anyone'.

Elsewhere, threads were teeming with retreads of longstanding scrounger imaginaries. An SEO-friendly www.telegraph.co.uk article headlined 'Claim suicidal thoughts for benefits' (Croft 2024) attracted a comment brimming with clichés about beery benefit cheats that recalled anecdotes from scrounger-bashing interviews quoted in Golding and Middleton's seminal *Images of Welfare* (1982). The poster in question suggested that 'cash in hand drug using pub goers' should be 'first for the gulags' (an historical allusion to Siberian labour camps for undesirables Josef Stalin introduced to the Soviet Union). Moreover, even milder cliché tropes invariably projected a normative scrounger discourse, with posters parroting the 'doxa' of 'welfare commonsense' voiced by right-wing pundits (Jensen 2014). One reader responding to Littlejohn's column elaborated on his sentiments thus: 'The British public know the reason why, our benefit system is too generous that's why the scroungers can go abroad on holiday, having multiple tattoos, smoke, go down the pub, gamble and that's why people are pouring in'.

The montage of images of fecklessness contained in this near stream-of-consciousness tirade not only (again) conflated exploitative benefit recipients with migrants – through the water metaphor describing them 'pouring in' (Mujagić 2018). It also bore the imprint of deep-rooted intertextual associations with media and popular cultural archetypes ranging from Frank Gallagher, the hard-drinking, chain-smoking patriarch in the comedy-drama *Shameless*, to the denizens of James Turner Street, the Birmingham neighbourhood featured in controversial docusoap *Benefits Street*. There were also further echoes of encounters with beer-swilling 'scroungers' quoted by Golding and Middleton – notably their record of an interview conducted with a 50-something slaughterhouse worker, who estimated that six out of ten claimants were scrounging, judging by his experience of spotting '40 or 50 of them in the pub' (Golding and Middleton 1982: 172).

Self-identified deservingness and the symbolic annihilation of 'active' inactives

One of the starkest takeaways from the comment sample was the near-total absence of posts acknowledging that many people classed as economically inactive are (by any measure) useful social contributors – for example, by working as unpaid caregivers or volunteers. On the contrary, on the rare occasions unpaid carers were mentioned at all, they were often cast as *undeserving*, usually on the basis of sweeping assumptions that they misused this status as a tool to further exploit the benefits system. This image of *feigned* virtuousness – people's assuming carer status under false pretences – was exemplified by two comments posted on *Telegraph* threads during event 9. In one, a poster from Great Yarmouth used othering terms to deride 'these people' who 'ensure their children are diagnosed with some kind of mental disability so they are entitled to carer's allowance, PIP etc'. The other drew an explicit opposition between (deserving) taxpayers and (undeserving) benefit recipients – framed as 'people perfectly fit to work but [who] know the system', who 'get their dole topped up with PIP payments, attendance allowance, carers allowance' and 'live their best lives courtesy of us mugs who pay taxes'.

Meanwhile, on the rare occasions that any post appeared *defending* inactive people, these very rarely adopted overtly counter-hegemonic positions. Instead, they tended to be posted by individuals self-identifying as part of this or that deserving subgroup who portrayed themselves as atypical of inactive people in general – in other words, explicitly defining themselves *against* the undeserving 'others'. Any deserving recipients of out-of-work benefits such posters identified were invariably 'people like them', who had worked hard all their lives previously and/or were inactive now only due to genuine sickness or disability, or because they had chosen to retire early (a subject to which we return in Chapter 5). A number of comments reflecting such sentiments appeared in response to two articles published during event 9: the 26 November 2025 *Telegraph* story headlined 'Starmer dodges crackdown on sickness benefits' (Gutteridge 2024b) and a *MailOnline* column published two days earlier in which Leo McKinstry ranted against the 'bloated monster' of the welfare state (McKinstry 2024). Several of these posts directed their resentment towards migrants and asylum-seekers. One suggested the Labour government would 'take from the British people who...need it' to give to a 'family of 15 from Algeria to pretend they are all unwell'. Another predicted that ministers would 'free up money for the asylum system' off the backs of 'the farmers, the pensioners, the small businesses' – an allusion to a slew of controversial measures announced in the recent budget, including inheritance tax changes affecting farms, a cut to Winter Fuel Payments for most pensioners, and a rise in employers' NI contributions. Self-identifying 'deservers' included a 'single mum' who 'worked' and 'never got free nursery places', but worried Starmer would 'target...the single mums', not 'the drinker or the obese or the shirkers'.

Those who chose to speak up for deserving groups – regardless of whether they considered themselves to belong to them – included a man describing himself as 'an older guy, who works out, still works, runs 5 miles 3 times a week, trains much younger people and I am studying for a masters in AI'. While decrying the 'good proportion of this country' he considered 'weak and feeble minded' because 'consecutive governments' had 'pandered to and promoted the mental health/PTSD nonsense that is used like a crutch and excuse', he conceded 'there are also those individuals in society who are genuinely afflicted with serious and long standing mental health conditions, both psychological and psychiatric' who 'should be given the greatest care'. Meanwhile, the tiny minority of more overtly counter-discursive posts (most appearing during later discursive events) tended to focus on contesting the accuracy of scrounger myths by asserting their own, direct or vicarious, experience of inactivity and/or unemployment. Thus one poster responding to a *MailOnline* story headlined 'If people refuse to work they WILL lose benefits' (Tapsfield 2024) stating that they 'had been in employment for over 20 years, but found myself out of work after redundancy and a serious illness'. Another claimed to have 'applied for over 500 jobs in the last 7 months', leaving them 'feeling... that at 51 I am being overlooked for younger people'. A third gave a shoutout for 'the woman facing us' who had 'a brain tumour and can barely walk', forcing her 'elderly husband' to do 'literally everything for her'. Both had previously 'worked all of their lives paying taxes and bringing up three kids'. A further poster adopted a more overarching lens, by posing the question, 'why force those out of work to come off benefits?', and adding that 'benefits is peanuts' and it was 'not as if they are driving lamborghinis [*sic*] in mansions'.

Of the few posters expressing empathy towards benefit recipients who gamed the system (comments that, by definition, implicitly bought into scrounger discourse) these, too, were often couched in divisive terms: positioning the gamers in relation to (even) *less* deserving others (often migrants). One such remark, responding to the story comparing Britain's inactivity rates to those of Chile and Colombia, began by asking whether we should 'blame' someone brought up 'in a heavily taxed country' who had 'watched their parents and grandparents work all their lives and pay taxes', only for 'consecutive governments' to 'just give it to whoever rocks up here'. Extending this allusion to the mythic imaginary of overseas benefit/NHS 'tourists', they asked, 'why not take a leaf out of the new arrivals book' and 'demand it free and get it', before ending with a morbid image lamenting their own plight and that of other (virtuous) 'people like them': 'I have worked all my life [and] never claimed benefits and I am now resigned to the fact I will work till they are putting the nails in the lid'.

This, then, is the landscape of contemporary media, political and public portrayals of economic inactivity – and of those individuals who (rightly or wrongly) are tarred with labels like 'inactive' and 'workless'. Viewed collectively, the three interwoven discursive fields – the news media, Parliament and the court of (selective) public opinion – represent a hostile and unforgiving social space. They amount to a febrile, frequently toxic, political public sphere characterized by stigma, suspicion, distrust and (most unjustly) the symbolic annihilation of all those *classed* as inactive who are actually *working* – principally as volunteers and/or carers – and often also managing their own illnesses and disabilities. The next chapter begins the task of unravelling the inequities and inaccuracies inscribed into these stigmatizing narratives, by relating them to the personal (hi)stories and lived experiences of those who, though seldom given a voice in news stories or parliamentary debates, know better than anyone else what it is like to *be* inactive: the people themselves.

3

Inactivity and Intersectionality: The Lives of the Economically Inactive

Terry[1] and his wife have been joint full-time carers for two of their four children for more than twenty years. As a boy, their eldest son was diagnosed with Asperger's syndrome and oppositional defiant disorder – a behavioural condition that manifests itself in unpredictable bursts of anger and aggression. Their 18-year-old daughter has Chiari malformation, an abnormality causing part of her brain to protrude through the back of her skull. Another of their daughters, in her early twenties, 'really wants to go to work' but was recently diagnosed with severe anxiety and 'two types of depression' – triggered, in part, by the release from prison of someone who subjected her to a childhood trauma.

Despite facing round-the-clock pressures to look after his children, when Terry was last in paid work he met immovable resistance from his employer as soon as he asked for flexible hours. 'Until 2005 I was in full-time work, but my daughter was born with an illness which meant she was in and out of hospital a lot', he recalled, chuckling morbidly: 'I got a written warning and was told that work was more important than my family!'

Yet unpaid caregiving responsibilities, dismissive and intransigent employers, and the challenges of supporting children with complex physical, mental and emotional needs are not the only barriers preventing Terry and his wife returning to paid employment. This hardworking 'inactive' couple also have serious health problems of their own. After being signed off with a cardiovascular condition from his last job, as a warehouse worker, Terry had a heart attack. He is now undergoing tests for problems with his lower oesophagus. His wife suffers from spondylitis (inflamed vertebrae), which means she struggles to walk without assistance, and has a stoma requiring her to wear a colostomy bag.

The intersectional factors affecting Terry, his wife and three of their children are exacerbated by a mix of severe financial hardship and seemingly endless waits for NHS treatment and assistance from a creaking social care system. Theirs is a not-untypical tale of life at the sharp end of the UK's chronically underfunded, oversubscribed mental and physical health services, and its increasingly officious and inadequate benefits system.

At the time of our interview, the latest of these relentless pressures was the suite of cuts to sickness and disability-related benefits then being proposed by Keir Starmer's Labour government. Despite their daughter's Chiari diagnosis – a condition that causes muscle weakness, neck pain, balance problems and headaches, and prevents her from taking part in any sports – she stood to lose half her income under initial proposals contained in the Department for Work and Pensions' controversial 2025 'Pathways to Work' green paper. If enacted, these changes would have frozen the disability component of Universal Credit – the £416-a-month benefit top-up she received to compensate her for being unable to work. And she was also facing a more drastic cut to her income, under ministerial plans to increase the frequency of reassessments, and tighten eligibility for, the daily living component of PIP – which is meant to help with additional daily costs disabled people face whether they are in or out of work. Campaigners' main line of attack against this particular 'reform' was that it risked preventing disabled people who *were* working from continuing to do so, while undermining the efforts of others to upskill, attend job interviews and enter employment.

The proposed PIP eligibility conditions would also have affected Terry's wife. At the time he relayed their story, she was receiving the higher rate of both living and mobility components, reflecting difficulties she had walking and carrying out basic tasks because of a fused disc at the base of her spine. But under the plans unveiled in the green paper, future claimants would have had to 'score' at least four points against a single everyday activity to continue qualifying for the benefit. Previously, tasks such as being unable to wash beneath the waist without assistance received only two points. Terry himself would almost certainly have lost out, as, even under the existing regime, he had only ever qualified for the lower rate of PIP. And if his daughter's future PIP entitlement had been threatened, he and his wife would have been penalized further, as this payment tends to act as a 'gateway benefit' to Carer's Allowance – a weekly payment of around £82 received by anyone who looks after someone with an illness or disability for 35-plus hours a week.

As if their illnesses, disabilities and financial challenges were not difficult enough to manage, Terry and his family had also put up with years of stigma and distrust arising from their enforced reliance on the benefits system. His experience of feeling constantly scrutinized, monitored and eyed judgmentally by others led Terry to sound defensive at times as he described some of the costly items his family needed to make their lives bearable. 'She's on the high rate care and high rate mobility [PIP]', he said of the benefits used to fund his wife's costly day-to-day expenses.

'People say, "oh that means she gets £600 a week", but the problem is she has a stoma, so she has the [colostomy] bags all the time, so it's buying clothes that fit the bags'. He was equally self-conscious about his daughter's expenditure – in her case, on vital equipment enabling her to stay fit and exercise without worsening her condition. 'It's the sort of thing that if someone came in and they saw she had a treadmill, they'd think she doesn't deserve it', he reflected, using the impersonal 'they' to denote the assumed disdain and suspicion of the wider public.

The imagined chorus of disapproval to which Terry alluded speaks to the climate of distrust towards people with no option but to rely on a welfare state that (despite popular myths) has become increasingly grudging and conditional after more than fifteen years of austerity-driven 'welfare reform', legitimized and enabled by the stigmatizing and annihilating media and political discourses examined in the last chapter. It was little wonder that families like Terry's had been left feeling paranoid about knocks on the door and demands for repayment when contemporaneous news reports continued to raise the prospect that money they had received to support them with caregiving duties might be clawed back by the DWP as part of a widely publicized drive to correct years of supposed 'overpayments' in Carer's Allowance (Carers UK 2025a). 'I worry every day that I'm going to get a letter through the post telling me I owe thousands', Terry explained at the time, recalling a story about 'a woman with Alzheimer's they're ordering...to pay back because she didn't fill something out on a form'. Criticizing the complexity of the application process, he said the forms were made 'as hard as possible' to complete, adding, 'it does feel deliberate – quite often they'll ask the same question three different ways'.

While each one of the 9.3 million 16- to 64-year-olds then listed as economically inactive will have their own unique personal story, many of the pressures and prejudices Terry relayed would doubtless resonate with large numbers of them. In particular, he and his wife are among the growing, but little-discussed, minority of people who are both disabled and full-time carers. According to Carers UK, Britain's leading caregiving charity, carers 'were more likely than non-carers to be disabled' in December 2024, with more than a quarter of those in England (27.5%) and 29.8% in Wales having their own disabilities – compared to 17.8 and 21.4% of non-carers respectively (Carers UK 2024). And this was to say nothing of the 870,000 children likely to have been affected by the cuts to PIP announced in March 2025 because they were living in households with at least one disabled benefit recipient (Child Poverty Action Group 2025). Indeed, the latter fact was particularly inconvenient for Labour ministers straining to frame as a 'moral duty' (Morrison 2025) the overarching package of 'welfare to work' reforms of which these cuts were a part. How 'moral' was it for a government elected on a pledge to reduce child poverty – which, according to its own figures, had come to affect nearly a third of all UK children by 2025 – to plunge many of them further into it, especially when 46% of those living in families in receipt of PIP were in *working* households (Child Poverty Action Group 2025)? More broadly, how compatible was the government's moral mission to lift disabled people out of poverty through 'work' if so much of the weight of their welfare cuts was due to fall on a benefit that had no direct link to individuals' employment status – and one that, for millions of people with disabilities and long-term illnesses, made the difference between their being able or unable to afford the equipment they needed *in order to* enter the workplace?

The tightening of eligibility conditions for PIP was also likely to have more extensive, and sinister, consequences for individuals' entitlement to wider forms of support on which many had historically depended. According to expert consultancy Policy in Practice, the removal of PIP would have left as many as 830,000 people 'invisible' to the NHS and local authorities, by removing a crucial 'marker of need' they require to access everything from adult social care to priority status in homelessness assessments (Butler 2025). In a briefing document published shortly after the green paper and ensuing Spring Statement, it warned that, while the benefits system had 'always recognised and supported those too ill to work', the reforms would have had 'the unprecedented consequence of illness being unrecognised, unsupported and invisible'. This would 'effectively erase some of the most vulnerable people' from the system entirely (Butler 2025: n.pag.), symbolically annihilating them from the discourse and practice of public policy.

The focus of this and the next chapter is on exploring the complex and varied barriers to work experienced by a wide-ranging group of people classed as economically inactive, or (in the eyes of government at least) *under*-active: that is, not employed for as many regular hours as they might (or supposedly *should*) be working. They range from individuals forced to manage debilitating, sometimes life-threatening, chronic illnesses to people with complex physical disabilities and others with comorbid combinations of these and other conditions – including those affecting their mental health. Yet, despite being classified as 'inactive' in the cold, hard bureaucratic language of official statistics, almost all of the eleven individuals who agreed to share their experiences actually *do* work – very hard – by any sensible and civilized measure of what that term means (as we shall see in more detail in Chapter 4). Two-thirds of the interviewees (seven in total) were unpaid carers for children and/or other relatives, while almost all the remainder offered their labour, again without payment, as volunteers. Some worked as charity campaigners or peer mentors, while others volunteered their time for food banks or other community initiatives. Several had spent years juggling both caregiving *and* volunteering.

To illustrate the range and pervasiveness of the intersectional inequalities affecting inactive people, interviewees were drawn from cities, towns and villages spanning the length and breadth of the UK – from Guildford in South-East England via North Wales, Lancashire and Edinburgh right up to the far north-east of Scotland. Interviews were arranged with the help of several charities working with marginalized groups, principally people affected by economic disadvantage. These charities were Heard, a charity that amplifies the personal stories of people from minority groups by connecting them with the media; ATD Fourth World, a campaign group dedicated to giving a voice to people experiencing poverty; Volunteer Scotland, an umbrella organization for third-sector groups that rely on voluntary workers, many of whom are classified as economically inactive; and the Glasgow-based Poverty Alliance.

We begin by exploring the multi-dimensional barriers that prevent many people from undertaking or sustaining conventional paid employment – from disability and illness through caregiving responsibilities to inflexible employers offering only unsocial hours, poverty pay and an unwillingness to provide them with the (often simple) adjustments they would need to enter or remain in the workplace. The next chapter will then go on to unpack the experiences of carers in more detail, as well as exploring the contributions to the public good of volunteers – drawing on sociological critiques of the concept of 'work' to conceptualize the efforts of both these groups as unpaid, unrecognized forms of labour. But let us begin by examining the complex life challenges that lead many people to become (and remain) inactive in the first place.

Physical disability, long-term conditions and mental ill health

Of all the obstacles impeding interviewees' efforts to obtain or hold down regular employment, the most commonly cited were disability, chronic physical conditions and mental ill health. Most of those interviewed had worked in conventional paid jobs at one point or another – until being driven out by a combination of work-related sickness, injury and mental health conditions, or worsening symptoms for existing health complaints. Many of these health issues (as we shall see in coming sections) were driven or exacerbated by aggravating factors, from low pay to long hours and inflexible working conditions.

Gloria, who has myalgic encephalomyelitis (ME - also known as Chronic Fatigue Syndrome), was forced to give up her career as an occupational therapist (OT) more than a decade ago after her debilitating condition was inflamed by a virus diagnosed as probable glandular fever. 'I had swollen glands and was feeling unwell. I never really recovered from it', she recalled, describing how she was reduced to being 'housebound for about four or five years', before managing 'very, very slowly ... to get out of the house a little bit more'. She described how 'a day out of the house might mean three days in bed afterwards', necessitating that she spend her mornings 'really just doing things to help getting my body going', such as 'a bit of very gentle yoga', meditation and stretching. She added that, during the afternoon, 'I have to lie back down and I'll go to bed usually about 4, half 4, for a couple of hours. That period of time in between, that's where I "live", that's where I do normal things that other people do'.

For Gloria, the loss of a specialized job for which she had trained over many years was upsetting on many levels – not least because it deprived her of a long-held professional identity. Such widely experienced trauma is rarely reflected in sweepingly generalized media and political narratives like those explored in Chapter 2, which tend to portray economically inactive people as a mass of 'career' non-contributors. 'There's...the role loss', she reflected, ruefully. 'You've gone from being an NHS member of staff. Now I'm a scrounger. Now I'm a benefit claimant. Now I'm a piece of shit on the bottom of someone's shoe, because that's what we're almost told to believe'.

Gloria's reflections on her path from working taxpayer to workless benefit recipient are indicative of a curious ambivalence about self-image that was discernible in a number of the interviewees' musings about their inactive status. By explicitly criticizing prevailing media-political discourse, she signalled her disdain for tabloid labels like 'scrounger'. Nevertheless, by vocalizing her belief that society now viewed her (and other disabled people) in this way, she showed herself to be acutely aware of, and deeply affected by, stigma – despite also being at pains to *reject* such labels. This curious tension is a subject to which we return in more detail later in this chapter.

Similar journeys from the status of valued social contributor to (supposed) social dependant were described in some detail by a number of other interviewees. Single parent Esther, 35, graduated with an Oxbridge degree and had the makings of a promising career as a case worker for a national domestic violence charity until being diagnosed with the debilitating musculoskeletal illness fibromyalgia, alongside attention deficit hyperactivity disorder (ADHD). As she grew progressively weaker and more easily fatigued during the day, it became impossible for her to continue holding down a full-time job – though she had continued to do as much work as her conditions allowed, volunteering for human rights charities. 'I was working in domestic violence, was living in a basement flat, was underground all day and starting to feel awful. After about 1, I couldn't do anything and was just lying on a bed', she recalled. 'I was full time and the first issue with working full time was lack of childcare. I didn't have any option so I moved to part time'.

Esther's employer was understanding up to a point, but over time pressure began mounting for her to decide whether she was fit enough to return to working longer hours. It was at this stage that she began to realize her condition had only become more manageable because she had reduced the length of her day – and that going back full time would worsen her symptoms. By this stage, work 'was still Monday to Friday – just 9–1', but 'was still aggravating my health', she reflected. After taking two months off, she 'felt a lot better, going to the gym', but 'when I had the conversation with work, "oh are you feeling better now?" I thought, "I *am* feeling better but it's because I'm not working!" '

Though a replacement job as a teaching assistant seemed to suit Esther better for a while, even this eventually became too much for her limited energy levels:

> I found that even that was difficult to do five days a week. Then I started wrestling with the fact that I couldn't work more than about two days a week. I couldn't do anything or make dinner. I couldn't get dressed. It wasn't anxiety-related – it was just heavy fatigue.

While deteriorating health had forced both Gloria and Esther to reduce their hours and, ultimately, give up work, Bryony's working life ended before it had ever really begun. At the age of just 15, she 'started showing signs of endometriosis', which rapidly 'became quite chronic'. 'I was hospitalized over 100 times, it lost me my job, a lot of friends', she recalled, adding that 'every job I ever applied for there was, "we can give you sick days", but I had to take all my sick days, so no job ever kept me on'. As with Gloria and Esther, her symptoms had become ever more limiting over time. Bryony, who had a habit of referring to her endometriosis condition by the shortened, near-personified nickname 'endo', explained that 'the annoying thing with endo is that it can cause other conditions too'. In her case, these included 'lesions and adhesions in my bowel and abdomen'. 'Endo has caused quite a bit of trauma over the years', she added, leaving her 'highly anxious' and with 'brain damage' that caused her to repeatedly fall and break her knees. 'It feels like being stuck in the body of an old person – it drives me bonkers!'

Although long-term illnesses and disabilities were interviewees' most commonly cited work-inhibiting conditions, several people were also managing complex mental health issues – including some whose primary diagnoses were physical. These stories reflected the strong association between physical and mental comorbidities among the general UK population. According to the Centre for Mental Health charity, 30% of the English population (15.4 million) at any one time have one or more long-term physical health conditions – and three out of ten of these people (4.6 million) also have a mental health problem. Conversely, at least one in five people in England (10.2 million) has a mental health issue – and nearly half of these individuals (46% or 4.6 million) also have chronic physical conditions. 'Mental health and physical health are closely interrelated', explains the charity in its literature, adding that, because 'people living with a physical health problem are twice as likely to have poor mental health', this can create a vicious circle of one condition negatively impacting the other – as mental ill health also tends to 'have a detrimental effect on their physical condition' (Centre for Mental Health n.d.).

Another group disproportionately affected by mental health comorbidities are those living with neurodiverse conditions (Mind n.d.). Ian, 27, who has both autism and ADHD but had managed to hold down a demanding full-time job as an administrative assistant in his local council's adult social care department until his fixed-term contract ended, also struggles with his mental health. He said his symptoms were often brought on by the stress of knowing society regards him as inactive. 'I know disabled people have been made to feel like they're a burden in various ways and that's really ingrained...It is really personal and really emotional', he explained, adding:

> When the recent benefit cuts and the conversation around it really blew up, it was really scary in many ways – it felt kind of surreal, like the voices inside of my head had kind of broken free and were now in the real world, and everyone else was talking about things I had been talking about with myself.

He recalled how, on the night (in March 2025) when Chancellor Rachel Reeves announced she was going to extend cuts to disability benefits previously announced by then Work and Pensions Secretary Liz Kendall, 'it was very difficult for my mental health and it's probably safe to say I had a bit of a meltdown'. He added:

> I just completely broke down and cried and had to wake my parents up at 2am because I just needed a hug – I felt targeted. I was being made to feel like a villain and misunderstood. It made me kind of feel how I used to feel at being bullied at school and being made to go back to school. It's like injustice and 'the powerful' targeting us.

Ernest, 66, was forced to give up his job in forestry after suffering an injury at work that had been partially triggered by his underlying condition, 'Gulf War Syndrome' – an illness suffered by many veterans of the 1990–91 Gulf War that has since been linked to symptoms ranging from chronic fatigue and muscle pain to hypertension, diarrhoea and severe skin rashes. 'I'm one of about 25,000', he said of the syndrome, which was only formally recognized in 2005 following a widely publicized Pensions Appeal Tribunal case – and, even then, not as 'a discrete pathological entity', but 'an umbrella term' for various conditions (Ministry of Defence 2012). While Ernest felt 'comparatively lucky' not to be among the ranks of people who had 'passed away' due to health complications caused by the syndrome, including serious heart and liver disorders, he did hold it responsible for ultimately bringing his post-war career to a grinding halt. Recalling the accident that had ended his working life, he said:

> I was trimming a bank and tripped on a rabbit hole [and] ended up rolling down this bank and couldn't get up. Over the course of 18 months my doctor said, "that's it – you're finished with work". I couldn't physically walk. I couldn't do anything.

Inflexible and/or prejudiced employers

If there was one overarching factor that had undermined interviewees' ability to hold down work, or return to it after periods of ill health, it was the long hours, unreasonable demands and inflexible working conditions imposed by employers. This strongly echoes the findings of a slew of recent reports, including a longitudinal analysis of the 'work journeys' of 9169 16- to 60-year-olds published by the Work Foundation in December 2024. This found that workers in declining health were four times more likely to leave the workplace, and become unemployed or inactive, if their employers offered them little or no flexibility in relation to where, when or how they worked – whether through home working, a hybrid home/workplace split, or hours that fitted in around their routines and wider responsibilities (Work Foundation 2024).

For those with physical disabilities and/or managing debilitating medical symptoms, the biggest obstacles to work were employers unwilling to make basic adjustments they needed to be able to access it – from investing in simple physical adaptations, such as wheelchair ramps, to offering them flexible work patterns to fit in around GP and hospital appointments or their need to manage fluctuating symptoms. While Ernest felt that 'things *have* got a lot better for the disabled now', largely because of the introduction of equalities legislation (most recently the Equality Act 2010), he recalled how '30 years ago you weren't employed because you'd cost the company money'. Even today, he said many employers would still 'find an excuse not to employ you', especially if this meant they could avoid 'the cost of changing a building to make it more wheelchair-accessible'. Bryony was blunter. She recalled the farcical experience of being employed to help one organization (a national charity) 'write their disability policy', only to be 'laid off' once she had completed it – and replaced by 'an able-bodied person who had studied disability'. 'These companies don't want to make the adaptations: we're here to make them money', she said bitterly, before adding:

> They don't want to spend money. Whilst talking about 'getting back to work', they're cutting everything...These things are so frustrating but they're such a

> common experience for people who are long-term sick or disabled. Employers will not give an inch. They want you working as many hours to make them as much money as possible.

In Gloria's case, an inability to commit to rigid working hours due to her often dramatically fluctuating symptoms ultimately led to her dismissal – ironically, from her role as an OT (in which she had spent her time helping other sick and disabled people live active lives). After a prolonged period off work due to a downturn in health, she had briefly tried returning to work 'doing six hours a week', but rapidly found herself 'too ill even to do that'. 'That failed and eventually I was dismissed on grounds of ill health' and 'prior to that my sick pay had run out, so I was already claiming benefits even when I was still technically employed', she recalled. Referring to the current media and political debate about the benefits and virtues of rewarding employment, she added:

> I was an occupational therapist: of course work *is* good for people - but you don't have businesses, organisations, that will employ people in the way that we need it to. If you said to me, 'do ten hours of work over a few months', I could do that.

By contrast, for ME sufferer Andy, 37, having access to work that offered a degree of flexibility had made all the difference in enabling him to remain in the workforce – though the pressure of juggling part-time jobs to make ends meet continued to take a toll on his health. 'I've been teaching for about five years', he said of the role he had first taken up as a visiting part-time lecturer while studying for a doctorate at the University of Oxford. 'I have a condition where it's like ... if I don't have flexibility ... Working 9 to 5 would make my condition worse', he expanded, adding that 'without the flexibility, my capability to work would decrease more over time – so there's sort of an investment angle, where it would be worthwhile [for the government] to subsidize partial economic activity'.

Andy tended to lecture about '26 weeks of the year', perhaps spending two to three hours marking essays on Thursdays and a similar time teaching on Fridays. When health allowed, he might also boost his earnings by picking up 'shifts at a call-centre ... as and when I need money', which could be anything from two to three times a week to 'a couple a month'. On occasion, he had had no choice but to take on extra hours, to cope with the ever-escalating cost of utilities, rent and food bills during Britain's post-pandemic inflation spiral. 'I had to take on the part-time job to get over the cost-of-living crisis', he reflected, adding that 'doing two days a week part-time work, one day a week teaching, and then four days a week a DPhil, is a bit of a disaster when you've got ME!'

For some disabled interviewees, the difficulties of working long hours and unsocial shifts, sometimes in physically demanding work, were compounded by intersectional pressures relating to their responsibilities as caregivers for dependents – including children and/or other relatives with their own disabilities. 'It's very difficult to find a job where you were saying, "hopefully I can do five days a week, but I can't commit" ', reflected Terry, because 'bosses don't want that – they want a full-time employee'. He added that, in his most recent post as a warehouse worker, he had run into difficulties because he 'was having to take my daughter to appointments ... I was having to ring and say, "I can't come in today: my daughter's had a turn and she's in hospital" '. Although 'none of them actually sacked me because of it I got written warnings', he added, recalling the point when 'it got to the stage where it wasn't worth the grief and I had to become a full-time carer'.

For others, the biggest obstacle was the UK's chronic lack of affordable and/or round-the-clock childcare – and this was especially the case for those with their own care needs. 'The first issue with working full time was lack of childcare', reflected Esther on her struggle to find reasonably priced nurseries and juggle daily drop-offs and pick-ups as a low-earning single parent. These were sentiments echoed by several other interviewees – and not only those who, like her, were managing their own disabilities or health conditions.

Jean (an elective inactive) retired from her senior management position at a Midlands further education college in her late 50s, partly so that she could offer her grandchildren childcare that was more affordable and flexible for their parents than the costly provision available through most nurseries and childminders. It was only because of the support offered by both their sets of grandparents, she argued, that her son and daughter-in-law had been able to hold down their jobs. 'That enabled my daughter-in-law to go to work', she recalled, adding that, 'at that point at least one of the children was still out of school, so they would have had to try to find childcare, and then, once they had started school, it's working around school hours'.

Marie, a retired headteacher who now volunteers in an Edinburgh mothers' and toddlers' group, said it was increasingly commonplace for children to be brought along by 'older people in their 70s', because the ever-escalating cost of paid nurseries and childminders meant that it was only financially viable for many parents to work if they had access to unpaid familial childcare. She recalled how at least four out of six of her former school colleagues in their 50s 'were going to have to think about leaving to do granny duties – because the parents can't afford the childcare'. 'It was cheaper or better for an older woman teacher to leave work, to then become the granny to look after the children – so the daughter could go back to work', she sighed, with a shake of her head.

These anecdotes and experiences open up a whole new arena of pressures impinging on many people classed as economically inactive in today's Britain. This is a chronic shortage of affordable childcare, which – most independent observers agree – has the country lodged firmly near the bottom of the international affordability league. According to 2023 data compiled by the World Economic Forum, the UK's typical childcare costs were the fifth highest in the world that year – with only Czechia, Cyprus, New Zealand and the United States charging more. The analysis, based on figures from the OECD, found that net childcare costs for a UK couple on an average joint salary accounted for a quarter of their entire household income – forcing many to consider whether it was viable for both of them to stay in work at all, in cases where marginal gains from additional earnings were matched, or outstripped, by the extent of these outgoings (World Economic Forum 2023). Indeed, for many parents it is not illness or disability, but the sheer impracticality and/or unaffordability of accessing childcare around their (often variable and/or unsocial) working hours, that forces them into the position of being 'inactive' in the first place. This is to say nothing of the injustice of labelling those who choose to remain 'stay-at-home parents' inactive in the first place, given the extensive hours they spend caregiving and performing other unpaid domestic labour – not to mention the long history of revering traditional gender roles and family structures (especially on the political Right).

Indeed, the UK's affordable childcare crisis has been a longstanding and persistent problem. It was, after all, this issue that underpinned the challenges facing out-of-work lone parents back in the 1990s, at the time of that earlier moral panic about worklessness promoted by right-wing agenda-setters discussed towards the end of the last chapter. Back then (as now), political diagnoses and prescriptions varied – with the Conservatives deriding 'young ladies who get pregnant just to jump the housing queue' (Lilley 1992), while Labour despaired of a 'generation of young women' for whom 'early pregnancies and the absence of a reliable father almost guarantee a life of poverty' (Blair 1997). One outcome of the growing political focus on an inactive grouping widely framed as morally deviant was (then, as now) to make life even more challenging for them – by 'incentivizing' them off welfare and into work, largely through benefit cuts.

It is with this thought in mind that we turn to one of the other common experiences uniting almost all the people with disabilities and long-term illnesses interviewed for this chapter: financial hardship and problems with the benefits system.

Financial hardship and a punitive benefits system

Payment delays, inadequate entitlements and the trauma of being put through repeated reassessments to validate the authenticity of their disabilities and illnesses were among the commonest experiences of the welfare system relayed by interviewees. A frequent complaint was that – contrary to popular myths – benefits themselves were woefully inadequate to live on, especially after years of on-off freezes and real-terms cuts imposed by governments and amid the ongoing 'cost-of-living crisis' caused by rising inflation in food, energy and housing costs. The insufficiency of Housing Benefit (Local Housing Allowance/LHA) was a particular gripe, with numerous interviewees emphasizing how they invariably had to top up their rent payments to landlords out of the benefits they were meant to use for food and other basic essentials. Bryony received only £846 a month in LHA, but explained that 'my rent is £1400 a month, which means I pay £500 a month on top of LHA – so if I wasn't getting PIP I couldn't pay my rent'. Esther had a similar story, describing how her landlord charged her £1600 a month for a small basement flat in London – 'so it's above the local housing allowance' – but adding that she had managed to boost her LHA beyond the £1325 she was initially awarded by applying for a discretionary housing payment top-up. But this, she said, was only because she had the confidence to persist in finding out about such under-advertised avenues, thanks to her 'position of privilege' as an assertive Oxbridge graduate. By contrast, most people were 'delegitimized by the system to the extent that they won't pursue things – they'll just get by and treat themselves like trash because they are treated that way'. Testimonies like these echo the findings of recent research by the housing and homelessness charity Crisis, which found that just 2.5% of private rented properties listed in England, and 2.7% of those across the UK, were affordable to Housing Benefit recipients (Crisis 2025).

The most disturbing stories, however, had less to do with financial hardship itself than with the trials and tribulations individuals faced in applying for support, and being required to 'prove' their disabilities and health conditions (often repeatedly). Without exception, every one of the eight interviewees who was inactive for health-related reasons had been subjected, at one time or other, to WCAs – which are used to determine individuals' (in)eligibility for benefits relating to their incapacity for employment – and/or separate tests to consider whether they should be awarded PIPs (which are supposed to assist with the costs of managing disabilities and other conditions, including for people who are in work). The ordeals recounted made these tests sound more like military interrogations than sensitively handled medical assessments, with most resembling performative trials that might have been deliberately designed to ensure that genuine claimants slipped up – typically by demonstrating a higher degree of physical and/or mental fitness than they claimed.

Memories of being forced to answer 'trick questions' or ordered to parade around assessment rooms and carry out seemingly random (and irrelevant) physical tasks to demonstrate their degree of discomfort had left many interviewees feeling extremely wary about the true purpose of these tests. This was particularly true of those with fluctuating and/or less visible conditions, notably relating to neurodiversity and mental health. And it was not just the spectre of the assessments themselves that had caused them stress and anxiety, and left them feeling perpetually on trial. Another common complaint was the Kafkaesque modes of questioning on the forms they had to fill out to qualify for tests in the first place. Describing the sequence of traps she had had to avoid in navigating this part of the process, ex-OT Gloria reflected that the only reason she had managed to score 'full points' was because, 'as a health professional, I knew what language to use to help me describe a particular task'. 'If I hadn't had my degree and studied what I'd studied I don't know if the average individual can fill out this form and truly fully answer in a way that really articulates the difficulties they have', she mused.

While Gloria's inside knowledge carried her through the process successfully, she said the experience of being put through the third degree herself, rather than just witnessing it vicariously as a case worker, had 'definitely changed my perspective' on the benefits system – leaving her feeling much more sceptical about both the processes used to assess claimants and the motivations underpinning them. 'Most of the people I'd worked with were people with severe and enduring mental health problems', she said of her former caseload, adding:

> Although I'd had people say to me, 'can you help me? I'm being reassessed for benefits', really I had *no* idea at the time of ... how the ... the assessments were actually done, that people were even scored, that people would score points for each question and you had to be careful how you worded it.

This had also led her to re-evaluate some of the past cases with which she had been involved as an OT:

> I remember one person quite well, and the DWP phoned me and said, 'you filled out part of this form, can I ask you about one of these questions?' I said 'yes'. That person was denied benefits. I think now, 'was that actually my fault'? I maybe should have done more work on exactly what these forms were asking for. It was only when I came to do it myself that I became aware ... Here's what it's *actually* asking. You need to be very careful about what words you use, as to whether you get two points or whether you get four points. Be careful not to say 'sometimes I'm like this ...'. I didn't know anything when I was working, and when I was helping people fill out the forms. It's really changed my outlook on what I believed about the system.

Bryony had a similar perspective, having spent time during the pandemic working as a volunteer benefits adviser with other sick and disabled claimants trying to navigate the system – many of whom had since fallen victim to efforts by the DWP to claw back supposed 'overpayments'. To her, the potential pitfalls of incorrect form-filling could be even more sinister, with genuine claimants sometimes facing accusations of fraud and threats of legal action, in addition to sudden and unrealistic demands for repayment. 'During lockdown I was helping so many people apply for things', she recalled, describing the predicament of 'two friends who had signed on during lockdown but had worked for years, but they're now going to court'. 'If you put the wrong information down...you can literally end up in prison for filling the form out now, because you can end up being paid the wrong amount and that's "fraud" ', she reflected, adding:

> They're cracking down: even when it's their error, that mis-payment will be on your record forever ... what they are going after now is people who went on to benefits during COVID, because they didn't have the knowledge – they're going for those people.

The problem of any such pandemic-era overpayments, she argued, stemmed from a mix of steadily rising demand for incapacity and disability-related benefits, especially for people laid off and/or suffering from mental ill health during lockdowns, and a severe shortage of DWP staff adequately trained to administer an already complex and overwhelmed system. 'During COVID they didn't have the staff to do everything, and there was such a demand that they basically went "yes, yes, yes" ', she sighed, so 'they're actually looking at those people ... for overpayment or mis-payment, or a mistake on their part. It will be the poor person with the claim who will suffer'.

The advice that both Gloria and Bryony were keen to share to help others without their knowledge and personal experience of assessment processes negotiate this Byzantine system would doubtless cast them as 'sickfluencers' in the eyes of many critics. However, both saw themselves in very different terms: as genuinely disabled claimants who just happened to understand the unspoken logics, priorities and agendas underpinning Britain's under siege, under-resourced, oversubscribed welfare state. These included the increasingly narrow definition of the *degrees* of physical and mental incapacity that individuals had to demonstrate to qualify for exemption from the work-based system and acceptance into the need-based one, and the stigma and condemnation faced by anyone judged to be trying to acquire this privilege under false pretences.

As a father of three adults with work-limiting illnesses, the husband of someone with severe physical disabilities, and a long-term recipient of incapacity-related benefits himself, Terry's main ordeals at the hands of DWP had been associated with WCAs and PIP assessments. He vividly recalled how, at one PIP appointment, he had 'noticed a security guard going outside', and 'every time people left, the security guard was filming people walking away'. Direct and vicarious experiences of this kind were common to a number of stories recounted by interviewees, underlying a pervasive sense of suspicion and distrust towards the underlying motives behind DWP policies; the true basis on which benefits were awarded and withdrawn; and even the honesty and integrity of individual assessors. Gloria relayed a similar experience of being 'tested' to see if she tripped up (almost literally) when she had to attend a job centre interview after being accused of benefit fraud. The accusation had arisen because she was seen to have too much money in her bank account – a result of being reimbursed by her ex-employer for unclaimed holiday pay after being forced to leave her OT job because of ill health. 'The job centre was in a pedestrianized area and I didn't have a wheelchair at the time, [so] my husband had to carry me in', she recalled, adding that staff then casually told her, 'it's upstairs'.

In Ernest's case, one of the biggest obstacles to claiming the benefits to which he was entitled was the length and complexity of the application forms. This left him feeling so baffled and intimidated that he had to organize an appointment with the Citizens Advice Bureau (CAB) charity to help him decipher them. He remembers this occasion all too well – not least because of the fact that 'the lady who was helping me was helping somebody else' who, despite having 'lost a leg in a motorcycle accident', had been 'told by the DWP to get a job as a floor walker in a shop'. Describing the forms themselves, he recalled how, 'in the space of six questions they asked the same question six times in a different way' and 'if you answered no to one of them they then questioned why you answered yes to any of the others'. He added that 'the form for the people with learning disabilities was actually 64 pages long – it was a book, it wasn't a form'.

The payment for which Ernest was applying at the time was the legacy benefit that preceded PIP, and is still used to this day for children up to the age of 16: Disability Living Allowance (DLA). He only managed to qualify for it, on appeal, after initially being forced to attend an assessment centre to which he was barely able to gain physical access. 'The doors to the centre where the medical was held were so heavy that there was no way I could have opened the doors, and couldn't have attended the meeting – it took two people to open them', he recalled. He also recalled that 'the lift was broken, and I was told I had a choice: "you can either climb these stairs or you can come back in a week's time"'. 'I had to go without the money for a week – I think that was the plan!' he added.

But horror stories about the way the system was (mal)administered extended well beyond the indignities of disability assessments. Several interviewees relayed direct and vicarious experiences of various measures used to threaten or punish people claiming out-of-work benefits, including those receiving payments relating to sickness or disability but nonetheless placed in a 'work-related activity group' – which classified them as having some (if limited) ability to work. Most commonly, sanctions (the reduction or withdrawal of benefits for anything up to six months) are imposed when claimants are judged to have failed to meet their contractual commitments to apply for jobs, attend interviews or arrive punctually for appointments with job coaches. 'At the moment, decisions are taken by people who haven't had any training – it's people in a job centre who might have had a bad day', reflected Terry of his own past travails. Expanding on this point, he added:

> If they're in a bad mood, then they sanction you. I know people who've been sanctioned for silly things like being 10 minutes late for an interview - they've lost 50 per cent of their benefits. But they were stuck on a bus behind a car accident. Apparently, that wasn't acceptable – they should've got an earlier bus. To me, if they'd been stuck behind a car accident, it sounds like they'd got an earlier bus! I got to the point where I started getting two trains or buses before I needed to get somewhere... I'd end up at places over an hour earlier and things like that.

As a recipient of Employment and Support Allowance/ESA (the legacy sickness benefit preceding the introduction of incapacity-related Universal Credit/UC), at the time of her interview Gloria was in the 'support group', which technically exempted her from activities designed to prepare her for returning to work. But while she felt more insulated than others from 'pressure from the job centre and the DWP', she said this had not always been the case. 'My actual experience of having to go through the benefits system was actually traumatic', she recalled, adding that 'the services you think are there to help you are really unhelpful – that fear always lives there and you're not always thinking about it because I'm not at the point of needing another assessment yet'. While evidently relieved at being off the DWP's radar for now, she had vivid personal memories of the creeping dread even the most disabled claimants experienced at times when they were due for a PIP reassessment. 'There's a lot of fear, and sometimes where you've had a letter and you know an assessment is coming that really resurfaces', she said, adding that 'it's always there at the back of your mind – there's always letters coming through the door. Just seeing the envelope – and you can see the address is from the DWP – is, "oh my God, what is it *now*?" ' The peculiar terror emanating from the faceless formality of this Kafkaesque DWP bureaucracy has been conceptualized elsewhere as 'fear of the brown envelope' by sociologist Kayleigh Garthwaite (Garthwaite 2014) and as 'Brown Envelope Syndrome' by Growing Rights Instead of Poverty Partnership (GRIPP), a group of activists working to promote entitlement to social security as a human right (GRIPP 2024). In a 2024 pamphlet entitled *Untold Realities of Poverty in the UK*, it wrote:

> Can I ask you a question? When you go to bed tonight will you simultaneously breathe a sigh of relief but, at the same time, fear what the morning will bring – caused by something that happens to nearly everyone around the world and doesn't cause a seconds' [sic] thought from most people? Unfortunately, for thousands of people on welfare benefits this is a daily reality. 'What is this cause of trepidation?' I hear you ask. Simple, the daily post being delivered!!
>
> But why should the daily postie cause such fear? Well, it's a condition called 'Brown Envelope Syndrome (BES)' and I am a sufferer.

Brown envelopes, and the understandable phobias to which they give rise, are a potent symbol of one of the most disturbing aspects of the inactive experience: the coldly dispensed conveyance of state-sanctioned stigma. Regardless of its contents, for these sick and disabled interviewees (and millions of others like them) every brown envelope bearing the DWP postmark carried with it the stigma of being repeatedly reminded of one's enforced reliance on 'welfare' – and the threat of being cast into penury should this threadbare, ever more conditional safety net be withdrawn. It is to the subject of stigma and its equally disempowering bedfellow, symbolic annihilation, that we now turn.

Social insecurity and social isolation: Life as an invisible inactive

If one subject united all the interviewees, without exception, it was the sense that they were forever being judged, even informally 'assessed', by other people – for no other reason than that were out of work (or only doing small amounts of it) and/or receiving sickness or disability benefits. It's 'the money, the money and… it causes arguments', said Bryony of the tensions her status as a benefit claimant had caused, even among her own friends. 'People don't realise they can say something quite dismissive, ableist', she said, reflecting on how 'I don't look disabled without my sticks'. Yet, she added, 'if I was in a wheelchair…if anything, it's worse', recalling how

> my mum was in a wheelchair for nearly 20 years before she died [and] she was spat at – literally one person threw rubbish at her because they said she was rubbish and that's where she belonged, in front of a child!

Bryony recalled one specific incident, on a train to Leeds, when 'very loudly a man complained that he'd paid for a chair and so he sat on my disabled mother'. On other occasions she had 'heard people scream at her that she was a fake and a fraud and could probably walk'. Reflecting on recent rises in disability hate crimes (see, for example, Disability Rights UK 2025a), she said 'visible disabilities' could 'add a whole new layer to being disabled, because then you've got the stares and people pointing'. She added: 'I often worry, "is someone watching me? Is someone recording me?" ' explaining that she felt 'constantly scared of, "am I being judged?" I feel like I have a neon sign screaming "vulnerable" over my head. I have people standing behind me planning to mug me. Who's going to knock her stick away?' She added, 'sadly, we are vulnerable and we're more likely to be attacked. I tried sitting down in a disability seat the other day and someone said, "you can fuck off: you're not disabled, you can buy that stick in a chemist!" '

When asked who the main culprits were for spreading distrust and suspicion towards disabled people, most interviewees broadly agreed about who was responsible for the prejudice and negativity: journalists and politicians. 'When that stuff started getting pushed more in the media the atmosphere did change – it became very scary', recounted Bryony, adding that 'the amount of verbal attacks, even from people we know – people became quite hard and mean and judgmental and would just make really broad, misinformed, assumptions – "oh, your mum must be rich" '. By promoting narratives portraying benefit recipients as 'a bunch of scroungers', added Ernest, the tabloid press and other news outlets had made it easier for successive governments to win support for increasingly dystopian policies, from sanctions to benefit fraud hotlines. 'There was an incentive a few years back whereby people were getting rewarded for dobbing people in', he recalled, describing this as 'scary', because 'all of a sudden you feel that you could end up with no money'. He knew 'people who were dobbed in, who weren't doing any work, but were getting penalized for weeks at a time – it's guilty until proven innocent!'

For Gloria, what was 'really unhelpful, and what brings the fear back up, is all this talk about benefit claimants – "we need to reduce the number of people" – all the political rhetoric'. She described how reading such portrayals 'fires up a lot of anger' in her, and that she would 'frequently shout and swear at the telly' at portrayals of 'these lazy people that won't go to work'. But more pernicious still was the fact that, for all the outrage she instinctively felt about them, these stereotypes and caricatures were so persistent that she sometimes found herself internalizing the stigma they projected. 'I think people do...start to believe it almost', she said, reflecting on how she had 'always had this sense, since I went off work, that I *should* be doing work – I should be able to do more – even though I know what my symptoms are on a daily basis'. She added, 'we're living in a society where to not be working is not proper...and not right'.

But not everyone was so sanguine about allowing stigmatizing media and political discourses or intolerant social attitudes to dent their own self-esteem. 'I've been looking at setting up my own charity, and working with parents and de-stigmatizing benefits', said Esther, outlining her aspiration to do 'more policy work in terms of challenging the narrative'. 'I just reject it full out – I don't listen to those voices', she said of labels like 'scrounger' and 'shirker', and the wider inactivity debate. Though she acknowledged that she found it 'more difficult' to cope with stigma 'when it comes from friends or people I know', her conclusion was that the main reason 'working people' disapproved of those on benefits was because, in truth, 'they don't like the system themselves, and don't like going to work – so they just resent people who don't want to do it'. She added:

> Normally it's people without children, to be honest, or men – they don't "get" it – or they would be like a mum who does work and is finding it incredibly difficult, and they're just doing that to get by ... A lot of people are unhappy with work, so they have an issue with the jobless, because they are not doing what they see themselves as *having* to do.

Andy took a similar view. He described prevailing anti-benefits discourses as 'miserly' and responsible for making people feel as if they were 'being attacked', and dismissed 'punching down' as 'undignified', adding that he refused to internalize the barbs because (like many others on benefits) 'I know more than these ministers do'. However, he conceded that the reason he had managed to insulate himself was because he was fortunate enough to be 'a "credentialled" person', as someone able to maintain at least some paid work. Yet while he recognized this status bestowed a certain amount of privilege on him in comparison to wholly inactive claimants, Andy was still disturbed by what he saw as a dark turn in societal narratives towards poverty and benefits in recent years that he saw as 'regressive compared to 1000 years ago'. 'Historically, it's been considered there were some social groups who were sort of seen as "deserving"', he said, reflecting that, while he was 'not one for the principles of "deserving" and "undeserving"', it 'shocks me that there is no longer a category of "deserving"', such as those who are genuinely sick and disabled – which he described as 'becoming an erased category'.

The possibility that we have entered an era in which certain categories of vulnerable person once viewed as intrinsically deserving are slowly being 'erased' – symbolically annihilated both discursively and in terms of public policy – is a disquieting undercurrent that runs throughout much of this book. In the context of this chapter, this idea is important because it speaks to another dimension of anti-welfare stigma: its role as a vessel for *promoting* symbolic annihilation. Besides contributing to a sense of shame and worthlessness, stigma was described by interviewees as having real-world consequences, by compounding the lack of opportunities and material disadvantages resulting from individuals' financial hardship, and contributing to their marginalization – isolation and even exclusion – from mainstream society. 'If they [inactive claimants] go to see someone, people will complain cos they go to the pub', reflected Terry – echoing the substantial body of social research that has exposed disapproving attitudes towards out-of-work benefit recipients who dare to try to maintain social lives (see, for example, Golding and Middleton 1982). 'The trouble is', he added,

> that pub trip might be the only time that week they see anyone – it's the only way they get to see anyone and stay sane and enquire with people if there are any odd jobs that they know about ... They're networking!

Others explained how they themselves had come to feel ever more disconnected from, or invisible to, their erstwhile friendship groups through a process of stigmatization, creeping marginalization and, ultimately, annihilation. 'My family life was suffering because I felt that I was worthless to the kids', sighed Ernest, adding that his 'social life went completely out of the window', leaving him feeling that he 'was a waste of space'. This, in turn, led him to 'consider ending it all'. For Bryony, meanwhile, being inactive had 'caused massive problems'. 'If you can't go to things like dinner parties, birthdays – if you're not physically present – people stop inviting you', she said, reflecting on how her friends 'don't want to have to make allowances – they just want to go on with their lives' and 'don't want to have to worry about someone fainting or passing out at a dinner party'. She said she had 'gone from being very sociable and going out to things to...nothing':

> I don't get messages because people don't want to keep in touch. It gets to the point where you don't have anything to contribute. My life is nothing like theirs: there's no children. If it wasn't for my allergies, I'd be using food banks! I'm on a strict, limited diet, which means I can't eat out. Even if I do, my support dog isn't allowed.

Although Andy had held on to most of his friends, he lived with his grandfather, and conceded there was 'a sort of independence issue' with that. But his 'main problem', psychologically, was his 'battle with weight', which he found 'very easy...to put on' because it was so 'difficult for me to exercise'. 'As you can imagine, you get quite miserable, so it's very easy to comfort eat', he said of the mental health impacts of spending so much time (living and working) alone. 'Mostly it's more than a mourning of the past – it's a fear of what you might lose in future', he reflected, describing 'a fear that maybe I won't have a family – or I'll have to trade off other things other people might have'. This felt to him like 'a pre-emptive mourning of the future'.

We return to some of these ideas in the Conclusion, when we consider the concept of economic inactivity as a form of partial existence or 'half-life': a liminal state of survival somewhere between living, with the full sense of social acceptance and belonging this brings, and being ignored, shunned, excluded – or annihilated. But before coming back to these uncomfortable themes, it is time to consider the concept of inactivity from two more positive and myth-busting perspectives. In the next chapter we debunk some of the enduring misconceptions of the economically inactive by exploring the role many of them play as valuable social contributors – whether through caregiving or offering their unpaid labour as volunteers to benefit the common good. In the short chapter that follows, we then turn to exploring the lives and perspectives of another unsung group that, barring the brief explosion of coverage around the late-COVID 'Great Retirement' or 'Great Resignation', tend to be similarly discursively invisible, or symbolically annihilated: 'elective' and/or 'new inactives' who have consciously chosen to quit the workplace.

NOTE

1. Aliases are used for interviewees throughout Chapters 3–5.

4

Caring, Volunteering and Disabled Labour: The Hardworking 'Inactive'

Kirsty's typical day starts at 5 a.m., when she steps in to relieve her sister Amelia at the bedside of the second youngest of their eight siblings. The 3-year-old's major bodily organs are affected by a genetic disorder that, says Amelia, is 'so rare it doesn't have a name' – forcing her to constantly lie in a prone position, connected to an oxygen tank. But the punishing 24/7 shifts needed to care for her are only part of her sisters' unpaid routines. While Amelia, 19, watches over her, Kirsty, 21, is responsible for three other disabled siblings, among them a 4-year-old with multiple conditions including spina bifida.

Though Amelia, Kirsty and their family live in north-east Scotland, their mother (a single parent) still juggles her role at a local charity with a longstanding position as a Cambridge University researcher. This often requires her to work away from home – leaving caring responsibilities, in her absence, to her two eldest children. If either sister manages to wangle a half-hour or so for themselves during the course of a day, it's only then that they can squeeze in their studies – or, in the case of Kirsty (who recently completed an Open University degree in politics, philosophy and economics), efforts to find a job with an employer flexible enough to allow her to work from home full time.

'My siblings come first, always', Amelia explained, during a video call conducted over a shaky Wi-Fi connection in autumn 2024, before adding, 'typically it's them, then my studies, and then whatever else falls beneath it. I just study when she's [youngest sister] asleep – when she's napping, I'm studying'. Her youngest sister, she said, 'needs constant supervision' – especially when their mother is on a 'work week', which involves her being 'out and about a lot', rather than analysing data, writing reports or handling video calls from home. As a result, 'being able to be flexible about when I work is vital'.

Amelia and Kirsty are on call round the clock, and every day is much the same – with no weekends and very rare holidays. The nearest they normally come to any respite is during twice-yearly visits to a hospice in Kinross, in Scotland's 'central belt', where they can catch their breath while their 3-year-old sister receives a few days' specialist care.

Yet according to ministers, statisticians and the media, Amelia and Kirsty are both economically inactive – or (to use the term's more disparaging synonym) workless. This is despite the fact that they, and the 5.8 million other unpaid carers like them, work night and day for no wage and collectively save taxpayers £184 billion a year – equivalent to the combined budget for the National Health Service across all four UK nations (Petrillo et al. 2024). As Amelia put it, 'if someone else took care of our siblings, they'd need specialist training that would take months – and spending their entire lives here [in north-east Scotland] would cost a fortune too'. She added, 'We do it because we love them'.

Drawing on experiences such as these, this chapter contests the entire premise of contemporary bureaucratic and political definitions of what constitutes 'work' and 'economic activity' – terms it purposely problematizes as much as work*lessness* and *in*activity themselves. It does so by exploring a multitude of meaningful ways in which people categorized as inactive contribute to the common good. As well as supposedly inactive people providing unpaid care (many of them with their own disabilities and health conditions), we also hear from those working long hours as volunteers in a range of other capacities – including as community workers, benefit advisers and charity campaigners.

Annihilating 'unsung heroes'? Poverty, invisibility and the lives of unpaid carers

Every year, on 21 November, news organizations and the government dutifully wheel out commentators and senior ministers in performative displays of admiration for Britain's least-celebrated workforce: unpaid carers. True to form, Carers Rights Day 2024 saw everyone from Scottish First Minister John Swinney to UK Social Security Minister Sir Stephen Timms pay their respects with high-profile visits to local carers' charities. A week later, Stephen Kinnock, then Minister of State for Care in the Department for Health and Social Care, unveiled a £22.6 million funding boost designed to 'give carers much-needed breaks and greater flexibility, as well as technology to make their lives easier' (Department of Health and Social Care 2024: n.pag.). In so doing, he doubled down on an apparent shift towards recognizing the value of the contributions made by unpaid carers signalled weeks earlier, when the newly installed Labour government had confirmed the biggest rise in the 'earnings threshold' for receipt of Carer's Allowance since the 1970s, by granting eligibility to 60,000 carers previously disqualified for earning too much money from paid employment. In a flattering statement accompanying his department's announcement, Mr Kinnock declared unpaid carers 'the country's unsung heroes' – praising them for providing 'invaluable support to vulnerable people every day' and emphasizing how it was 'vital they too have the support they need so they can look after their own health and wellbeing', assisted by their local councils.

Yet within four short months, his sister ministry, the Department for Work and Pensions, was announcing plans to impose the biggest cuts in state support for unpaid carers in living memory. It did so through twin-pronged proposals making it harder for sick and disabled people to claim benefits, on the one hand, and, on the other, implicitly making ongoing support for unpaid carers conditional on engagement with the wider job market – both by them and (wherever possible) by those for whom they cared. In its controversial March 2025 'Pathways to Work' green paper, the DWP announced a suite of proposals that, if enacted in full, would have left both carers and cared-for people severely financially penalized. These ranged from tougher eligibility requirements and more frequent reassessments for many people already receiving PIP relating to their personal care needs to tighter conditions for new claimants applying for either or both of PIP and the health-related top-up to Universal Credit.

While ministers were unabashed about their underlying agenda for cutting health and disability payments – to save money and boost economic growth by getting 'more people off welfare' and into their vanishingly narrow definition of productive 'work' (Department for Work and Pensions 2025b) – one largely unacknowledged knock-on effect of these measures was to punish carers themselves. As someone's entitlement to PIP and/or other health-related benefits often acts as a 'gateway' for their *carer's* ability to access financial support – specifically Carer's Allowance (CA) and the Carer Element in Universal Credit – the planned changes were destined to deprive some 150,000 'unsung heroes' of their main or only sources of income (Carers UK 2025b). Not only this: as many people providing unpaid care for others are disabled themselves, and have historically received PIP and/or incapacity-related payments in their own right, tens of thousands of carers faced being penalized twice over, by losing their own access to benefits. Analysis by Carers UK calculated that many affected households stood to lose more than £8000 a year (Carers UK 2025b). All this came at a time when, according to the Joseph Rowntree Foundation, both carers and disabled people were already more likely than those from almost any other groups to be living in 'deep poverty', and families 'with an unpaid carer' were 'more likely to move into very deep poverty than those without' (Joseph Rowntree Foundation 2025: n.pag.).

So why are so many people labouring as unrecognized and unpaid carers when one of the founding purposes of the welfare state was to provide state-funded, 'cradle-to-the-grave' support for anyone unable to look after themselves? Problems with Britain's ailing benefits system aside, there is also an ongoing, and escalating, crisis in its social care system at a time when the country's population is rapidly ageing (Barton et al. 2024) while fertility rates are declining among the working-aged adults whose labour and taxes are needed to support their elders (Office for National Statistics 2024b). As a result, today's social care provision is being squeezed by a pincer-movement of persistent financial strain (bequeathed, in part, by fifteen-plus years of real-terms austerity cuts) and ever escalating demand – including as a result of the increase in disability-related economic inactivity since the pandemic. The levels of provision available – and the precise criteria for accessing it – have always been something of a patchwork across England alone, let alone the four separate nations, as local authorities often set their own criteria for precisely how (and whether) particular individuals might qualify for assistance with care relating to their physical and/or mental health needs. Today, though, there is an ever-present sense that care is being effectively 'rationed', and, in practice, the ability of children and adults of working age to access help with tasks such as washing, dressing and cooking (let alone anything else) from someone outside their own family is largely contingent on whether the former are able to access Disability Living Allowance (DLA) and the latter PIP – and, if so, at what level(s). If a DLA or PIP assessment concludes that someone is fit enough to work and/or look after themselves, or uses its highly contested points-based system to award minimal support, that individual will either be left to their own devices – or, if they happen to live with someone else, the burden will fall on them. Otherwise, the only recourse to accessing professional care is if the individual or their family has its own money to pay for it.

Alongside the *economic* drivers of Britain's (over-)reliance on unpaid carers, there are also cultural factors at work in many cases, with traditions of caring for sick, disabled and elderly relatives hardwired into the customs of certain ethnic communities. One result of this is to introduce a racialized dimension into the more widespread disadvantages faced by unpaid carers, as the social contributions of particular minority communities are rendered disproportionately invisible, and therefore unaddressed, in public policy and discourse. While the overall ethnic breakdown of people providing unpaid care at the time of the UK's 2021 censuses broadly reflected that of the general population (Eley 2023), academic research has pointed to stark differentials in the number of hours per week devoted to this work by carers from different groups. According to recent analysis of data from the UK Household Longitudinal Study (2009–20), seven out of ten Pakistani carers and three quarters of those from the Bangladeshi community looked after someone within their own household, compared to just two in five of those from White backgrounds. The disproportionate intra-familial focus of care within Pakistani and Bangladeshi households translated into much longer hours spent on unpaid care – with a little over a quarter of White carers devoting twenty-plus hours a week to these duties, compared to just under 41% and more than 43% of Pakistani and Black African carers respectively (Wells et al. 2024). Hardly surprising, perhaps, that a study of the pandemic experiences of Black, Asian and minority ethnic carers found that, during lockdowns, they had been left more heavily impacted by the closure of essential services in their areas, more materially disadvantaged and more anxious about their finances than those from White groups (Carers UK 2022).

It is a measure of the ongoing invisibility – or symbolic annihilation – of unpaid carers in public discourse (and policy) that, over its well-thumbed 79 pages, the 'Pathways to Work' green paper had almost nothing to say about them – that is, apart from reiterating the government's previously announced pledge to raise the amount carers were permitted to earn from paid work before forfeiting their Carer's Allowance. This was pointedly framed as a device designed to 'support unpaid carers to combine caring responsibilities with some paid work' (Department for Work and Pensions 2025b: 12). Other than this, Britain's loudly lauded 'unsung heroes' merited only a single mention, on page 79 – in which ministers undertook to 'consider the impacts on benefits for unpaid carers' as part of their 'wider consideration of responses to the consultation as it develops its detailed proposals for change' (Department for Work and Pensions 2025b: 79). And yet, according to an early analysis by the respected social security advisory service Benefits and Work, the paper's proposal to remove PIP from anyone who did not score at least four points for one daily living activity in a future reassessment – the so-called 'four-point rule' – could have led to nine out of ten recipients losing up to £9,600 a year in benefits by 2029–30. Physically disabled people who were most likely to suffer because of the changes included those whose primary disability was back pain or arthritis – with eight out of ten and three-quarters of all claimants with these conditions, respectively, at risk of losing their PIP daily living components, according to a Freedom of Information Act request (Disability Rights UK 2025b). There was also cause for concern for people whose primary conditions related to their mental health: the FOI request found that nearly half of those with anxiety and depression and more than a quarter with other psychiatric disorders were unlikely to achieve the minimum qualifying four points, judging by previous assessment outcomes (Disability Rights UK 2025b).

The discursive invisibility of unpaid carers (especially those providing full-time care, with no room to take on additional work) offers governments the protection of plausible deniability for the negative impacts of cold, hard cuts like those proposed in the green paper. It also acts as a further form of symbolic annihilation of the experiences and perspectives of many people classed as economically inactive – and a denial of the intersectionally disadvantaged lived realities of many of this book's interviewees.

A succinct summary of the unrewarded and unrecognized sacrifices made by full-time carers came from Ernest, when recalling the long years of round-the-clock labour his son had put into caring for him. 'He's virtually unpaid', Ernest explained, adding that 'he gets Carer's Allowance, which is about £60 a week', which 'gets topped up with income support' (a further £30) taking him up to about £90 a week all told – 'for which he has to effectively work thirty-five hours, for £90, which is well below the minimum wage!' Responding to what he saw as the popular image of carers – on the rare occasions they manage to gain any visibility – he reflected that 'people...think that they sit around and do nothing a lot of the time – which is not the case at all'. He added that, though he was 'a lot more independent than some people', allowing his son to 'get a lot of time off that others wouldn't', he knew others from his time working in the disability sector 'who were working not far short of 24/7, and the chances of them getting respite was very slim'.

A similar perspective was relayed by Terry, who remarked on how a short spell working as a volunteer outside the home seemed to count for much more, in the eyes of the DWP and job centre staff, than his many years providing round-the-clock care for his disabled wife and children. 'Whilst I was an unpaid carer, I still had to go to certain meetings to see a job coach or go to training', he recalled, noting how 'they [DWP] calmed down...with me going to these appointments once I started volunteering'. The performance of physically going out to work (albeit as a volunteer) seemed to satisfy the authorities that Ernest was 'keeping myself prepared for the workplace' in a way that did not apply when he was a lowly carer. 'That was what they were worried about – me losing touch with the workplace', he said, adding that 'they seemed to think that even if you were caring for someone else you only had to do so for a limited amount of the day'.

Terry's experience speaks to the symbolic violence to which unpaid carers are subjected, as an informal, largely invisible labour force so often excluded from media-political discourse. For Esther, redress for this historical under-recognition of individuals providing unpaid care needed to be extended well beyond those looking after sick or disabled relations – to people choosing (or, in many cases, forced by their circumstances) to stay at home to care for dependent children. As a lone parent herself, she viewed 'unpaid domestic labour' as 'surely the most useful thing' to society as a whole, because it was 'making sure we have good health and not criminalization – that comes from raising kids, right?' 'I took the view that the best thing I could do was raise my kids well, but that work – and it *is* work – is not recognized as work', she said of her time bringing up a son while also volunteering for a succession of charities and campaigns, and managing the fluctuating and often debilitating conditions (fibromyalgia and ADHD) that had prevented her from holding down more rigid and/or full-time paid work. 'I think mothers should be paid for work', she went on, suggesting that

> if you have a kid you get paid, like, two grand a month – you either get someone to do the childcare, and do something else, or you get paid to be a mother, because being a mother is work in itself.

The inactive volunteer: Meet the 'workless worker'

Unpaid social care was only one form of unrecognized work being undertaken by the supposedly inactive individuals interviewed for this book. Almost all the interviewees also had stories to share about the considerable contributions they had made – and, in most cases, continued to make – to the public good by offering their unpaid labour through volunteerism. Though the range of voluntary 'jobs' and activities outlined was also expansive, many of them tended to be roles directly or indirectly related to their own experiences of Britain's hard-pressed welfare system – from working in foodbanks to dispensing benefits advice or campaigning for poverty and disability charities.

While the reasons for offering their unpaid labour varied – from a desire to stay active or relieve boredom to experiences of being required to do so, in return for out-of-work benefits – what united almost all interviewees was their belief in the intrinsic *value* of voluntary work, even if this was rarely publicly recognized by politicians or the media. For Ernest, it was important to do 'as much volunteer work as I can, because that's the way I can feel I can give something back', particularly as he was 'now at that lovely age where I'm properly retired' – and finally liberated from navigating his own ongoing battles with the benefits system. For Gloria, volunteering was, at least partly, about bolstering her own sense of self-esteem. 'As well as helping other people it's also helping me – with self-worth', she said, explaining how it stopped her feeling she was 'just a burden'.

Much of Ernest's earlier volunteering work involved helping out with local disability charities and community groups in his area, ranging from the Surrey Independent Living Council, for whom he assisted disabled people managing their household budgets, to Surrey Users' Network (later renamed Surrey Coalition of Disabled People), for which he was involved in inspecting care homes on behalf of the families of current and prospective residents. By contrast, Gloria's volunteering CV spanned the gamut of socially useful contributions – from those concerned with providing nuts-and-bolts support for vulnerable people to less utilitarian, but perhaps more mutually satisfying, endeavours. In addition to helping to man a phone line for the ME Association (a charity directly connected to her own condition), she was a member of the Patient and Public Involvement Panel for NHS Scotland's Mental Health Research Network. But her most rewarding contributions were those drawing on her expertise as a meditation teacher, including the groups or circles she organized for an online wellness group aimed at women. She explained:

> I upload meditations to Insight Timer, which is a meditation app. I can do that as and when I want - so if it takes me a week or it takes me two months, I can do that. If I can get comments from people that it's helped them sleep it makes me feel like I've done something.

Similarly diverse experiences of volunteering were relayed by Theresa, a 50-something textile artist whose working life had oscillated between short spells of paid work (largely in low-waged casual jobs) and longer periods of informal volunteering – often in return for 'bed and board', enabling her to largely sidestep the benefits system. 'I've put my energies into community projects, worked with asylum seekers and migrants, victims of domestic violence', she explained, adding that her choice of where to target her unpaid labour had been motivated by the fact that 'every day something shocks me: the way people are handled in the media and grouped together'. For three others – Annette, Bryony and (more recently) Ernest – voluntary work had been closely bound up with their own prior involvement, as beneficiaries, with the poverty charity All Together in Dignity (ATD) Fourth World. Ernest had helped out with everything from 'computer work' in the charity's Surrey satellite office to community gardening initiatives, while Annette's de facto roles as a helper at its South-East London offices was to contribute to administrative duties, including filing and basic paperwork, as well as acting as a 'meet-and-greet' for visiting members of its user network. Bryony's links with the charity had been more longstanding and extensive. 'I've been an activist with ATD since I was 11! I did loads of stuff in their youth movement, worked closely with the Council of Europe, did stuff for Oxfam, Amnesty International, Joseph Rowntree Foundation', she reeled off, breathlessly. The range of activities with which she had been involved over the years had ranged from campaigning duties – public speaking, fund-raising and 'help with research' – to hands-on grassroots work, including offering benefits advice and taking part in skills-sharing initiatives with other disadvantaged teenagers involved in the charity's youth movement. These had covered often mundane, but important, practical questions such as 'how to run a house, how to budget', she said, adding that 'no one's going to help you, so how do you decorate and fix up your house? It was stuff we thought we'd help out and teach each other'.

Yet, while the overwhelming consensus was that voluntarism was a positive thing – benefiting both wider society and volunteers' own personal well-being – not everyone offered it their unqualified praise. Bryony was particularly blunt in her criticism of what she saw as the tendency for larger national charities to plead poverty and exploit the voluntary labour of often hard-up people who would benefit from a modest wage. 'Proper jobs won't touch me with a broomstick, no chance – on paper, I'm an absolute mess!' she said, 'but I do all this voluntary work and community work, and I help all these people – but I can't do it for a job!' The worst offenders, she said, included some of the most respected charities. 'None of them will pay us – they're profiting off our labour but won't pay us', she said, accusing them of 'profiting from the disabled in that way, under the pretext of "we're giving you experience" '. She added angrily that 'they just profit off us – and because we're poor we tend to shop there too, so they get our money too!'

Ernest took a similar view, stressing how the efforts of Britain's unsung volunteer labour force saved government, charities and other employers 'a fortune'. 'People like myself volunteer to do gardening, [and] there was another lady who passed away who set up two or three youth clubs in their council estate, to get kids off the streets', he said, adding that this was 'all unpaid and it's all work that's done to keep the communities going', because 'otherwise the likes of running youth clubs you'd need to find paid staff to do it' and 'you'd need to find specific premises, whereas most of these clubs are run from within people's own homes'. 'The gardening jobs that I do you'd end up paying somebody £10 an hour, just to mow someone's lawn', he said, adding that he was happy to 'mow someone's grass for maybe 20p – that's how much petrol it costs me'.

There was also indignation, and some anger, at the lack of public recognition volunteering (like caring) received more generally – and the at best invisible, at worst stigmatizing treatment many people offering their labour for the common good, but classed as inactive, received from politicians and the press. Terry remarked:

> I wish them reporters ... would actually come and spend a day in the life of people who are doing the care – or people who have worked really hard to find work and are just doing voluntary work and things like that to stay active.

These views were echoed by Kirsty, who said media portrayals and the accompanying rhetoric on economic inactivity from government left her 'so frustrated', and wondering 'what happens if all the unpaid carers stopped caring'?

Informal economies, neighbourly relations and communitarian 'cultures of poverty'

As well as providing unpaid care and formalized types of voluntary work, some interviewees also engaged in forms of unrecognized labour – and informal economic activity – that did not fit neatly into either of these categories. These included reciprocal exchanges of social capital, entrepreneurship and cooperation comparable to those sociologists Oscar Lewis and Herbert Gans observed in their seminal 1960s explorations of slum communities in New York and Boston respectively: forms of contingent communitarian relation the former conceptualized as the 'culture of poverty' (Lewis 1966).

From her humble beginnings in Lancashire, North-West England, Theresa's life story reads like a one-person case study of how to make ends meet with little or no help from the state or taxpayer – despite having spent only short bursts in jobs that actually paid wages. 'When I left the college there wasn't anything lined up. I had about 37 pence in my bank account!' she recalled of the day in the 1990s she graduated with distinction in fashion and beauty therapy from a university 'down south'. In the first of many informal, mutually beneficial arrangements she went on to strike with vulnerable people needing help, she 'found free room and accommodation in exchange for help for a disabled lady' – a fellow artist with whom she 'stayed for ten years'. She went on to take on a host of other roles – from paid work in adult education and community teaching to volunteering in a food bank during lockdown. This contribution had brought with it practical fringe benefits that helped her get by without the need to claim benefits. 'I'd get to take the food home', she recalled, adding that during other spells as a volunteer, 'I was allowed to take some groceries and that would see me over a couple of weeks'.

These days Theresa was only able to 'keep the wolf from the door' because, during a past period of paid employment, she had managed to obtain an interest-only mortgage on a one-bedroom leasehold flat – ensuring that, however straitened her circumstances might become, she at least had a roof over her head. Even so, she could not 'afford to put on the heating' and was forced to 'sleep on boxes and a futon'. As for food, she was largely accessing this through her reciprocal relationship with the latest people for whom she was caring: a 'lady with Parkinson's' who was so disabled that she could not 'get up from where she's sitting even to walk to the door' and an 80-year-old pensioner who lived alone with her cat. On her visiting days, Theresa did all the cooking and, in return, got to have a warm meal herself. 'Some days I'll have an egg sandwich for supper', she said, 'or sometimes I'll visit the lady and stay over with her during the week', when she will 'cook for both of us'.

On top of his day-to-day role as an unpaid carer, Ernest also had extensive experience of offering his unpaid labour for the benefit of his wider community, and observing others doing likewise. 'If an elderly neighbour needed a shelf put up, you knew who to speak to and get that done – a lot of it goes on', he said, recalling how, during COVID, 'it became obvious that a lot of older people couldn't leave the house, so people brought food to them'. He added that 'even when COVID isn't going on, a lot of this is still happening but it's not spoken about because it's not so big'. The invisibility of these communitarian efforts, he said, denied the contributions made by those, like his neighbours, who 'were out of work but would go to the shops and do those runs' for other people – 'or even single mums', who would 'take the children of other mums so they can go to work'. 'They're just seen as scrounging single mums but they're helping the community running by picking up the kids for them so they could work', he said, adding:

> All these sort of things go on in communities but they're never seen or brought up: they're just seen as lazy people. They're doing all these sort of jobs that allow other people to live their lives. It's never talked about because the government just wants to portray these people as lazy people.

Terry's reflections on the invisibility of such forms of altruistic and/or reciprocal social acts in UK public discourse speaks to the wider symbolic annihilation of the material social contributions – and forms of economic activity – performed by people offering their services as unpaid carers and through more formalized channels for mobilizing voluntary labour. As with unpaid social care, many of the activities outlined were helping to fill the gaping holes left in Britain's increasingly threadbare welfare state safety-net after years of sustained government spending cuts. By volunteering in a food bank, and for various other charities involved in tackling food poverty, Theresa was helping to plug the growing chasm between dwindling levels of support available to unemployed, inactive and low-waged benefit recipients and Britain's ever-escalating cost of living – a gap one might expect to be addressed by taxpayer-funded social security. In picking up groceries and cooking meals for the elderly and disabled women she had befriended, she was relieving pressure on her local council's (doubtless overstretched) meals-on-wheels service and stepping in where formally employed paid carers might otherwise have been needed.

More importantly, considered through the prism of social value, rather than 'pounds and pence' cost savings, Theresa, Terry and others like them were contributing immeasurably to the well-being of vulnerable, isolated and often very lonely people. Such forms of communitarian cooperation and charitability evoke political scientist Robert Putnam's conception of 'social capital' (Putnam 1994), or what Gans memorably described as a virtuous 'spiral of reciprocal obligations' in *The Urban Villagers*, his classic 1962 ethnographic account of the lives of people struggling to survive in a deprived area of Boston (Gans 1962: 84). Specifically, the small acts of altruism and compassion Theresa and Terry described bore close comparison to what Gans defined as 'latent' forms of obligation, whereby people are motivated by 'a desire to give and receive, and enjoy the resulting reciprocity'. These contrast with the markedly more conditional and/or obligatory forms of social exchange Gans classed as 'manifest', which see reciprocity obligations become 'a duty' and 'a burden', and people trying 'to escape involvement'. Given this book's focus, it is highly significant that Gans explicitly elided these burdensome, conditional forms of reciprocity with those offered by 'representatives from the outside world, like welfare agencies', who only 'give aid in exchange for deference or loyalty to institutions' and, conversely, *withdraw* it when this is considered absent – much as today's DWP penalizes inactive non-contributors (Gans 1962: 84).

Gans's implicit juxtaposition of the humanity, camaraderie and enlightened self-interest displayed by those engaged in acts of latent reciprocity versus the bureaucratized, conditional and cynical deployment of state-directed manifest reciprocity was eloquently summarized in the following detailed anecdote from Terry:

> I remember quite a few years ago I helped a person paint their house and that I had to get called into a job centre and explain the situation. Then they wrote letters to the person to find out if I was getting paid anything, getting cups of tea, etc. They also questioned things like 'why would you bring someone in to help you do something they're not qualified to do?'

In a similar vein, Ernest described having to be discrete in applying his training in forestry to offer help tending the gardens of local people – in case he was 'dobbed in' to the DWP for helping out with physical activities while claiming disability-related benefits. 'This volunteer gardening that I do – I have to be careful that I don't do too much because someone could turn around and say, "oh he's doing all this work – he can't be disabled" ', he explained. For others, discussing such tensions opened up much wider questions – to which we return in both the next chapter and the Conclusion. These include fundamental conundrums around how society defines terms like *social value*, *contribution*, *work* and *activity* (economic or otherwise). 'The way we conceive of work is insane and it doesn't fit actual work or societal well-being at all', observed Esther, reflecting on her journey from high-flying Law graduate to homeless single mother to her current position, as a disabled person moving between modestly paid jobs with the CAB and human rights charities (helping other vulnerable people) and bouts of what the state would doubtless define as economic inactivity. She said:

> I really do think that when it comes to work we need to start to think, 'what are we working for? What are we placing value on here? It's work if it's profiting someone else – right'? Why do we think someone is contributing if they are ultimately ... wrecking the environment?

She added (in a nod to her sense of latent, not manifest, obligation) that, through her proposed charity work, she would 'like to be doing more policy work in terms of challenging the narrative' around 'economic inactivity' and critiquing the environmental impact of economic growth.

Disability as hard work: Towards an understanding of 'disabled labour'

Beyond all the forms of socially valuable unpaid labour this chapter has already explored, there is another – even more frequently ignored, less publicly visible – aspect of many inactive people's lives that merits consideration, as a corrective to the narrowness of society's conceptions of 'work'. This relates to the significant day-to-day efforts people with work-limiting disabilities and illnesses need to muster simply in order to manage – or cope with – their own impairments and health conditions. As Bryony explained exasperatedly:

> Being sick and disabled *is* a full-time job – between the medical equipment, the time spent with the condition, being sick is a full-time job because we don't get time off. It doesn't stop at the weekend. It doesn't stop at five o'clock. In the end, being disabled is a full-time job.

One of the most vivid descriptions of what might best be termed 'disabled labour' was relayed by Andy. Though he had successfully obtained a degree, and held down demanding jobs for much of his adult life, the trauma of managing a debilitating bone marrow condition, and the compromised immune system it engendered, had taken a serious toll on his personal and professional stamina. 'I can work but my energy levels, pain levels, are up and down a lot and I get sick, [so] I need to structure where it [work] can get done', he explained, reflecting on his dependency on employers willing to let him work from home – and at times of his choosing. He recalled how, at one point during childhood, he had been forced to go through such a prolonged period of regular medical appointments that his school attendance was severely disrupted – and he was often too tired and weak to study. 'I noticed that I was having a lot of problems with my blood – I was bruising just from basically sitting down or moving, I was having blood coming out of my skin', he recalled, describing how a test for leukaemia led to his diagnosis with a haematology condition and the start of an unrelenting four-year period of outpatient care. 'I was tired all the time – I was in pain', he said, adding, 'I just never got better ... There was a five-year period when going to hospital was just a part of my life'.

Andy's description of how his energy-sapping immunity-compromising condition interfered with the most basic day-to-day aspects of his life and work strongly echoed the experiences of single mother Esther, who had also battled for years to hold down jobs. She described sometimes experiencing such intense 'fatigue' that she could not even 'make dinner' or 'get dressed'. Recalling the period when her symptoms had first started becoming acute, she described how she 'was working in domestic violence, was living in a basement flat, was underground all day and starting to feel awful', and that, 'after about 1 [p.m.] I couldn't do anything and was just lying on a bed'.

Others described how they had been forced to end periods of employment – or take prolonged time out – because of debilitating and/or fluctuating symptoms, often triggered, at least in part, by workplace pressures. 'If I had to pick one single thing that has caused me the most anxiety in my adult life it might be employment in various ways', said Ian of his struggle to overcome acute ADHD and autism symptoms on graduating from university to seek out, and then hold down, his first job. 'Even before I knew I was neurodivergent', he said, 'I just felt this huge dread at the idea of joining the workforce, because I knew there were lots of things I couldn't do or couldn't do as easily'. Recalling his sense of jubilation on landing his post as a local authority administrator ('it was like imagining what it might be like to become an astronaut or an Olympic athlete'), he described how the first few months of pride and relief soon gave way to bouts of exhaustion, as his eagerness to impress took its toll on his mental and physical health. 'It was extremely intense in terms of being in that job – the first six months or so were relatively easy and I was just kind of constantly in disbelief that I actually had a job and it was going relatively well', he said, adding, 'as things got on I got really burned out [and] I had to take about two months off with medical leave because I was really burned out'.

The pressures of disabled labour were not confined to those with caring responsibilities for others or who had continued trying to hold down jobs. Almost all the interviewees with one or more disability or chronic illness had anecdotes describing the sheer amount of hard work involved in managing their conditions – and the barriers they often presented to carrying out even the most mundane day-to-day activities. In Bryony's case, her main illness – 'endo' – had the habit of hitting her so badly on any given day that she could spend up to 'eight to ten hours a day stuck in my toilet' – forcing her to rely on 'a fall-over alarm' that she even had to 'wear at home'. 'If I go for a walk, I will need an eighteen-hour nap', she added.

But beyond their battles to complete what most able-bodied people would consider everyday tasks, the most significant form of disabled labour interviewees complained about was their frequent, at times continual, battles with 'the system' – especially the health, social care and welfare-related services on which they depended to access vital support. This applied to everything from problems applying (and being assessed) for benefits and social care to protracted waiting times for specialist medical appointments on the NHS. Of all the hard-pressed services they were forced to grapple with, few were more labour-intensive and difficult to access than appropriately qualified mental health professionals. Describing his 21-year-old daughter's then ongoing battle to find the support she needed to enable her to re-engage with the workplace – an intention one might have expected government agencies to enthusiastically facilitate, given their ongoing crusade to move as many inactive people as possible off benefits and into paid jobs – Terry described how she had found it 'impossible to get the help she needs'.

For others, the main focus of their disabled labour was expressed through exasperation at the effort it took them to navigate Britain's increasingly conditional and complex benefits system – and being forced to repeatedly 'prove' their disability just to retain their access to existing (and often inadequate) financial support. Describing the tangled odyssey she had taken through multiple iterations of legacy disability benefits over more than two decades, Bryony explained how it was only by threatening to take her own life that she managed to prompt the DWP to complete her migration from the legacy incapacity benefit Employment and Support Allowance (ESA) to Universal Credit – a process that proved so Byzantine and protracted that it left her for months with 'no income at all'. 'The only reason they sorted out my claim, I'm sorry to say, is that I tried to kill myself – I tried to jump out of that window, on the third floor', she recalled, adding that, 'when they finally paid it, they basically admitted that they hadn't read the paperwork'. Even then, her battles with the benefits system were not entirely over. Although her overall income today 'can be okay' (largely because she now also qualified for PIP), her support with housing costs fell well short of her actual rent, as she was no longer eligible for 'discretionary housing benefit' – a higher level payment that is only available to people on legacy benefits. 'If your rent is over the local housing allowance, you have to pay the shortfall for your rent – and council tax', she explained. As outlined previously, Bryony's local housing allowance (LHA) – set centrally by DWP on the basis of the average rent in her area – only came to £846 per month, while her rent was £1400. This forced her to pay '£500 a month on top of LHA' out of the income-replacement benefits she ostensibly received to pay for all her other outgoings.

In one sense, then, disabled labour can be understood in relatively simple terms: as the *additional* strain experienced by people with disabilities and long-term health conditions over and above the tiredness (and occasional burnout) to which everyone is prone, particularly if juggling demanding jobs and/or caregiving duties. In other respects, it represents a distinct, often multifaceted, form of toil – or category of work – that is simply not an issue for anyone fortunate enough not to have to manage a condition or ailment that interferes with the most basic aspects of their everyday lives.

Considered as an aggravating factor to any one (or more) of the other types of hardworking 'inactivity' explored in this chapter, disabled labour represents a significant form of intersectional disadvantage. We have already seen how unpaid caring responsibilities are unequally distributed across the populace – with those working long hours as informal carers disproportionately likely to be women and/or to have their own disabilities or chronic health conditions. But in circumstances where individuals are also wrestling with Britain's unforgiving social security and social care systems, to access everything from the most basic carers' assessments to which they are entitled, to respite, benefits and the Carer's Allowance to which these offer a 'gateway' or 'passport', these already intersecting pressures coexist with the most onerous drudgery of all: the burden of disabled labour.

We return to the subject of disabled labour and the lack of recognition surrounding it in the Conclusion. For now, though, it seems sadly appropriate to consider this most invisible and thankless form of 'work' – as we have so much else – through the theoretical prism of symbolic annihilation. Throughout the book so far, we have seen how so-called inactive people are subject to a near-constant and invidious combination of stigma on the one hand and symbolic annihilation on the other. When they surface in public debate, it is too often through denigrating media discourses casting them as 'scroungers', 'shirkers' and/or 'work-shy' – or barely more dignified political rhetoric accusing them of 'gaming the system' (Starmer 2024b) or 'taking the mickey' (Nevett 2025) for daring to claim even the most meagre out-of-work benefits. At the same time, they are largely *absent* from public debate when it comes to recognizing – and, by rights, celebrating – their significant day-to-day contributions to their families and communities, and the wider public good. These are the contributions they make through unpaid caregiving and childrearing, volunteering, and other altruistic and neighbourly acts.

Above all else, though, there is the ceaseless toil of disabled labour. It is disabled labour that represents the single most denied (or ignored) aspect of the lives of those too physically and/or mentally impaired to engage with conventional paid employment. Its range and breadth is extensive: from the effort it takes some people to get out of bed, to wash, to dress, to prepare themselves simple meals, to go shopping (or even to order it online), to the infinitely more complex and labour-intensive business of applying for benefits, or even just working out for what help (if any) they might be eligible. This is before one factors in the myriad, ever more intrusive ways in which sick and disabled people are subjected to continual surveillance, repeated reassessment, and demands to submit themselves to performative displays of sickness and disability by state agencies determined to account for every grain of support (financial and otherwise) they receive.

The lived experience of disabled inactives is, then, one of conflicting, even contradictory pressures: that of endless, monotonous, *invisibility* from the public gaze on the one hand, and continual, forensic *scrutiny* and *surveillance* by the state on the other. Moreover, the present trajectory of public policy suggests this paradoxical picture is likely to continue over coming years. Not only are disabled people likely to face more frequent benefit reassessments (and, potentially, less generous entitlements) – leaving them stranded in an unceasing limbo of insecurity and uncertainty about when their eligibility might end. Not only will this leaner, meaner welfare state probe further into their private lives – both through the clinical assessment process and new measures requiring banks to comb their accounts in fishing expeditions to root out 'welfare fraud' (Department for Work and Pensions 2025a). But their sense of constantly having to 'prove' their disability while shouldering the onerous burden of managing it day to day (whether alone or helped by unpaid carers who may themselves be disabled) is unlikely to be ameliorated any time soon, given ministers' stubborn refusal to make the case for overhauling Britain's chronically underfunded social care system with as much speed and energy as they seem intent on cutting the social security safety-net (Department of Health and Social Care 2025).

In the next chapter, we explore the lives and perspectives of a very different group of inactive people. These are individuals we conceptualize as 'elective inactives', because they have consciously chosen to step away from the workplace before reaching retirement age, in many cases because they have sufficient financial security to do so. Yet as we shall see, even in these cases the shadow of inadequate social care – and underfunded, understaffed public services more generally – looms large. While growing numbers of older workers might well be retiring early to enjoy 'the good life' while they can, few of these individuals seem to be non-contributing inactives. Far from it: in addition to being active consumers, travellers and hobbyists, and using their spending power to boost the wider economy, many elective inactives are significant social contributors who use much of their newfound 'spare time' to enrich the common good through unpaid caregiving and volunteering. It is to exploring this further subcategory of the economically inactive that we now turn.

5

Opting Out of the Rat Race? Meet the 'Elective' and 'New' Inactives

It finally sank in that Jean had actually retired on the day she bought herself a camper van. 'It's an old T26, quite an elderly lady', she said of the Volkswagen she acquired eighteen months after bringing her 30-year further education teaching career to a premature end, for the sake of her sanity, at the age of 56. 'We try to do one big trip a year, where we go away for a month', she explained, describing how she and husband Phil (also retired, after being made redundant at 60) had since 'been up to the Outer Hebrides, down the whole length of Spain, up to Finland, off to the Grand Prix – little things like that'.

To Marie, the impetus to step away from work came after the earliest, most intense phase of the COVID pandemic – a period during which, in addition to being headteacher of a large primary school, she was put in charge of registration in a centralized 'hub' for key worker parents and vulnerable families set up by her local authority, in lowland Scotland. 'I was doing two jobs', she explained, describing how her school had to be 'reset' in June 2020 to accommodate the changes, 'and then had to change again in July and then August, because guidance repeatedly changed' – meaning that the process of adaptation 'was constant'. This allowed her space for 'no holiday that year' and left her unable to 'switch off at the weekend' because changes in COVID guidance were emailed to her every Friday evening and she 'never knew when the next thing was coming in'. After a prolonged period when she had been almost constantly on call for children and parents who were 'stressed out of their minds' with home-schooling, Marie's decision to retire early, at 57, ultimately came down to the necessity of preserving her own mental health. 'My family said they were worried about my own health and my own well-being', she recalled, adding that, despite having 'officially retired' in August 2022, 'it took me from the August to the November to feel well'.

For Jack, retirement beckoned still sooner. Aged just 52, he was recently forced to call time on his three-decade medical career, first as an accident and emergency doctor, then a general practitioner (GP), because of his own declining health. Though he has not ruled out the prospect of returning to some form of employment in future – 'something uncomplicated', like working part time in a DIY store, for a local upcycling charity or even returning to a hospital in a more junior capacity – for now he is content to potter round the sprawling garden at his farm in 'deepest Dorset', go fishing, build kit cars and hone his woodworking skills (his latest creation being a sixteen-foot-high dovecot).

What Jean, Marie and Jack have in common is the fact that all three are *elective* inactives: people who have taken rational decisions to step away from the labour market, in some cases years before reaching pensionable age, in order to slow down, explore new horizons and, most importantly, safeguard and improve theirs (and their families') quality of life. In this short final chapter, we consider this under-explored subgrouping of people who, while they would officially be categorized as economically inactive, are invariably very far from that – and often strongly object to this label, on the basis of their lengthy prior working lives and the social contributions many of them continue to make in retirement. As well as considering Jean, Marie and Jack's stories in more detail, the chapter takes an exploratory look at how the concept of elective inactivity was deliberated in the online public sphere at the height of the (ultimately short-lived) period between late 2021 and early 2023 popularized as the 'Great Retirement' or 'Great Resignation'. It does so through the lens of below-the-line comments published beneath newspaper articles around four discursive events, during which media narratives chronicling government measures to stem the flow of older workers out of the labour market were both responded and contributed to by posters including self-identifying early retirees – here conceptualized as 'new inactives'.

Push versus pull: The drivers of elective inactivity

A feature of all three interviewees' personal stories was their complexity. While Jean, Marie and Jack had each taken conscious, carefully considered decisions to step away from senior professional roles long before time, and all three had seen their incomes drop significantly as a result, their reasons for doing so were driven as much by the push-factors of ever more demanding (and, in some cases, less rewarding) jobs as pull-factors like the lure of increased leisure time, lengthier holidays and improved quality of life. In this respect, their rationales for retiring early offered implicit critiques of 'normal' working life in post-COVID, post-Brexit, post-austerity Britain – another rejoinder to the worship of work promoted by today's political and media elites. Moreover, far from being selfishly motivated by 'lifestyle choices' alone, all three had other considerations in mind besides their own well-being and fulfilment – from the growing care needs of partners and ageing parents to the contributions they could be making as volunteers or campaigners. None of these stories was a simple case of a well-off person luxuriating in their ability to cast off the shackles of employment and put their feet up. Although all three had been fortunate enough to be able to make their moves from positions of relative financial security (a privilege not available to everyone), they also did so with a sense of responsibility to others and (for Marie and Jack at least) an element of reluctance and uncertainty.

For Jean, the stimulus to start weighing up the pros and cons of early retirement began shortly before the pandemic, during a period of upheaval and escalating demands at the Midlands FE college where she had worked for 25 years. She recalled how she had been given 'responsibility for the whole curriculum' at a time when 'things were changing a lot in further education' – a situation that left her thinking 'do I want to carry on doing this until 67?'. She explained:

> The other reason [for retiring] was that my principal had retired the year before and we had a new principal who had completely different ideas, whose background wasn't education as such – they'd been a finance director – so they were relying on me hugely.

She added that she was 'working ridiculously long days, weekends, whatever', so 'I just thought, "I don't want to do this for many more years" '.

Escalating work pressures were also central to Marie's decision to resign from her headteacher position in 2022, especially after her townhall bosses declared, 'COVID has gone, just get back to normal'. At the time, her position on the front line convinced her that the devastating impact on children of lockdowns meant they would benefit from the continuation of 'soft starts' to help them re-engage with school after spending so many months at home. 'I was told to get back to normal because it [soft starts and staggering play times] was wasting too much time', she recalled, adding that her managers 'didn't seem to understand' that many children 'weren't ready to learn' again so quickly. As pupils had only experienced mixing and socializing in small groups since August 2020, she also felt it was important to phase in any return to the 'old normal' more gradually than her employers wanted. It was a combination of this ramped-up working environment and advice from concerned family members who saw the toll her responsibilities were taking on her that convinced Marie the time had come to step down, however regrettably – though, she said, 'once I'd made the decision I was actually much happier in myself'.

Jack's predicament was more urgent. Despite holding down a succession of intensely pressurized medical jobs over the past 30 years, he had done so while managing type 1 bipolar disorder – a condition forcing him to rely on antipsychotic drugs and ongoing psychiatric treatment. By the time he had reached the end of 2024, with memories of the pandemic finally receding, his psychiatrist advised him to apply for early medical retirement. This was finally approved by an NHS panel in spring 2025 – nine months after he had been forced to give up his most recent GP post, owing to a combination of mental and physical exhaustion. 'Workload was very gradually and very slowly piled on top of me, [so] it got to the point that we decided to move to the country and have a relatively quiet life', he recalled of his earlier years working as a doctor in Accident and Emergency. Eventually Jack became so desperate to restore some work-life balance that he quit his permanent full-time job to become a locum GP. But this decision backfired when he found himself 'working six days a week, driving two hours each way to make up the hours, leaving home at 6 a.m., getting back at 10, and falling asleep on the sofa' – a punishing routine that 'was just too much'.

But while Jack's retirement decision was primarily motivated by a need for self-preservation, in Marie's case there were also other family care needs to consider, and these had only become more acute since she gave up work. Although her husband still worked full time, he had developed his own 'medical issues', meaning that she needed to be 'around for him'. She also helped her brother look after their elderly parents, with whom he lived. Describing herself as one of 'the squeezed middle' – a generation of middle-aged people sandwiched between legacy childcare duties and the pressures of caring for elderly parents – she believed that it was only by taking early retirement that she had been able to 'give more support to them and my brother, by not working'. 'If you've got people who are 55 to 70, they've got either childcare responsibilities for grandchildren or elderly parents they're responsible for', she said, adding that, among other things, this meant 'they can't put themselves out there for work' – however much the government might want to coax older, skilled and experienced workers back into the labour market.

The time dividend that came with their early retirement had also enabled Jean and her husband to help out other family members – in their case, providing vital childcare for their grandchildren. Without this their own children would have struggled to hold down jobs – and 'to enable them to have a mortgage they need to work'. Being on hand to mind their son's children, in particular, had 'enabled my daughter-in-law to go to work', Jean said, recalling how, at the point her husband was made redundant (and began to offer his help), 'at least one of the children was still out of school, so they would have had to try to find childcare' for whole days at a time, while in later years they would have faced the problem of 'working around school hours'. 'Both sets of grandparents helped out tremendously, with looking after the children before they went to school', she added.

However, while other people's needs certainly featured in all three interviewees' decisions to scale back (and ultimately quit) work, perhaps more important was their cold, hard weighing-up of the risks versus benefits for their own health and well-being of ploughing on towards state retirement age. 'The statistics are quite shocking, particularly in certain sectors – that people retire and then, when they stop, that's it', reflected Jean, referring to the mix of anecdotal knowledge and official data that had informed her decision to opt out while she was still young enough to enjoy a long and lively retirement. 'I could see that happening to me', she added, recollecting how 'the amount of pressure in my job was such that I was thinking, "if I get to 60 at this rate I'll be lucky" '. 'If people need to carry on' working until an ever-later retirement age, she suggested, then 'one lesson for employers' might be that 'maybe people should be looking at more flexible working', with a steadily declining 'work rate' in later life that bears more resemblance to how many people 'start off in your teens, doing a Saturday job or whatever'.

In Jack's case, mid-life mortality born of overwork and other exacerbating lifestyle factors was something he had seen too often with his own eyes – not least when, towards the end of the pandemic, his surgery was suddenly flooded with patients who had ignored early symptoms during COVID, only to present with organ failure or cancers that were too advanced to treat. 'When it finished, the level of work went from being just a normal GP to being a consultant GP', he said, recalling how 'we had people with end system failure for a lot of diseases that they hadn't been seeing the GP about – they were coming in with end kidney disease or heart failure'. For Jack, 'the worst things of all were patients coming in with terminal cancer' who had 'just left their symptoms for two or three years'. Returning to his own situation, he recalled reading one alarming statistic showing that 'GPs that retire at the age of 65 have an average life expectancy of 66!'

Volunteering and giving back: The social labour of 'active inactives'

Aside from their familial caregiving commitments, all three interviewees spent variable amounts of time contributing to the common good in other ways, notably through more or less structured forms of volunteering. Despite being nominally retired, both Jean and Marie had gradually become so heavily involved in running crucial local amenities that if they had withdrawn their labour, their communities would have faced the loss of vital lifelines. Jean recalled how she had been so used to running around during her professional working life that on stepping down from her college job, she initially wondered, 'how are you going to fill your time?' This was a question she rapidly answered by volunteering to become a trustee of a community library in Leicestershire. 'If you like, it was still contributing – but in the volunteer sector', she reflected, explaining how this pattern was to continue even after she and her husband took a decision to up sticks and move county. 'When I moved down here I was going to give myself … take a step back and enjoy life, [but] we did that for about nine months and then got collared one day to be trustees of the community shop', she chuckled, reflecting on her latest role managing another vital social hub in the Hampshire village where the couple recently relocated.

Adopting a more serious tone, she suggested that volunteering was one of a number of ways in which the ongoing *economic* contributions of many retirees were conveniently ignored or downplayed by politicians and the media. 'It is still being active, economically, in the community – because in the library it does add an economic sort of aspect', she argued, adding that 'we had people come in and research how to get jobs – people who were unemployed or didn't have a computer at home – so I felt I was contributing in that social sense'. In fact, by the point Jean began volunteering in her local library in Leicestershire, the county council had become so desperate to make cost savings after years of Whitehall-imposed austerity that it 'would have closed the library in the village if the community hadn't taken it on'.

Though far from being the only volunteer involved in saving the library – she described how 'the nature of that village' ensured there was 'uproar', and 'a very good parish council that twisted arms, including mine, to start the process of keeping it open' – her own contributions involved everything from fundraising ('at least £10,000 a year to cover costs') to contract work drawing on expertise gained during her years working in further education. Volunteers' collaborative efforts eventually managed to double the number of people using the library, by offering 'all sorts of activities in that space', from an art and craft group to 'little talks' and 'a toddlers' reading group'. Jean had since seen a similar turnaround of fortunes, over time, in the local shop where she now worked, which had become 'more than just … a shop in the village – a social enterprise as well'. 'We do have a paid manager and two paid people in the Post Office part of it, but the PO is subsidized by the shop to pay those staff, and everybody else is a volunteer', she observed, adding, 'again, I don't think it would continue if it didn't have that support'.

Marie's volunteering efforts provided a similarly essential service, by helping to plug gaps in both state and private-sector childcare provision for low-income parents without convenient family networks to hand: hardworking people who might otherwise have been forced to quit their jobs. In this way, she was using her own retirement (as Jean and Phil had with their own children) to enable younger people, unrelated to herself, to remain *in* work – and not be forced into inactivity.

Aside from running a Sunday school at her local church, Marie's biggest contribution was looking after working parents' children at a weekday toddlers' group – a role she had taken on within months of stepping down as a headteacher. 'It was meant to be for five weeks, while the community worker was away, but I'm still there!' she joked. As with Jean, Marie's role drew heavily on skills and experience honed in her prior professional career. 'You're almost in a health visitor role, because you're checking in on their mental health and the children's milestones', she ventured, explaining that, because of her previous roles as an experienced educator, she sometimes found herself looking out for children's wider social and emotional well-being – and signposting their parents to other support services in the community.

Though Jack's more recent retirement had been forced on him by health concerns, even he was already contemplating ways of using his newfound free time to 'put back' into society. 'I feel a little bit impotent not working, because I've worked to excess all my life – so I need to fill that vacuum', he reflected, adding that he anticipated 'looking for different work' in the future. The freedom afforded by a recent inheritance from his late father, combined with a lump sum from his early retirement pension, had bought him time 'to explore different avenues' at his leisure. Nonetheless, he had already signed up to help out a local charity that 'repairs old things from the dump, like radios and so on, and sells them for charitable purposes'. This determination to stay active was, Jack conceded, fuelled by a certain amount of self-interest. 'In my experience, of people who retire early, the ones who keep active are the ones who live longer', he said.

While all three interviewees clearly valued being in a position to offer their services voluntarily, and found these experiences rewarding, their efforts often demonstrably involved very hard work – and (for Jean and Marie at least) considerable time commitments. For this reason, both gave short shrift to dominant media-political discourses depicting inactive people as idle and/or lumping them all together – especially those who might be volunteering or caring for dependents. 'I genuinely don't think that, as a society, we recognize and value it [volunteering]', said Jean, admitting that she could 'get quite on my high horse about it', because 'I think society doesn't actually appreciate the contribution of volunteers'. She gave as an illustration an incident the previous day in which there had been a power cut at the village shop, forcing volunteers to scurry round removing perishable food from the chillers to ensure customers' safety once the shop was able to reopen. 'People didn't understand', she said of the impatient attitude of some fellow villagers irritated by the shop's temporary closure, who seemed unaware that those trying to manage this tricky situation were doing so in their own time – unpaid.

For Marie, feeling under-appreciated as a volunteer was bound up with her frustrations at the ongoing financial impact of her decision to leave paid work prematurely – just a handful of years before reaching her official headteacher retirement age. 'I haven't had an income in three years', she said, explaining that she had rejected the option of claiming her teachers' pension three years before time, at the age of 57, as she would have lost 'a lot of money'. As a result, she and her husband had 'gone down a whole wage', forcing him to continue working full time, despite his own medical issues. By the time Marie reached 60 (the age at which she would finally be able to access her pension without penalties), she would have been 'retired for three years with no income'. She was equally critical of the suggestion – repeatedly floated by governments – that skilled professionals like herself belonged back in the paid labour force, paying taxes and contributing to Britain's ongoing push for economic growth. As she would neither have wanted nor been able to return to her previous role as a headteacher, the kinds of jobs she 'could possibly go for' would have been better used to help 'young people who need to get on the job ladder'. 'I think a lot of people my age think, "well we've done our working bit – let other people have their chance" ', she reflected, adding that there were many upcoming experienced teachers 'who want to be in promoted roles such as headteachers', but could not find those jobs 'because someone like me is there in the role'.

Marie added that dominant media representations of inactive people as non-contributors made her feel 'angry', because 'it makes me think ... in a normal working week I was meant to work 35 hours a week, but it was 70', leaving her feeling that 'I've already given you more than I was paid or recognised for, how dare you!' And, in a comment that might have spoken for the ambivalent feelings of tens of thousands of other elective inactives weighing up the costs and benefits of early retirement, she added:

> I didn't just suddenly decide, 'I want to finish work' – and it was *hard* to finish work. It's my money that I've earned – it's my money that I've been sensible with. We [early retirees] have a choice to go back to work if we want to, but a lot of the time we can't do it because of our own health or caring responsibilities - or because we don't want to take other people's jobs.

Here, then, in their own words, are the stories of those fortunate enough to be able to leave the formal workplace before their time: individuals motivated by a range of issues and incentives, from the lure of increased leisure time to exhaustion and declining health after long years of demanding paid labour. Though only snapshots, they exemplify what it means to belong to yet another symbolically annihilated grouping whose lived experiences give the lie to the label 'economically inactive'. But how has this particular variation on the socially constructed concept of worklessness been deliberated in the online public sphere? In the closing section we examine this question through the prism of below-the-line comments posted beneath articles published during a very specific period in the evolution of the UK's great inactivity debate: the much-storied (but short-lived) 'Great Resignation'.

Deliberations of the deserving? Self-identified new inactives on the 'Great Retirement'

An intriguing subgrouping of posters that emerged from the chatter and debate published on newspaper comment threads in the earlier stages of Britain's inactivity panic – a period during which much of the emphasis of media and political discourse was on the problem of the late/post-COVID 'Great Resignation' (or 'Great Retirement') – was the small but significant minority who *self-identified* as 'new' or pre-pandemic elective inactives. Although neither of these terms was explicitly used by posters, a number of those who stood up for and/or praised middle-aged and older workers taking conscious decisions to quit the labour market went further – by outing *themselves* as early retirees. Moreover, far from adopting defensive or apologetic postures, many such posters exhibited a sense of angry defiance in response to much of the contemporaneous media-political framing, which they saw as portraying people who had worked hard all their lives before opting for early retirement as part of the wider problem of working-aged inactivity.

In this sense, the collective stand taken by these self-identifying elective inactives represented a curious variant of the *counter*-discourse(s) disputing the hegemonic positioning of inactivity (and inactive people) detailed in Chapter 2. Rather than adopting a *united front* with those airing more conventional counter-discursive views – for instance, commentators contesting stigmatizing narratives labelling disability benefit recipients as 'scroungers' – they often pointedly distanced themselves from such people. They did so by (explicitly or implicitly) constructing themselves as a deserving in-group, and distinguishing people like them from the imagined mass of nameless others (the undeserving out-group) that were widely castigated in the media for exploiting the welfare system – a system they often vocally emphasized they did not use themselves.

This final section offers a series of selective snapshots of online conversations and commentaries taken from (often lengthy) threads posted beneath articles published over a nineteen-month period between September 2021 and April 2023. The snapshots were drawn from an overall sample of thirteen threads clustered around four discursive events during the period when the inactivity panic first began: the late/post-pandemic phase popularly known as the 'Great Resignation'. The sampled threads were all lifted from the two news sites that devoted the most space, and most frequent coverage, to the inactivity debate: *MailOnline* (6) and www.telegraph.co.uk (7). The sampled moments included three of those examined in Chapter 2's discourse analysis, as well as an additional initial discursive occurrence that took place just over a year beforehand (in November 2021). Numbering 2142 in total, the size of the overall comment sample was significantly larger than the one examined from a more selective range of articles in Chapter 2 (1378). The four moments were as follows:

- November 2021 – the publication of data from employers and the Office of National Statistics showing the number of UK job vacancies at an all-time high;
- December 2022 – the publication of international comparative data from the OECD ranking the rate of 'economic inactivity' in the UK as the highest in the world;
- February 2023 – the launch of new DWP benefits crackdown on 'economic inactivity';
- March 2023 – Chancellor Jeremy Hunt's unveiling of his 'back-to-work Budget'.

Before examining some of the comments more qualitatively, it is worth giving an indicative quantitative overview of the overall balance of sentiments across the whole discursive field contained in the sampled threads. The overarching picture is shown in Table 5.1, while Table 5.2 gives a granular breakdown of the sentiments in *counter-discursive* posts: the subset of comments containing those posted by self-identified elective inactives.

As can be seen, even at this early stage in the increasingly hysterical national conversation around Britain's unfolding inactivity 'crisis', comments adopting a

TABLE 5.1: Overall balance of audience sentiments across events 1–4.

First-order hatred	**Second-order hatred**	**Soft negative**	**Hard negative**	**Empathy**	**'Soft' counter**	**'Hard' counter**	**Total**
70	22	13	1332	62	401	242	**2142**

TABLE 5.2: Breakdown of counter-discursive sentiments across events 1–4.

Hard counter-discursive	**Soft counter-discursive (identifying as elective inactives)**	**Other soft counter-discursive**	**Total**
242	343	58	**643**

counter-hegemonic position – in this case, to question or challenge the suggestion that elective inactivity was a problem – were very much in the minority. Amounting to 643 in total, they represented just three in ten of the total included in the overall sample of 2142. This is perhaps all the more notable for the fact that the problem group(s) in this particular case were not the usual suspects that right-wing *Mail* and *Telegraph* commentators love to pillory – feckless/fraudulent welfare claimants – but relatively well-heeled older workers taking a rational decision to get out while the going was good: in essence, a demographic very much aligned with the income and age profiles of these papers' own core audiences.

For all this anomaly, it is worth noting that of those posters prepared to speak out against the dominant pro-worker/anti-workless discourse both papers chose to amplify, nearly one in ten (58) went well beyond merely criticizing it, to instead directly and explicitly self-identify as being among the targeted group(s). In so doing, they risked staining themselves and their own reputations with the stigma ascribed to Britain's latest popular folk-devil during a period of rapidly escalating moral panic. Moreover, of the wider majority posting counter-discursive comments, most positioned themselves as firm allies and defenders of those electing to retire early. A typical example was a poster who suggested (in a sideswipe at more stereotypically inactive people) that 'the people retiring at 60ish have probably been working their socks off for 40-plus years and paying tax to a succession of spendthrift Govts', adding that 'most are not workshy' but 'possibly have caring responsibilities or volunteer or simply want to enjoy life'. Another observed that it 'sounds more like people with spare money have chosen to get out the rat race for a while', before adding: 'Good on them. Life is short'. Others strongly disputed the use of the term inactive to describe people who had worked hard, paid taxes and contributed for long periods prior to retiring. In a throwback to Jean and Marie's criticisms of the binary contributor/non-contributor distinctions embodied in hegemonic discourses lumping all inactive people together, one asked, 'How does stepping back from work while continuing to spend lots of money in the economy make one "economically inactive" '?

Of the posters who self-identified as newly inactive themselves, one opened their comment with the unashamed declaration 'I'm one of them', before setting out the contrast between the risible '3.75% pay rise' they had been offered by their employer in the face of the then ongoing cost-of-living crisis and the 'anticipated 10.1% uplift in pension' they stood to earn by retiring early. 'What would you do?' they signed off rhetorically. Theirs was one of a number of posts that largely contented itself with expressing joy and relief at the blissful prospect of being able to quit the workplace prior to pension age, or preparing to do so shortly. In doing so, these often displayed a self-satisfied, even gloating tone in reeling off the freedoms their lifestyle choices had bought them (or soon would do). 'I have just stopped at 63. Life couldn't be better', said one, before reeling off the benefits of an 'NHS pension, some savings and an inheritance', 'no mortgage' and 'sons living in their own place'. Declaring themselves on the cusp of retirement (aged 59), another reader responded to a lengthy exchange between fellow posters by jokingly urging them to 'move over', as they would be 'joining you for relaxing breakfasts at the garden centre in 312 days' time'. After that, they added, the 'only building work I plan to do is in my garden!' Yet another described 'the worst days Bass fishing at my sea edge Scottish 2nd home' as beating 'hands down' their 'best day ever at the world of work'.

An intriguing subdiscourse running through many gloating posts, as well as those that focused on justifying their authors' early retirement decisions, was an 'anti-woke' agenda – a sentiment strongly echoing the positions of the sites on which they appeared. Such comments often expressed a vocal aversion to equality, diversity and inclusion (EDI) policies, and other contemporary workplace practices which they framed as evidence of a wider societal drift towards politically correct norms and attitudes – approaches that had invariably impacted on the working lives of their posters, and thereby further legitimized their decisions to quit the rat-race early. In one of the most expansive and colourful of these broadsides, a self-described '58 year old with a good pension' railed against the insidious creep of 'diversity and unconscious bias training' in the following terms:

> Why would I, a 58 year old with a good pension, want to work? Hmm let's ask some simple questions: Will I be penalised by the tax system for doing so? Yes – absolutely hammered by it. Can I work part time? Not in my profession where it's 5 days a week or nothing. Do employers value people of my age, experience and skill set? No, they think we are dinosaurs who need to be re-educated with diversity and unconscious bias training. Can I work from home? Only a couple of days a week for my prospective city job so I'd have to face the horror of what passes for our train service. I keep reading these articles about labour participation and they always say the same thing. Somehow its [sic] our fault that we no longer wish to work. What is needed is some long overdue reform and a change in attitude to the over 50s. Plentiful cheap labour has been abused by the big corporates. They've used it to feather their own nests and stiff the workers, ultimately, you reap what you sew. Howl at the moon as much as you want but the die is cast now.

For others, though, any renewed sense of *joie de vivre* was modified by their irritation, even contempt, for politicians they blamed for promoting the prevailing inactivity narrative. One said they had spent '35 years slogging away in a job with long hours followed by 10 years caring for my disabled elderly mother to keep her out of going in a care home', so 'if [Jeremy, then-Chancellor] Hunt thinks I'm going back to work he'll have a long wait'. But while some reserved their criticism for the elite actors they held responsible for promoting the dominant discourse – including the very news-sites on which they posted – others trained their fire on various distinct types of inactive people they saw as their less-deserving bedfellows, including those signed off work due to illness and disability. 'Whether it's luck, good judgement, hard work or a mix that enables you to retire early, if you can do it without claiming benefits etc then go for it', argued one, before adding that it 'seems lazy reporting to me to lump these various groups in together'. This us-and-them discourse was echoed by another poster declaring themselves '60 and retired', with 'a comfortable lifestyle', who pointedly emphasized that they did 'not claim any benefits and never have', and had 'no intention of going back to work to pay tax to support those on benefits who in many cases have a better lifestyle than I do'. And, in a longer post that mobilized a montage of othering stereotypes to construct a smorgasbord of undeserving recipients of taxpayer-funded largesse, another wrote:

> Why would I go back to work when most of my hard earned pay is pinched by a government that won't sort its own house out, flirts with re-joining the EU, continues to spaff billions on public systems that don't work, welfare and not stopping the French channel taxi service ??? No thank you very much. Getting the garden sorted is far more important.

For anyone unfamiliar with the strawmen shibboleths of right-wing elites, this read as a useful digest of the full litany of evils reviled by www.telegraph.co.uk, *MailOnline* and their political fellow travellers throughout the post-austerity/Brexit/COVID era. Moreover, each of the disparate issues it conflated could be seen as a proxy for a particular group of deviant and exploitative others. While the 'French channel taxi service' represented the asylum-seekers supposedly besieging the beaches of southern England (the target of a separate moral panic unfolding contemporaneously with that around inactivity), the allusion to the cost of the UK's erstwhile membership of 'the EU' carried connotations critical of everything from the fabled European Union liberal elites to the economic migrants who had historically moved to Britain under free movement rules. Above all, though, it wheeled out that most abject of floating signifiers, 'welfare': the one-word catchall for abjection and deviance so often used to sow the seeds of distrust and division among social groups with supposedly competing claims to deservingness.

This, then, is how we leave the discourse on economic inactivity as we approach our Conclusion – at the end of a chapter specifically designed to recognize (and celebrate) the social value of contributions made by many people who are *classified* as inactive but who often strongly dispute this designation, on the basis of their prior (and ongoing) endeavours. The discursive framing of inactivity *in general*, as manifest through the term's normative usage as a synonym for worklessness, is one that constructs anyone not in conventional paid work, particularly unwaged people receiving social protection, as (worthless) non-contributors. The existence of a narrative continuum positioning 'non-workers' in this way has been demonstrated throughout the book, perhaps particularly strongly through Chapter 1's historical review and the critical discourse analysis of contemporaneous texts deployed in Chapter 2. As we have seen, this is a discourse that is rendered all the more divisive and pernicious by the hardwired distinctions between deserving and undeserving inactives – retired *ex*-workers and the 'career' workless – that emerge through the lived experiences shared between people self-identifying as new/elective inactives online.

By contrast, it would be unfair to characterize any of the elective inactives interviewed for this chapter as being judgmental about those who claim out-of-work benefits because of their *inability* to participate in the paid labour force. Nevertheless, even among them there were glimpses of indignation at any suggestion that, by taking decisions to retire early, they were freeloading on taxpayers or shirking their responsibility to contribute. As Jean put it, when standing up for under-appreciated volunteers, 'people commit an awful lot' – and 'a lot of those people are retirement age'. And while Marie was similarly careful not to condemn anyone forced to rely on social security, she was at pains to stress that she did not see herself as 'a burden to anybody'. As she put it, 'I'm not claiming benefits or causing anyone harm: I'm just not working'.

The coming Conclusion attempts to bring together all the strands examined in this book, from the historical evolution of discourses on worklessness and the factors leading to it – especially various forms of incapacity – to the hegemonic assumptions underpinning Britain's current panic about economic inactivity. Beyond this, the intention is to round off on a more hopeful and forward-looking note – by proposing some small steps that might help us rationalize and rethink what we define as work, with the aim of placing more value on the multifarious forms of social contribution we currently deny and annihilate.

Conclusion: Towards Redefining Work and Recognizing 'Active Inactives'

Scroungers, malingerers, parasites, leeches. 'Economically inactive' people have weathered every conceivable slur in recent decades – and remain routinely stigmatized in populist political speeches, tabloid and conservative news outlets and the 'wild west' terrain of social media. To pundits, they offer a clickbait-friendly punchbag: a strawman scapegoat channelling popular myths about fraudulent disability claimants and workless non-contributors. To politicians, they offer a convenient discursive tool for displacing blame for rising welfare costs onto over-generous benefits and inactive people *themselves* – not the austerity, NHS waiting-lists, cuts to mental health services, poverty wages and punitive working conditions that drive so many out of the workplace to begin with.

Recently the stigma and othering endured by out-of-work sick and disabled people (and full-time carers) has entered a sinister new phase. In one sense, the prejudices of old have merely morphed into new iterations. History's sturdy beggars, Clapperdudgeons and counterfeit cranks have been supplanted by *Little Britain*-style caricatures of chancers hopping in and out of wheelchairs or on and off mobility scooters, while young adults scarred by a post-COVID spike in mental ill health are dismissed as slackers and snowflakes. But these explicit expressions of popular disdain and cynicism now sit alongside newer, more deeply othering discursive constructs. In their performative deference to 'working people' – or 'hardworking' households – politicians of Left *and* Right have mainstreamed what amounts to the worship of work. Theirs is the indiscriminate, unthinking collective delusion that employment of *any* kind, no matter how pointless, mundane, monotonous and/or exploitative, is intrinsically worthwhile – and virtuous. By the same measures, those they define as 'workless' are implicitly cast as worthless.

And yet ministers apply only the narrowest definition of what work *is*. In their literal-minded, monetized imaginary – one that seems to know the price of everything and the value of nothing – the only people who qualify as 'workers' are those fortunate enough to be paid for their labour (however poorly). Put simply, while there is room in the ranks of 'working people' for Uber drivers, factory workers, property developers and (presumably) hedge fund managers, there is no place for food bank volunteers or unpaid carers.

In framing their entire prospectus for government as a mission to serve 'working people' – and excluding from their embrace anyone not earning a wage – Britain's present Labour government (like others before it) has engaged in repeated acts of symbolic annihilation, including towards some of its most vulnerable and disadvantaged fellow citizens. Indeed, the discursive downgrading – at times erasure – of such citizens constitutes a form of *double* annihilation. The deserving/undeserving binary of worker-versus-workless annihilates people classed as inactive by denying their intrinsic worth as human beings – consigning those with work-limiting disabilities, illnesses and caring roles so demanding that they leave no time or energy for paid employment to a status portrayed as, at best, inferior; at worst, morally deviant. But inactive people are also annihilated through denial of the various forms of work and other socially useful activities many of them *do* perform. In this way, the virtues of community-based volunteering, familial caregiving and other forms of unpaid endeavour that bring no financial reward but often entail substantial personal sacrifice are annulled. In essence, all recognition of their value (and acknowledgement of those who perform them) is obliterated from the public sphere. The extent to which individuals are recognized or valued at all depends on myopic assessments of what they contribute, in pounds and pence, to economic growth – not their wider contributions to the public good, let alone their intrinsic worth as human beings.

All this is to say nothing of the most discursively invisible form of work performed by these and other 'active inactives': disabled labour. As the personal stories recounted in Chapters 3 and 4 demonstrate, for people managing complex disabilities, physical illnesses and mental health conditions, life itself is hard work. Basic daily tasks like washing, dressing, shopping and cooking can be painful and energy sapping, involve serious pain and discomfort and take far longer than they do for able-bodied people. This is why Personal Independence Payments have become such a lifeline for many disabled people – and one of the few sources of financial and material support, from adapted clothing to accessible cars, allowing them to engage with paid work (the end goal that governments consistently claim they want to achieve!) All of this is what has made Keir Starmer's (at time of writing, unfulfilled) 'moral mission' to push through 'welfare reforms' that could *withdraw* PIP from hundreds of thousands of people, perhaps even those unable to wash their lower bodies without assistance, feel as counterproductive as it is morally indefensible.

Yet the travails associated with disabled labour go far beyond the effort involved to perform mundane but essential day-to-day tasks. Those whose illnesses and disabilities are so debilitating that they are unable to undertake paid work – and forced to rely on benefits and/or carers – also face endless battles with bureaucracy to ensure they receive their social security and social care entitlements. Many are also expected to performatively 'prove' (and re-prove) their disabilities – subjecting themselves to 'fitness-for-work' and/or PIP reassessments that are so Kafkaesque and clinically intrusive they can feel more like police interrogations than tests designed to assess their social and medical needs and ensure they are offered appropriately tailored support. All the while, seriously disabled people are left living in perpetual 'fear of the brown envelope' (Garthwaite 2014): the Damoclean threat of suddenly being cut off by the state and (more importantly) having their conditions, and by extension identities, invalidated.

In this way, many inactive sick and disabled people are locked out of mainstream society: too 'poor' to participate in 'normal' social life and marked with the stain of social invalidation. This is the truest form of stigma. To spend one's life struggling to afford basic essentials, to be repeatedly required to demonstrate one's physical, mental and material needs (not to mention one's honesty), is, in every sense, to be marginalized – socially, economically, existentially. It is to be condemned to leading a liminal existence that renders one, by turns, invisible and highly, *publicly* visible: symbolically annihilated by ableist social attitudes that ignore, or refuse to accept, the reality of one's everyday life challenges and, alternately, problematized by the neoliberal norms and prejudices inscribed into a public discourse that incessantly obsesses over the cost of economic inactivity and 'welfare'. This was what Bryony described when she recalled her 'social life' going 'completely out of the window' at the point when her disabilities became so acute she was forced to claim out-of-work benefits. Once you can no longer go to 'dinner parties, birthdays', she recalled, 'people stop inviting you'– in her case, reducing her from 'being very sociable' to 'nothing', because 'people don't want to keep in touch'.

But while these might be the most egregious forms of stigma and symbolic violence directed at economically inactive people, they are not the only ones. Just as problematic as the term 'inactive' is its bedfellow: the oft-misused word 'economic'. Alongside the million or more people unable to 'work' because they are unpaid carers (Department for Work and Pensions 2022), and nearly 3 million classed as inactive owing to disability or long-term illness, a growing number of middle-aged and older workers are consciously opting out of the labour force some years before reaching pension age. Unlike those claiming sickness and disability benefits, many of these individuals are far from economically disadvantaged – their relative affluence having provided the cushion enabling them to quit the labour market in the first place. These early retirees – many of them 'new inactives' who have taken rational choices to leave the workplace, post-COVID, so they can enjoy their lives while they can – are too wealthy to claim benefits, and/or have no need or desire to. This makes them an uncomfortable fit for time-worn tropes portraying inactive working-aged people as trapped in cycles of welfare dependency. Moreover, these (suddenly) time-rich, financially comfortable, often physically fit individuals tend to be highly active in the broader sense – using their extended leisure time to travel, play sports and pursue vigorous hobbies. And, as they tend to be relatively affluent, elective inactives make significant *economic* contributions – including by spending money saved or invested during their working lives.

Yet though the various segments that collectively constitute the so-called economically inactive are (in many ways) highly diverse, they are far from mutually exclusive. Just as many of those unable to work because of disability also experience the intersectional disadvantage of having to care for someone else, those fortunate enough to be able to opt out of the workplace are not all solely motivated by self-interest. As we have seen, post-pandemic 'new inactives' – and other early retirees – take their decisions for a mixture of reasons. While quality-of-life considerations are often involved, so too are concerns about ageing and vulnerable relatives. Many of today's 50- and 60-somethings find themselves in sandwich generations, still recovering from long years of child-rearing while also supporting – and, in some cases, directly caring for – ailing parents. With Britain's population rapidly ageing, and the costs of paying for professional social care soaring by the year, these pressures are only likely to intensify in decades to come. And neither do the efforts of the country's elective inactives stop there: beyond caring for elderly dependents, many early retirees contribute in other ways, too – by giving their time and sharing the knowledge, skills and expertise they have accumulated during their prior decades of employment, as volunteers, charity fundraisers and campaigners.

From moral missions to moral mirage: The illusion of deserving vs undeserving poverty

In a previous book on the subject of welfare discourses, this author observed that media and political narratives about social security often seek to distinguish not just between the deserving and undeserving poor in *general* terms (e.g. genuine versus fraudulent/idle claimants) but also between more- and less-deserving *types* of poverty. Recent years have seen these subgroups defined in all manner of ways – for example, generationally or in relation to specific aspects of poverty they experience that are popularly framed as being more morally offensive than others (or, indeed, than poverty full-stop). These include – but are not limited to – food, fuel, funeral and period poverty.

Of all the various groups to have experienced hardship in recent years, three are consistently portrayed as more intrinsically deserving than the others: children, pensioners and the 'working poor'. In the latter case, championing the plight of those experiencing *in-work* poverty – people unable to put food on the table or pay their bills, *despite* the fact they are working – implicitly runs the risk of othering and dismissing the suffering (and legitimate appeals for empathy) of the '*work-less* poor': inactive people and that other grouping with which they are so often (inaccurately) conflated, the unemployed. And yet – quite apart from arguments that many 'inactive' people *are* working – it is impossible to honestly separate 'child poverty', 'food poverty' or 'fuel poverty' from the hardships experienced by many of those classified as inactive. In the first place, many children living in poverty are in homes where at least one adult is out of work because they are sick or disabled – or, to put it another way, many households affected by any cuts to sickness and disability benefits contain at least one child. Until the point that the Starmer government was forced to abandon its plans to drastically toughen the eligibility criteria for PIP (at least temporarily), even its own estimates projected that the effect of doing so would have been to plunge a further 50,000 children into relative poverty (Department for Work and Pensions 2025c).

Disingenuous discursive distinctions between deserving and undeserving types of poverty, and the groups they affect, are all the more troubling because they are not just promoted by the usual suspects – right-wing politicians, libertarian media commentators and free-market think-tanks. Rather, in their justifiable efforts to spotlight specific problems at particular times, many charities and campaigns fall into the trap of constructing 'single-issue' (and therefore compromised) countervailing responses to dominant deserving/undeserving discourses of the moment. A single-minded focus on the evils of child poverty, in-work poverty or specific *manifestations* of poverty is the understandable *raison d'être* of many (highly commendable) interest groups and/or initiatives – from successful recent period poverty campaigns to the Child Poverty Action Group, a charity that does much to combat poverty beyond the parameters of its narrowly framed moniker. However, in training their fire so selectively on the poverty experienced by this or that deserving demographic – and implicitly excluding from their embrace all of the others – such otherwise noble causes open up space for welfare state naysayers and hardened scrounger-bashers to continue promoting their narratives of stigma, division and distrust.

Not only are discourses that implicitly pit one form of poverty against another pernicious; they also often contain deeply dishonest and misleading representations of the nature and costs of existing social security *policies*. How did Labour's plans to toughen the eligibility criteria for PIP and the incapacity-related Universal Credit top-up – styled as a 'moral mission' to save claimants who wanted to work from the scrapheap and 'get Britain working' – square with its other great moral crusade: to rid Britain of the scourge of child poverty? There can be no child poverty 'taskforce' or 'strategy' worth the name that does not simultaneously recognize and address the hardships experienced by the economically inactive – just as no drive to reduce pensioner poverty can ignore the commonalities between challenges and inequalities experienced by many older people and those affecting others with disabilities and chronic health conditions. Likewise, 'welfare reforms' designed to reduce levels of economic inactivity will never do anything more than inflict further poverty and misery on already vulnerable people as long as ministers continue to insist on making short-term savings *before* putting in place the conditions necessary to enable people to return to work. They are even less likely to do so if they involve the slashing of benefits, like PIP, that are specifically designed to *facilitate* work.

In the end, one can mount a 'moral mission' about almost anything – from protecting property or, conversely, taxing extreme unearned wealth to fighting terrorism and defending a nation's borders (the latter two being priorities repeatedly emphasized in Starmer's strongman posturing). But surely the most important moral mission of all is to build a society that is *worth* defending in the first place – by protecting the vulnerable (including people inactive owing to serious illness and disability) and lifting all of one's citizens out of poverty, hunger and want. Moreover, while Britain's moral missions of the moment would benefit from a serious reset, a good interim starting point might be to at least rethink the various policy solutions proposed for delivering them. In order to ensure the success of any drive to increase employment among inactive people, governments need to be prepared to spend *more* money on 'welfare' in the short term – not less. People with complex disabilities and illnesses who have spent long periods out of the labour market need intensive support that is sustained, meaningful and individually tailored. Equally importantly, employers must be prepared to take a chance on people with 'work-limiting' physical and mental conditions (and gaps on their CVs) – and, where necessary, make bespoke adjustments to their working environments, demands and routines in order to ensure that their workplaces are genuinely accessible.

In short, if we are serious about asking people with complex disabilities and long-term illnesses to work sufficient hours to be able to earn a living – and benefit from the 'dignity' and 'purpose' so blithely ascribed to employment by politicians – then training, apprenticeships and new forms of work entirely all need to be thrown into the mix, and in serious, sustained and imaginative ways. How tenable is a drive to get millions of inactive people into the workplace if even the government's own data shows there were only 736,000 vacancies in the UK economy as of May 2025 (ONS 2025c) and respected think-tanks point to a stark mismatch between the nature of those jobs and the knowledge and skills of those currently out of work (Department for Education 2024)? In short, there need to be enough dignified, appropriate and accessible jobs to accommodate people to begin with.

Unless or until *all* these strands of support and opportunity are addressed, any attempt to coerce large numbers of long-term sick and disabled people (back) into work – by removing supposed 'incentives' encouraging them to remain on benefits – are likely to achieve nothing beyond plunging them and their families (including children) deeper into poverty. Yet throughout Britain's inactivity panic, the dominant discourse from government and media – the public conversation that tends to both shape and reflect policy responses – has insisted on maintaining the delusion that the most significant driver of stubbornly high levels of incapacity-related inactivity is the 'ease' with which people can claim sickness and disability benefits. In other words, the dominant discourse is driven by a concern about the mounting *financial cost* of providing for people too sick or disabled to enter employment and the supposed incentives that 'trap' them out of work – not the challenges and obstacles testified to by the lived experiences of those individuals themselves. It is, then, this rising benefits bill that is framed as the primary problem – not the fact that so many people suffer from work-limiting illnesses (including mental ill health) to start with; nor the years-long delays they endure while waiting for the consultations, surgery and/or counselling that might enable them to enter or return to work.

Reframing inactivity: The way forward

So how can we change the national conversation about economic inactivity? Moves towards treating inactive people with more respect should ideally start with ministers and policymakers: actors with the power to reshape dominant discourses if they so wish, and with no excuse to be ignorant about the realities of inactivity and the barriers that promote it. But in the absence of this leadership (and it *is* woefully absent) the march towards dignity might also start with the language the media uses to frame and discuss issues of public concern.

The popular vocabulary used to describe people is important because it signifies what society collectively thinks of them and the position they occupy – and, by extension, how they should be treated. To put it another way, discourse is important because it not only *reflects* public opinion and social attitudes but also helps to *shape* them. In turn, public perceptions and concerns both legitimize existing policy approaches and (occasionally) 'demand' alternative ones, including (at times) more progressive steps to correct inequalities.

In seeking a corrective to popular myths about the economically inactive, an obvious starting point would be to bring the ethical codes of Britain's main media regulators, the Independent Press Standards Organisation (IPSO) and Ofcom, in line with that of the only regulatory body to have fully adopted the recommendations of the 2012 *Leveson Report into the Culture, Practices and Ethics of the Press*: the Independent Monitor of the Press (IMPRESS). While all three codes contain explicit clauses prohibiting journalists and news organizations from publishing content that is discriminatory or prejudiced, both IPSO and Ofcom confine themselves to safeguarding groups with legally protected characteristics under the Equality Act 2010: i.e. they offer little or no direct protection to people experiencing socioeconomic inequality. Although Ofcom adds to its list a prohibition of hatred relating to 'social origin', only IMPRESS explicitly protects 'socio-economic status', further qualifying this protection to encompass those 'receiving welfare and benefits payments' (IMPRESS 2024: n.pag.). However, as legacy newspaper owners are free to decide which (if either) code to sign up to, only a handful of smaller publishers adhere to the stricter IMPRESS standards, with the overwhelming majority opting for IPSO's light-touch oversight – ostensibly in defence of their rights to wider press freedom. Unsurprisingly, these include the worst offenders in stigmatizing the economically inactive: *Express* newspapers, *MailOnline* and www.telegraph.co.uk.

Indeed, if IPSO and Ofcom's attitude towards stigma and invective based on social status is lax, even worse is the 'nothing-to-see-here' approach enshrined in the 'community rules' and moderation policies news publishers themselves use to monitor and maintain civility on their below-the-line comment threads. These rely on red flags being raised by audience-members who have willingly immersed themselves in these self-selecting discursive echo-chambers: people overwhelmingly more likely to endorse than dispute the (often stigmatizing) views fellow community members express. *MailOnline*'s current 'House Rules' confine themselves to urging readers not to 'make or encourage' comments that are 'offensive, racist, sexist, homophobic or discriminatory against any religions or other groups' (*MailOnline* 2011). In its 'community guidelines', www.telegraph.co.uk professes to 'not tolerate religious abuse, racism, sexism, homophobia, minority abuse, hate speech or any offensive generalisations', while outsourcing it to readers to 'be the creators' of their own discursive 'environment' and promising its moderators will only then 'review reported comments' (*The Telegraph* 2025). The legacy press and broadcast media are, then, as under-policed a discursive environment as social media, where – for all its lawless reputation – major platforms like X and Facebook are nominally *stricter* about encouraging users to flag or report stigma and invective, including towards economically disadvantaged groups.

Regulators and publishers would, no doubt, respond to such criticisms by asserting that they *do* protect many inactive people from discrimination – if only through rules and policies prohibiting hate speech against the disabled (a protected group). Yet how does this explain away the mass of stigmatizing content published in opinion columns, other articles, and below-the-line comments analysed in Chapter 2? For editors, journalists and posters, the get-out clause is simple: their target, they would doubtless argue, is not people with *genuine* disabilities, but those who are *faking* them. There is, then, no easy redress for the invective to which people experiencing povertyism, classism and benefits stigma are routinely subjected in the UK media, in the absence of more wide-ranging statutory and regulatory protections.

From myth to reality: Reshaping the narrative through lived experience

If regulators, news publishers and social media companies cannot be relied on to prevent the circulation of stigma and hatred towards 'workless' people, how else can we change the national conversation around economic inactivity? In one sense, modifying the language used to 'describe' inactive people is – and only ever was – one part of the struggle. The task of changing popular discourse is not just a matter of addressing the question of how we speak *about*, or *on behalf of*, those affected – but ensuring we speak *to* them. In other words, journalists and politicians need to extend the range and scope of 'expert' sources they cite in their output (and, in the government's case, use to inform policy), by embracing those with the greatest expertise: inactive people themselves.

Even after a fifteen-year period spotlighting the narrowest imaginarics of 'welfare reform' – various prescriptions for how best to cut the benefits bill (and fast) – there *is* precedent for more inclusive approaches of this kind. During the pre-COVID period when it was preparing to start accumulating incremental devolutionary powers over the country's benefits budget, Nicola Sturgeon's Scottish Government convened a succession of 'experience panels' to guide its approach to 'welfare' policy. This was a consultation genuinely worthy of the name, particularly when compared to other recent governments' approaches to welfare reform. Contrast it with the approach of Liz Kendall who, despite offering warm assurances that Labour would 'work closely with disabled people' to develop proposals based on its November 2024 white paper (Hansard 2024), mounted a consultation that officially ended on 30 June 2025 – nearly two weeks *after* the point that she had published a final draft bill, and barely a day before putting this to a formal vote in Parliament. In other words, the Labour 'consultation' was no such thing: it was a tick-box exercise to canvas views on what ministers hoped would be a legislative *fait accompli*. Only after being forced into a humiliating climbdown over its initial PIP proposals by a mass rebellion of its own backbenchers did the government finally agree to engage meaningfully with disability groups, by promising a review of assessments, prior to any future reform, that was genuinely 'co-produced' with disabled people (Hansard 2025b). Time will tell if this transpires.

By contrast, one outcome of the Scottish Government's consultation was a new Social Security Charter, first published in 2019 (and updated in 2024) – the abiding principle of which was a maxim that 'respect for the dignity of individuals' should lie 'at the heart of the Scottish social security system' (Social Security Scotland 2024). The semantic nuances of this sentence were significant enough. For once, the concept of 'social security' was being reclaimed, and re-emphasized, in place of a term that, for too long, had been mobilized as a shorthand signifier for the abject, feckless and undeserving working-aged poor: 'welfare'. But, beyond this, the charter also contained other notable steps forward in reframing the position of those forced to rely on social protection. Drawing on the work of campaign groups including the Poverty Alliance, this effort was preceded by a consultation with key stakeholders which asked them if there were 'any particular words or phrases' that 'should not be used when delivering social security in Scotland', and whether they were happy with the term 'user panels' for the focus-groups of existing social security recipients that were eventually christened 'experience panels' (The Scottish Government 2016). The consultation document also included the following highly significant passage:

> Users have told us that one of the key problems with the current system is the negative way it makes them feel. We are aware that, for many people, accessing support can feel difficult and disjointed, adding stress to what is already often a difficult situation. In order to address this, we will ensure that the language and tone that we use when communicating with people is respectful, considered and does not stigmatise. For example, we describe the powers that are being devolved to us as powers over 'social security' and not 'welfare'.
>
> (The Scottish Government 2016: 19)

There are precedents, too, for how to improve the quality and accuracy of media discourse – despite the clear deficiencies in current regulatory frameworks. Though the National Union of Journalists' code of conduct currently confines itself to upholding the same statutory protections for stigmatized groups as IPSO and Ofcom, it has published a widely cited guide to reporting poverty which goes much further – co-authored by people with lived experience and supported by charities including ATD Fourth World, On Road Media (now Heard) and Church Action on Poverty (National Union of Journalists 2022). The wording of the NUJ's formal code simply states that journalists should produce 'no material likely to lead to hatred or discrimination on the grounds of a person's age, gender, race, colour, creed, legal status, disability, marital status, or sexual orientation' (National Union of Journalists n.d.). But in its co-produced reporting guide it urges journalists to think sensitively about how they strike the right balance between 'statistics', 'individual people' and 'systems' in covering stories about poverty and benefits, by ensuring that they 'humanise a story', while also adding sufficient 'structural context' to 'make clear that their story illustrates a wider problem that society can choose to address' (or not) (National Union of Journalists n.d.: 7). This is a world away from what Shanto Iyengar terms the 'episodic framing' of sensational and/ or judgmental reports about 'welfare', in which individual 'human interest' stories are used to *stigmatize* benefit recipients in general, by portraying extreme, atypical cases as indicative of pervasive fecklessness and abuse of the system (Iyengar 1991).

Others have also taken steps to address the public language around poverty and benefits. During a period coinciding with the peak of austerity-era anti-welfare discourse, and the rise of 'poverty porn' TV, the Joseph Rowntree Foundation and the Frameworks Institute brought people with lived experience face to face with members of the wider public, and media content producers, through its 'Talking about Poverty' initiative. More recently, guidelines advising media professionals how to navigate the jargon around 'social security' (not 'welfare'), and report responsibly on benefits to avoid promoting 'stigma', were published by anti-poverty charity Turn2Us. Significantly, their timing coincided with the lead-up to the crunch parliamentary debate that ultimately derailed Kendall's ill-fated PIP Bill. 'We hear from people who feel ashamed or fearful after reading negative coverage', read the guide's introduction, before going on to stress the impact of 'stories that focus heavily on fraud' or portray benefit recipients 'as a burden' (Turn2Us 2025a). Reflecting the closely intertwined nature of media and *political* discourse, the charity paired this guide with a parallel one for parliamentarians, in which it emphasized MPs' and peers' 'huge power to shape our social security system' – both through 'the policy decisions they make' and 'the language they use to describe it'. In a targeted side-swipe at ministers, it added that, in ensuing months, it would be 'publishing innovative new research on how the government can remove stigma embedded in our social security system, as well as working with cross-sector partners to establish a more positive narrative around social security' (Turn2Us 2025b: n.pag.).

Listening to the inactives

There is, then, plenty of progressive pressure at work, as this book goes to print, to try to correct the longstanding inequities and inaccuracies that have up to nowbedevilled hegemonic popular narratives about economic inactivity, benefits and social security. But what of the perspectives of inactive people themselves? And how can we ensure that their stories and experiences are placed front and centre of future portrayals – rather than being ignored, distorted or (at best) appended as adjuncts and afterthoughts? One model from which journalists and other media producers might learn can be found in *The Roles We Play*, which started life as a photographic exhibition, then a film, and finally an exemplary booklet chronicling (in their own words) the caregiving, volunteering and other unsung social contributions made by people living in poverty. In the best traditions of showing, not telling, the booklet leaves the heavy lifting to those with lived experience, to relay what longstanding poverty scholar and campaigner Ruth Lister describes in her preface as the 'agency' they exercise in contributions from their own 'struggle to get by' to 'the ways they support family members, friends, neighbours and other members of their local communities and in their attempts to create better lives and conditions' (ATD Fourth World 2014: v). These moving tales of devotion and defiance testify to the wealth of different forms of unsung, unrecognized labour undertaken by 'inactive' people – from caregiving to cooking, decorating and volunteering in lunch clubs, playgroups and foodbanks. Drawing on such examples of personal sacrifice and disabled labour would offer a fertile ongoing source of case studies, and stories, for any forward-looking news organization chasing engagement in today's increasingly personalized, hyper-visual, people-focused attention economy.

As for charities and campaigners, traditional approaches to winning hearts and minds through media engagement have tended to adopt the top-down approach of leveraging space and airtime to 'broadcast' their messages to as wide (and immediate) an audience as possible. But with the mass media of old in retreat and legacy news audiences fragmenting – and increasingly bypassing traditional outlets entirely to access bespoke, targeted news diets via the side-door of social media – the time is ripe to reset legacy strategies for (re)shaping public opinion to more varied and narrowcast tactics, including by exploiting the affordances of digital algorithms. In this age of media atomization, what better time to experiment with new forms of framing and agenda-setting that work from the bottom up – beaming stories into the spaces where people *are*, not fighting against the tide to drag them to where campaigners (and journalists) might *like* them to be?

Insurgent start-ups promoting new forms of 'solutions journalism', 'constructive journalism' and 'pioneer journalism' around the world have a refreshing appetite for user-generated content, collaborative newsgathering, community participation and co-production – involving both audiences and sources. In Britain alone, fleetfooted news operations like *Bureau Local* are working directly and systematically with their community members to generate stories from the grassroots up. They are crying out for content that is newsworthy in its own right and, more importantly, tells 'the stories that matter' (Anderson 2025: 574) – including those that speak to (and *through the voices of*) the growing number of people whose own lives (or those of their relatives and friends) involve managing illness and disability, providing unpaid care, and tussling with the benefits system. With this latest disruptive turn come new opportunities to reshape elite-driven agendas and public attitudes, to better reflect the hopes, aspirations and lived realities of people from all walks of life – not least those formerly known as 'the workless'.

Appendix 1
Textual Analysis Methodology

The LexisNexis digital database of full-text UK newspapers was used to collect a series of relevant datasets spanning all national and regional papers across ten snapshot periods – or 'discursive "events" ' (Wodak 2001: 65) – spread over a 27-month timeframe spanning from 13 December 2022 to 22 March 2025. These were the weeks from 13–19 December 2022, when the UK was ranked as one of only seven OECD countries to have a higher economic inactivity rate than prior to COVID-19; 5–11 February 2023, during which new figures were published exposing chronic labour shortages across major sectors of the UK economy; 12–18 March 2023, encompassing Conservative Chancellor Jeremy Hunt's 'Back to Work Budget'; 19–25 November 2023, during which Work and Pensions Secretary Mel Stride launched a 'Back to Work' scheme to implement the Budget's measures; 13–19 February 2024, when new data from the ONS revealed the extent of the impact of rising long-term sickness on inactivity rates; 19–25 April 2024, during which Prime Minister Rishi Sunak launched his 'moral mission' to end Britain's 'sick-note culture'; 7–13 May 2024, when 'WorkWell' pilots were launched by the Department for Work and Pensions to spearhead government 'back to work' plans; 21–27 July 2024, during which former Health Secretary Alan Milburn launched his 'Pathways to Work' report that formed the template for Labour's proposed disability benefit reforms; 24–30 November 2024, when Liz Kendall published Labour's 'Get Britain Working' white paper; and 16–22 March 2025, during which Kendall published Labour's 'Pathways to Work' green paper.

Searches were conducted using the database's 'Europe' and 'United Kingdom' filters, with articles ordered from oldest to newest. The search terms used were 'economic inactivity' and 'economically inactive' and, following initial sampling, the datasets were manually cleaned to remove duplicates. The final size of the corpus was 1110 articles. A two-stage process was used to code articles' frames, beginning with the initial development of broad deductive categories, followed by a detailed read-through of articles. This process of fine tuning of categories through data immersion drew on Philipp Mayring's 'inductive category formation' approach (Mayring 2014). The approach to framing analysis was based on Todd Gitlin's definition of frames as the 'principles of selection, emphasis and presentation' underpinning texts (Gitlin 1980: 6), and Robert

Entman's methodological focus on four aspects of framing: the 'definition, causal interpretation, moral evaluation and/or treatment' of a 'problem' (Entman 1993: 53).

Six final categories of newspaper frame were identified: 'hard negative' (articles positioning inactive people and/or benefit recipients as workshy non-contributors, using explicitly stigmatizing tropes); 'soft negative' (articles framing inactive people negatively but in less overtly stigmatizing terms); 'hard positive' (articles adopting a strongly counter-hegemonic approach which explicitly defends inactive people); 'soft positive' (articles defending inactive people in more compromised terms – e.g. some but not all groups, such as genuinely disabled people or unpaid carers); 'balanced' (articles adopting a broadly neutral and/or descriptive approach to discussing inactive people) and 'incidental' (articles about other issues or topics – e.g. the state of the economy – that made reference to inactivity only in passing). The totals for each frame across the sample were as detailed in Table 2.1.

Following the initial coding of frames, CDA was applied to a selective subsample of the overall corpus to draw out deeper readings of the connotations and subtexts contained in key articles: i.e. to expose and unpack their latent as well as manifest content. The chosen form of CDA drew on Ruth Wodak's discourse-historical approach (DHA), which 'attempts to integrate a large quantity of available knowledge about the historical sources and the background of the social and political fields in which discursive "events" are embedded'. DHA applies three related 'aspects' of social critique: a 'text or discourse-immanent' approach, which focuses on identifying inconsistencies and paradoxes in texts; 'socio-diagnostic critique', which aims to decode the persuasive/manipulative character of discursive practices; and a 'future-related prospective' approach, which aims to improve communication by critiquing problematic discourse – e.g. stigmatizing language (Wodak 2015: 3). In supplementing framing analysis with CDA, the intention was to add a deeper layer of qualitative analysis to a small sample of texts chosen to illustrate various ways in which economically inactive people were problematized by the media-political commentariat. As it was not an objective to quantify *how many* articles/Hansard records adopted such approaches, this analysis was entirely qualitative, and no quantitative tabular data was produced.

Parliamentary texts (speeches, ministerial statements and other interventions) were sampled over the same snapshot periods as newspaper articles, with records drawn from the verbatim online record of Hansard. However, as Hansard produced only a handful of relevant texts in comparison to LexisNexis, analysis was confined to in-depth qualitative interrogation through CDA.

Finally, reader posts were sampled from comment threads posted beneath online articles published on the two national news sites that devoted the most space to discussing economic inactivity throughout the sample period: *MailOnline* and www.telegraph.co.uk. These were sampled from three snapshots positioned at the beginning, middle and end of this overall timeframe: event 1 (the week in December 2022 when data revealed Britain had one of the highest inactivity rates in the world); event 5 (the week in February 2024 when new figures exposed the scale of rising sickness benefit claims, especially among young adults); and event 9 (the week in November that year when Labour published its *Get Britain Working* white paper).

Initial datasets were manually cleaned up to remove comments irrelevant to the primary focus of analysis: views and attitudes towards economic inactivity and/or people classified as economically inactive or workless. This entailed the manual removal of all posts that did not express a clearly discernible viewpoint – or sentiment – about inactivity or worklessness. As some articles generated hundreds of comments, it was necessary to rationalize the datasets prior to analysis, by confining the final samples to only the first few pages of posts and prioritizing those that were 'most liked', 'most popular' or 'best rated'. The samples were initially coded (categorized) through manual sentiment analysis (Werner et al. 2017), using a similar high-level approach to the press and Hansard framing analysis. Stage one involved identifying the range of discursive categories present in the sample by applying Mayring's 'inductive category formation' approach (2014) and Pfeil and Zaphiris's rationale that this 'offers a way to capture the essence of the communication within an online community' (2010: 7). A smaller subsample of the extensive initial corpus was then subjected to more in-depth analysis through CDA.

The final dataset comprised a total of 1378 reader posts (comments): 252 from event 1, 327 from event 5 and 610 from event 9. Posts were eventually coded across eight categories, spanning the full spectrum of sentiments from the most aggressively stigmatizing (coded as 'hate speech') to those defending inactive people in the most uncompromising terms (coded as 'hard counter-discursive' comments). These categories were the following: 'first-order hatred', 'second-order hatred', 'hard negative', 'soft negative', 'empathy' (posts expressing some level of sympathy for people gaming the system), 'soft counter-discursive' and 'hard counter-discursive'. After fine tuning, the final tallies for each category were quantified. A full breakdown of reader sentiments across the two news sites and three discursive events is given in Table 2.2.

To ensure that initial quantitative coding of the frames of newspaper articles and reader comments was reliable enough to be replicated, one tenth of each sample (111 articles and 140 comments) was recoded six months after initial coding was completed. Recoding of articles produced a 97% match, with three pieces moved between adjacent categories: one from 'neutral' to 'incidental'; one from 'soft positive' to 'neutral'; and a third from 'neutral' to 'soft negative'. Recoding of posts produced a 100% match.

Appendix 2
Interview Methodology

Semi-structured interviews were carried out with a total of fourteen people classified as wholly or partially 'economically inactive', eleven of them because of disability, physical or mental ill health, caregiving responsibilities and/or intersectional combinations of two or more of these factors. The other three interviewees were individuals who had taken conscious decisions to downscale and/or leave the workplace for reasons ranging from their own or relatives' declining health to a desire to improve their work-life balance. Prospective subjects were initially approached for interview on the basis of characteristics that could be seen to qualify them as broadly 'representative' voices of the spectrum of factors leading to individuals' becoming economically inactive (Lavrakas 2008). The majority of interviewees were referred, directly or indirectly (e.g. via networks), by three charities: ATD Fourth World, Heard and Volunteer Scotland. Others were referred by the researcher's colleagues and/or personal contacts. Interviews were conducted on Microsoft Teams or telephone, depending on the expressed preferences of individual interviewees. Teams interviews were video-recorded and transcripts auto-generated within the program, whereas phone interviews were conducted on speakerphone, to allow them to be audio-recorded for manual transcribing with the help of open-source Audacity software.

Interviews focused on exploring the lived experiences of people classed as inactive, ranging from the circumstances that led to their 'becoming' inactive to their day-to-day routines and challenges. Subjects were also asked about their personal views on the nature and tone of dominant societal discourse(s) around this and related issues, including 'worklessness' and the benefits system more broadly. The semi-structured interview approach involved a mix of open questions, supplementaries and attempts to creatively rephrase enquiries that initially met with inconclusive answers or whose meaning was unclear to interviewees, in order to encourage them to expand on and/or rationalize views they expressed and/or add more detail or explanation to the background they had initially relayed about their lived experiences. Interviewees were encouraged to 'narrativize' their responses by describing their personal (hi)stories, using free association and illustrating their experiences with personal anecdotes (Hollway and Jefferson 2000: 35). For Teams interviews, the researcher drew inspiration from anthropologist Clifford Geertz's writings on 'thick description' – in particular, his contention that affectations, including 'winks and twitches', are often as significant as spoken words (Geertz 1973: 6–7). Moreover, in order to avoid making this process too extractive, all interviewees were invited to supplement their testimonies in their own time, if they so wished, by producing their own additional material – giving them platforms to articulate their (hi)stories and perspectives in their 'own words', whether in prose (e.g. follow-up emails) or in audio or visual form.

Interviews were conducted in full compliance with the research ethics framework of the researcher's home institution (the University of Stirling), and all subjects were asked to give their informed consent prior to interview – either in writing or verbally at the start of their interview recording. Given the sensitivity of some subjects discussed, initial flyers and social media posts advertising for interviewees were subject to prior approval by the gateway organizations (charities) who referred them. All interviewees were offered anonymity; provided with a detailed participant information sheet and outline of likely topics and areas of questioning ahead of interviews; and invited to attend the interview accompanied by someone else, if they so wished (e.g. a friend, carer or professional/charity key worker). Interviews were subject to thematic analysis – a process that draws together related strands of conversation from multiple individual datasets (in this case interview transcripts) in order to identify and explore common or recurring themes and the issues underpinning them (see, for example, Braun et al. 2014). Following this process, the researcher sent the interviewees copies of all their quotes he intended to reproduce in the book for sense-checking and final approval, offering them the chance to amend or retract any quotes with which they were not happy at this stage. Interviewees reserved the right to withdraw their consent for interview at any time during the process, including after being shown the material that the researcher intended to use.

References

Age UK (n.d.), 'Changes to state pension age', https://www.ageuk.org.uk/information-advice/money-legal/pensions/state-pension/changes-to-state-pension-age/. Accessed 10 July 2025.

Anderson, Bissie (2025), '"Join the coalition": How pioneer journalism communities reimagine journalistic epistemology from the periphery', *Digital Journalism*, 13(3), pp. 562–83.

Armstrong, Ashley (2025), 'Gen Z job slump: Brits under 25 drive up "worklessness" with almost 3 million now "economically inactive", damning figures reveal', *The Sun*, 12 March, https://www.thesun.co.uk/money/26644764/gen-z-unemployment-crisis-uk/. Accessed 10 July 2025.

ATD Fourth World (2014), *The Roles We Play: Recognising the Contribution of People in Poverty*, London: ATD Fourth World, https://www.atd-fourthworld.org/wp-content/uploads/sites/5/2016/02/20141017-The-Roles-We-Play.pdf. Accessed 10 July 2025.

Bangham, George, Finch, David and Phillips, Toby (2018), *A Welfare Generation: Lifetime Welfare Transfers between Generations*, London: Resolution Foundation.

Barton, Cassie, Sturge, Georgina and Harker, Rachael (2024), 'The UK's changing population', House of Commons Library, 16 July, https://commonslibrary.parliament.uk/the-uks-changing-population/#:~:text=An%20ageing%20population,but%20higher%20than%20some%20countries. Accessed 10 July 2025.

Bauman, Zygmunt (2013), *Wasted Lives: Modernity and its Outcasts*, London: John Wiley & Sons.

Bearden, Elizabeth B. (2019), *Monstrous Kinds: Body, space, and Narrative in Renaissance Representations of Disability*, Michigan: University of Michigan Press.

Bentley, David (2024a), 'Five new DWP benefit changes announced by Rishi Sunak and what they mean for you', *Birmingham Mail*, 19 April, https://www.birminghammail.co.uk/news/cost-of-living/five-new-dwp-benefit-changes-29028915. Accessed 10 July 2025.

Bentley, David (2024b), 'Labour work crackdown "fails to tackle soaring claims for DWP disability benefits"', *Birmingham Mail*, 24 November, https://www.birminghammail.co.uk/news/cost-of-living/labour-work-crackdown-fails-tackle-30440101. Accessed 10 July 2025.

Berry, Mike (2016), 'No alternative to austerity: How BBC broadcast news reported the deficit debate', *Media, Culture & Society*, 38(6), pp. 844–63.

Blair, T. ([1993] 2015), 'From the archive: Tony Blair is tough on crime, tough on the causes of crime', *New Statesman*, [29 January] 28 December. https://www.newstatesman.com/uncategorized/2015/12/archive-tony-blair-tough-crime-tough-causes-crime. Accessed 28 July 2025.

Blair, Tony (1997), 'Blair's speech: Single mothers won't be forced to take work', 2 June, https://www.bbc.co.uk/news/special/politics97/news/06/0602/blair.shtml. Accessed 10 July 2025.

Bodleian Libraries (n.d.), 'Disability history resources: Legislation', https://libguides.bodleian.ox.ac.uk/disability-history-resources/legislation#:~:text=Prerogativa%20Regis%20(1322)%20(17,allowing%20them%20license%20to%20beg. Accessed 10 July 2025.

Bogart, Kathleen R. and Dunn, Dana S. (2019), 'Ableism special edition introduction', *Journal of Social Issues*, online first, https://doi.org/10.1111/josi.12354.

Boileau, Bee and Cribb, Jonathan (2022), *The Rise in Economic Inactivity among People in their 50s and 60s*, London: Institute for Fiscal Studies.

Booth, William (2014), *In Darkest England and the Way Out*, Cambridge: Cambridge University Press.

Braun, Virginia, Clarke, Victoria and Rance, Nicola (2014), 'How to use thematic analysis with interview data', in A. Vossler and N. Moller (eds) *The Counselling and Psychotherapy Research Handbook*, London: Sage Publications, pp. 183–97.

Briant, Emma, Watson, Nick and Philo, Greg (2011), *Bad News for Disabled People: How the Newspapers are Reporting Disability*, Glasgow: Glasgow University Media Group.

'Britain's benefits scandal' (2024), *Dispatches*, Channel 4, 2 December, UK: Channel 4, https://www.channel4.com/programmes/britains-benefits-scandal-dispatches/on-demand/76935-001. Accessed 14 October 2025.

Brown, Gordon (1999), 'Speech to Labour Party Conference', *The Guardian*, 27 September, https://www.theguardian.com/politics/1999/sep/27/labourconference.labour7. Accessed 10 July 2025.

Bunbury, Stephen (2019), 'Unconscious bias and the medical model: How the social model may hold the key to transformative thinking about disability discrimination', *International Journal of Discrimination and Law*, 19(1), https://journals.sagepub.com/doi/10.1177/1358229118820742. Accessed 14 October 2025.

Butler, Patrick (2025), 'Ill and disabled people will be made "invisible" by UK benefit cuts, say experts', *The Guardian*, 8 April, https://www.theguardian.com/society/2025/apr/08/ill-disabled-people-uk-benefit-cuts-policy-in-practice. Accessed 10 July 2025.

Carers UK (2022), *The Experiences of Black, Asian and Minority Ethnic Carers During and beyond the COVID-19 Pandemic*, https://www.carersuk.org/media/c5ifvji0/carersukbamecovidreport2022.pdf. Accessed 10 July 2025.

Carers UK (2023), 'Census 2021 data shows increase in substantial unpaid care in England and Wales', Carers UK, 19 January, https://www.carersuk.org/press-releases/census-2021-data-shows-increase-in-substantial-unpaid-care-in-england-and-wales/#:~:text=Census%202021%20data%20shows%20increase%20in%20substantial%20unpaid%20care%20in%20England%20and%20Wales,-Press%20releases&text=152%2C000%20rise%20in%20number%20of,20%2D49%20hours%20of%20care. Accessed 9 July 2025.

Carers UK (2024), 'Facts about carers', Carers UK, 24 December, https://www.carersuk.org/media/ocxheq2c/facts-about-carers-dec-2024-final.pdf. Accessed 10 July 2025.

Carers UK (2025a), 'Thousands of carers receiving new debt letters as review into Carer's Allowance overpayments continues', Carers UK, 20 March, https://www.carersuk.org/press-releases/thousands-of-carers-receiving-new-debt-letters-as-review-into-carer-s-allowance-overpayments-continues/#:~:text=Thousands%20of%20people%20caring%20for,the%20Government%20in%20October%202024. Accessed 10 July 2025.

Carers UK (2025b), 'Briefing on pathways to work green paper: Impact on carers', Carers UK, 7 April, https://www.carersuk.org/media/cgiftoom/green-paper-policy-briefing-07-04-25.pdf. Accessed 10 July 2025.

Carroll, William C. (1996), *Fat King, Lean Beggar: Representations of Poverty in the Age of Shakespeare*, London: Cornell University Press.

Cates, Miriam (2023), 'Labour wants the state to bring up our children: The plan for graduate-led nurseries isn't just costly. It's a sinister attack on the role of parents', *Daily Telegraph*, 5 July, p. 14.

Centre for Mental Health (n.d.), 'Co-morbidities: Physical health and mental health problems together', https://www.centreformentalhealth.org.uk/co-morbidities-physical-health-and-mental-health-problems-together/#:~:text=health%20problems%20together-,Co%2Dmorbidities%3A%20physical%20health%20and%20mental%20health%20problems%20together,effect%20on%20their%20physical%20condition. Accessed 10 July 2025.

Checkland, S.G. and Checkland, E.O.A. (eds) (1974), *The Poor Law Report of 1834*, Aylesbury: Pelican.

Chhabra, Shakuntala (2016), 'Differently abled people and their life', *Global Journal of Medical and Clinical Case Reports*, 11 March, https://www.clinsurggroup.com/gjmccr/article/view/GJMCCR-3-122/pdf. Accessed 10 July 2025.

Chidwick, Tom (2023), ' "Back to basics": 30 years on', Miles End Institute Blog, 14 October, https://www.qmul.ac.uk/mei/news-and-opinion/items/back-to-basics-30-years-on.html. Accessed 28 July 2025.

Child Poverty Action Group (2025), 'Cuts to disability benefits would undermine government plans to tackle child poverty, warns charity', Child Poverty Action Group, 13 March, https://cpag.org.uk/news/cuts-disability-benefits-would-undermine-government-plans-tackle-child-poverty-warns-charity. Accessed 10 July 2025.

Clark, Kevin (2024), 'More than one-in-four North East workers is "economically inactive" ', *Sunderland Echo*, 13 February, https://www.sunderlandecho.com/business/more-than-one-in-four-north-east-workers-is-economically-inactive-4516278#:~:text=Economic%20inactivity%20in%20the%20North,the%20country%20as%20a%20whole. Accessed 10 July 2025.

Clark, Ross (2024), 'Long term sickness is costing taxpayers billions – we have to stop dishing out sicknotes and get people back to work', *The Sun*, 19 April, https://www.thesun.co.uk/news/27433732/ross-clark-sick-notes-cost-taxpayers-billions/. Accessed 14 October 2025.

Cohen, Stanley (1972), *Folk Devils and Moral Panics*, London: Paladin.

Coin, Francesca (2025), *The Great Resignation: The New Refusal of Work*, London: Bloomsbury Academic.

Corlett, Adam (2024), *Get Britain's Stats Working: Exploring Alternatives to Labour Force Survey Estimates*, London: Resolution Foundation.

Cox, Anthony (2013), *Empire, Industry and Class: The Imperial Nexus of Jute, 1840–1940*, Abingdon: Routledge.

Crerar, Pippa (2022), 'Leaked audio reveals Liz Truss said British workers needed "more graft" ', *The Guardian*, 16 August, https://www.theguardian.com/politics/2022/aug/16/leaked-audio-reveals-liz-truss-said-british-workers-needed-more-graft. Accessed 9 July 2025.

Crisis (2025), 'Fewer than three in every privately rented properties listed in England are affordable for people on housing benefit', Crisis, 1 April, https://www.crisis.org.uk/about-us/crisis-media-centre/fewer-than-three-in-every-100-privately-rented-properties-listed-in-england-are-affordable-for-people-on-housing-benefit-crisis-reveals. Accessed 10 July 2025.

Croft, Ethan (2024), 'Claim suicidal thoughts for benefits: Job centre staff show extent of UK's worklessness crisis', *The Telegraph*, 30 November, https://www.telegraph.co.uk/news/2024/11/30/worklessness-crisis-job-centre-sickness-benefits-dwp/. Accessed 10 July 2025.

Crowson, Isaac and Christie, Olivia (2024), '"Why would I want a job?" Shameless benefit scroungers in a seaside town boast they "chill out and enjoy life" while claiming "thousands a month" of YOUR cash as 10m go unemployed and 4,000 a day sign off sick in workshy Britain', *MailOnline*, 19 April, https://www.dailymail.co.uk/news/article-13327361/benefits-scroungers-seaside-town-workshy-Britain.html. Accessed 10 July 2025.

Daily Telegraph (2025), 'Cut welfare to size', *Telegraph*, 12 March, p. 15.

Davies, Nick (2008), *Flat Earth News: An Award-winning Reporter Exposes Falsehood, Distortion and Propaganda in the Global Media*, London: Random House.

Deacon, Alan (1978), 'The Scrounging controversy: Public attitudes towards the unemployed in contemporary Britain', *Social Policy & Administration*, 12(2), pp. 120–35.

Deans, J. and Hopkins, N. (1997), 'For all our benefit; The premier chooses one of Britain's bleakest housing estates to launch his drive to make the single mothers pay their way', *Daily Mail*, 3 June, pp. 12–13.

Deb, Pragyan and Li, Gloria (2024), *Upskilling the UK Workforce,* Washington DC: International Monetary Fund, https://www.imf.org/en/publications/selected-issues-papers/issues/2024/07/24/upskilling-the-uk-workforce-united-kingdom-552424. Accessed 10 July 2025.

Department for Education (2024), 'Skills England: Driving growth and widening opportunities', Gov.UK, 24 September, https://www.gov.uk/government/publications/skills-england-report-driving-growth-and-widening-opportunities. Accessed 10 July 2025.

Department for Work and Pensions (2022), 'The cost of working age ill-health and disability that prevents work', Gov.UK, 18 March, https://www.gov.uk/government/statistics/the-cost-of-working-age-ill-health-and-disability-that-prevents-work/the-cost-of-working-age-ill-health-and-disability-that-prevents-work. Accessed 10 July 2025.

Department for Work and Pensions (2025a), 'Fraud bill to save £1.5 billion progresses to the Lords', Gov.UK, 30 April, https://www.gov.uk/government/news/fraud-bill-to-save-15-billion-progresses-to-the-lords. Accessed 10 July 2025.

Department for Work and Pensions (2025b), *Pathways to Work: Reforming Benefits and Support to Get Britain Working*, Gov.UK, March, https://assets.publishing.service.gov.uk/media/67d84aa179f0d993dfb11f97/pathways-to-work.pdf. Accessed 10 July 2025.

Department for Work and Pensions (2025c), 'Spring Statement 2025 health and disability benefit reforms – Impacts', Gov.UK, London: The Stationery Office.

Department for Work and Pensions (2025d), 'Universal credit statistics, 29 April 2013 to 9 January 2025', Gov.UK, 18 February, https://www.gov.uk/government/statistics/universal-credit-statistics-29-april-2013-to-9-january-2025/universal-credit-statistics-29-april-2013-to-9-january-2025. Accessed 10 July 2025.

Department of Health and Social Care (2024), 'Unpaid carers supported by £22.6 million investment in innovation', Gov.UK, 28 November, https://www.gov.uk/government/news/unpaid-carers-supported-by-226-million-investment-in-innovation. Accessed 10 July 2025.

Department of Health and Social Care (2025), 'New reforms and independent commission to transform social care', Gov.UK, 3 January, https://www.gov.uk/government/news/new-reforms-and-independent-commission-to-transform-social-care. Accessed 10 July 2025.

Disability Rights UK (2025a), 'Disability hate crime: current situation', https://www.disabilityrightsuk.org/disability-hate-crime#:~:text=Key%20Evidence,of%20reports%20go%20any%20further. Accessed 14 October 2025.

Disability Rights UK (2025b), '90% of PIP Daily Living Component recipients would fail new Green Paper test', https://www.disabilityrightsuk.org/news/90-pip-standard-daily-living-component-recipients-would-fail-new-green-paper-test. Accessed 10 July 2025.

Draznin, Yaffa C. (2000), *Victorian London's Middle-class Housewife: What She Did All Day*, New York: Bloomsbury Publishing USA.

Duda-Mikulin, Eva, Scullion, Lisa and Currie, Richard (2020), 'Wasted lives in scapegoat Britain: overlaps and departures between migration studies and disability studies', *Disability & Society*, 35(9), pp. 1373–97, https://doi.org/10.1080/09687599.2019.1690428.

Duncan Smith, Iain (2014), 'Iain Duncan Smith's speech on welfare reform – full text', *The Spectator*, 23 January, https://www.spectator.co.uk/article/iain-duncan-smith-s-speech-on-welfare-reform-full-text/. Accessed 10 July 2025.

Dunn, Will (2025), 'Why Britain has a unique problem with economic inactivity', *The Economist*, 12 March, https://www.economist.com/britain/2023/09/14/why-britain-has-a-unique-problem-with-economic-inactivity. Accessed 10 July 2025.

The Economist (2025), 'Britain's worklessness disaster', *The Economist*, 13 March, https://www.economist.com/britain/2025/03/13/britains-worklessness-disaster. Accessed 10 July 2025.

Editors' Code Committee (n.d.), *The Editors' Code of Practice*, Independent Press Standards Organisation, https://www.ipso.co.uk/editors-code-of-practice/. Accessed 10 July 2025.

Eley, Sarah (2023), 'Unpaid care and protected characteristics, England and Wales: Census 2021', Office for National Statistics, 24 April, https://www.ons.gov.uk/peoplepopulationandcommunity/healthandsocialcare/socialcare/articles/unpaidcareandprotectedcharacteristicsenglandandwales/census2021. Accessed 9 July 2025.

Elgot, Jessica and Butler, Patrick (2025), 'Starmer decries "worst of all worlds" benefits system ahead of deep cuts', *The Guardian*, 10 March, https://www.theguardian.com/society/2025/mar/10/starmer-decries-worst-of-all-worlds-benefits-systems-ahead-of-deep-cuts. Accessed 9 July 2025.

Entman, Robert (1993), 'Framing: toward clarification of a fractured paradigm', *Journal of Communication,* 43, pp. 51–58.

Equestri, Alice (2022), 'Literature and disability in the English Renaissance', *Oxford Research Encyclopaedias*, 23 March, https://doi.org/10.1093/acrefore/9780190201098.013.1317.

Evidence and Information Department, Cancer Research UK (2025), *Cancer in the UK 2025: Socioeconomic Deprivation*, Cancer Research UK, https://www.cancerresearchuk.org/sites/default/files/cancer_in_the_uk_2025_socioeconomic_deprivation.pdf. Accessed 10 July 2025.

Fox, Aine (2023), 'Government told it must win trust of disabled people on back-to-work plan', *The Independent*, 15 March, https://www.independent.co.uk/news/uk/jeremy-hunt-government-mel-stride-chancellor-zoom-b2301490.html. Accessed 10 July 2025.

Francis-Devine, Brigid, Harari, Daniel, Keep, Matthew, Bolton, Paul, Barton, Cassie, Harker, Rachael and Cromarty, Hannah (2024), 'Rising cost of living in the UK', https://commonslibrary.parliament.uk/research-briefings/cbp-9428/. Accessed 23 October 2025.

Frayne, David (2015), *The Refusal of Work: The Theory and Practice of Resistance*, London: Bloomsbury.

Freud, David (2007), *Reducing Dependency, Increasing Opportunity: Options for the Future of Welfare and Work: An Independent Report to the Department for Work and Pensions*, Leeds: Corporate Document Services, https://www.mostewartresearch.co.uk/wp-content/uploads/2021/07/THE-FREUD-REPORT-2007.pdf. Accessed 10 July 2025.

Full Fact (2024), 'Inaccurate comparison of benefit fraud and tax losses circulates on social media', Full Fact, 26 September, https://fullfact.org/online/benefit-fraud-vs-tax-evasion/. Accessed 10 July 2025.

Gans, Herbert (1962), *The Urban Villagers*, New York: The Free Press of Glencoe.

Garland Thomson, R. (2017), *Extraordinary Bodies: Figuring Physical Disability in American Culture and Literature*, New York: Columbia University Press.

Garlick, Sarah (2022), 'Economic inactivity status, England and Wales: Census 2021', Office for National Statistics, 8 December, https://www.ons.gov.uk/employmentandlabourmarket/peopleinwork/employmentandemployeetypes/bulletins/economicactivitystatusenglandandwales/census2021. Accessed 10 July 2025.

Garthwaite, Kayleigh (2014), 'Fear of the brown envelope: Exploring welfare reform with long-term sickness benefits recipients', *Social Policy & Administration*, 48(7), pp. 782–98.

Geertz, Clifford (1973), 'Chapter 1/Thick description: Toward an interpretive theory of culture', *The Interpretation of Cultures: Selected Essays*, pp. 3–30.

Gentes, Andrew A. (2011), '"Completely useless": Exiling the disabled to Tsarist Siberia', *Interdisciplinary Journal of Siberian Studies*, 10(2), https://www.berghahnjournals.com/view/journals/sibirica/10/2/sib100202.xml. Accessed 10 July 2025.

Gentilcore, David (2006), 'The "golden age of quackery" or "medical enlightenment" Licensed charlatanism in eighteenth-century Italy', *Cultural and Social History*, 3, pp. 250–63, https://doi.org/10.1191/1478003806cs064oa.

Gerbner, George and Gross, Larry (1976), 'Living with television: The violence profile', *Journal of Communication*, 26(2), pp. 173–99.

Gitlin, Todd (1980), *The Whole World is Watching*, Berkeley: University of California Press.

Glover, Stephen (2014), 'Forget food banks: Why doesn't the church fight the evil of welfare dependency?' *MailOnline*, 17 April, https://www.dailymail.co.uk/debate/article-2606545/STEPHEN-GLOVER-Forget-food-banks-Why-doesnt-Church-fight-evil-welfare-dependency.html. Accessed 10 July 2025.

Godden, Richard H. and Mittman, Asa Simon (2019), *Monstrosity, Disability, and the Posthuman in the Medieval and Early Modern World*, London: Palgrave Macmillan.

Goffman, Erving (1990), *Stigma: Notes on the Management of Spoiled Identity*, London: Penguin Random House.

Golding, Peter and Middleton, Sue (1982), *Images of Welfare*, London: Wiley-Blackwell.

Goode, Erich and Ben-Yehuda, Nachman (2009), *Moral Panics: The Social Construction of Deviance*, 2nd edition, London: John Wiley & Sons.

Gov.uk (n.d.), 'Discrimination: Your rights', https://www.gov.uk/discrimination-your-rights#:~:text=you%20can%20do-,Types%20of%20discrimination%20. Accessed 10 July 2025.

GRIPP (2024), 'Untold realities of poverty in the UK', https://gripp.org.uk, GRIPP, 17 October, https://gripp.org.uk/2024/10/17/the-untold-realities-of-poverty-in-the-uk/. Accessed 10 July 2025.

The Guardian (2000), 'Did bad parenting really turn these boys into killers?' *The Guardian*, 1 November, https://www.theguardian.com/uk/2000/nov/01/bulger.familyandrelationships. Accessed 28 July 2025.

The Guardian (2024a), '*The Guardian* view on disability, illness and work: There is no "sicknote culture" in Britain', *The Guardian*, 22 April, https://www.theguardian.com/commentisfree/2024/apr/22/the-guardian-view-on-disability-illness-and-work-there-is-no-sicknote-culture-in-britain#:~:text=But%20there%20is%20no%20such,large%20number%20of%20unwell%20people. Accessed 10 July 2025.

The Guardian (2024b), '*The Guardian* view on Keir Starmer's speech: Serving working people, but what about others?' *The Guardian*, 24 September, https://www.theguardian.com/commentisfree/2024/sep/24/the-guardian-view-on-keir-starmers-speech-serving-working-people-but-what-about-others?CMP=Share_iOSApp_Other. Accessed 9 July 2025.

Gudkov, Lev (2005), 'The fetters of victory: How the war provides Russia with its identity', *Eurozine*, 5 March, https://zeitschrift-osteuropa.de/site/assets/files/4028/2005-05-03-gudkov-en.pdf. Accessed 10 July 2025.

Gullace, Nicoletta F. (2015), *International Encyclopaedia of the First World War*, https://encyclopedia.1914-1918-online.net/. Accessed 10 July 2025.

Gutteridge, Nick (2023), 'Lockdown "added to work crisis by making people scared to leave homes"', *The Telegraph*, 8 February, https://www.telegraph.co.uk/politics/2023/02/08/lockdown-added-work-crisis-making-people-scared-leave-homes/. Accessed 10 July 2025.

Gutteridge, Nick (2024a), 'Mental health culture has gone too far, says Mel Stride', *The Telegraph*, 20 March, https://www.telegraph.co.uk/politics/2024/03/20/mental-health-culture-has-gone-too-far-says-mel-stride/. Accessed 10 July 2025.

Gutteridge, Nick (2024b), 'Starmer dodges crackdown on sickness benefits', *The Telegraph*, 26 November, https://www.telegraph.co.uk/politics/2024/11/26/starmer-dodges-crackdown-on-sickness-benefits/. Accessed 10 July 2025.

Habermas, Jurgen (2022), 'Reflections and hypotheses on a further structural transformation of the political public sphere', *Theory, Culture and Society*, online first, https://doi.org/10.1177/02632764221112341.

Hagopian, Alicja and Maddox, David (2025), 'Welfare in numbers: The facts behind Britain's soaring benefits bill', *The Independent*, 25 March, https://www.independent.co.uk/politics/benefits-pip-welfare-numbers-reeves-spring-statement-b2721711.html. Accessed 10 July 2025.

Hall, Stuart, Critcher, Chas, Jefferson, Tony, Clarke, John and Roberts, Brian (1978), *Policing the Crisis: Mugging, the State and Law and Order*, London: Bloomsbury.

Hansard (1997), 'Child Benefit for lone parents', UK Parliament, 10 December, https://hansard.parliament.uk/commons/1997-12-10/debates/35c63adf-31d2-4aef-9a05-cb86e3fff563/ChildBenefitForLoneParents. Accessed 29 July 2025.

Hansard (2022), 'West Midlands economy', UK Parliament, 24 December, https://hansard.parliament.uk/Commons/2022-12-14/debates/2BAC9549-BFA2-4338-BC5B-7482D9220384/WestMidlandsEconomy. Accessed 10 July 2025.

Hansard (2023a), 'Payroll employees: Economic growth', UK Parliament, 7 February, https://hansard.parliament.uk/Commons/2023-02-07/debates/2E32B693-065D-413C-AB80-20456DCF16C6/PayrollEmployeesEconomicGrowth. Accessed 10 July 2025.

Hansard (2023b), 'Financial statement and Budget report', UK Parliament, 15 March, https://hansard.parliament.uk/Commons/2023-03-15/debates/5603C6A5-C487-4D37-8658-F6403BF9E5A5/FinancialStatementAndBudgetReport. Accessed 10 July 2025.

Hansard (2024), *'Get Britain Working' White Paper*, UK Parliament, 26 November, https://hansard.parliament.uk/commons/2024-11-26/debates/772B43CF-BC88-47A2-9199-8E30FD485B21/GetBritainWorkingWhitePaper. Accessed 10 July 2025.

Hansard (2025a), 'Welfare reform', UK Parliament, 18 March, https://hansard.parliament.uk/Commons/2025-03-18/debates/2863E51D-E53D-4444-9C51-6D064D94CC8A/WelfareReform. Accessed 10 July 2025.

Hansard (2025b), 'Universal Credit and Personal Independence Payment Bill', UK Parliament, 1 July, https://hansard.parliament.uk/commons/2025-07-01/debates/56F2EF7B-404B-44D4-865E-EA09FCD92EA4/UniversalCreditAndPersonalIndependencePaymentBill. Accessed 15 October 2025.

Hansen, Helena, Bourgeois, Phillipe and Drucker, Ernest (2014), 'Pathologizing poverty: New forms of diagnosis, disability, and structural stigma under welfare reform', *Social Science & Medicine*, 103, pp. 76–83, https://doi.org/10.1016/j.socscimed.2013.06.033.

Hardman, Isabel (2014), 'Even Iain Duncan Smith's critics can't reject his welfare reforms', *The Spectator*, 7 April, https://www.spectator.co.uk/article/even-iain-duncan-smith-s-critics-can-t-reject-his-welfare-reforms/. Accessed 10 July 2025.

Harman, Thomas (2008), *A Caveat or Warning for Common Cursetors, Vulgarly Called Vagabonds*, Whitefish: Kessinger Publishing.

Harro-Loit, Halliki and Josephi, Beate (2020), 'Journalists' perception of time pressure: A global perspective', *Journalism Practice*, 14(4), pp. 395–411.

Haylett, C. (2001), 'Illegitimate subjects? Abject whites, neoliberal modernisation, and middle-class multiculturalism', *Environment and Planning D: Society and Space*, 19(3), pp. 351–70.

Heffer, Greg (2022), 'Rise in Brits dropping out the workforce puts UK behind only Colombia, Chile and Switzerland in global league table of economic inactivity', *MailOnline*, 19 December, https://www.dailymail.co.uk/news/article-11553687/Rise-Brits-dropping-workforce-puts-UK-fourth-global-league-table-economic-inactivity.html. Accessed 10 July 2025.

Hickel, K. Walter (2001), 'War, region, and social welfare: Federal aid to servicemen's dependents in the South, 1917–1921', *The Journal of American History*, 87(4), pp. 1362–91.

Hollway, Wendy and Jefferson, Tony (2000), *Doing Qualitative Research Differently: Free Association, Narrative and the Interview Method*, London: Sage.

Hourihane, D.O.B. and McCaughey, W.T. (1966), 'Pathological aspects of asbestosis', *Postgraduate Medical Journal*, 42, pp. 613–22, https://pmc.ncbi.nlm.nih.gov/articles/PMC2466058/pdf/postmedj00406-0007.pdf. Accessed 10 July 2025.

Howe, Megan (2024), 'The rise of the "sickfluencer": How TikTokkers and YouTubers are telling their followers to maximise their sick and disability benefits – as more than 15,000 have their applications approved every week', *MailOnline*, 2 December, https://www.dailymail.co.uk/news/article-14148283/rise-illfluencer-TikTokkers-YouTubers-sick-disability-benefits.html. Accessed 9 July 2025.

Hughes, Bill (2015), 'Disabled people as counterfeit citizens: The politics of resentment past and present', *Disability & Society*, 30(7), pp. 991–1004.

Hunt, Jeremy (2023), 'Those who can work will … Those who can't we will help', *The Sun*, 12 March, p. 16.

Iacurci, Gregg (2023), '2023 was the "real year of the Great Resignation," says economist', *CNBC*, 1 February, https://www.cnbc.com/2023/02/01/why-2022-was-the-real-year-of-the-great-resignation.html. Accessed 9 July 2025.

IMPRESS (2024), 'Discrimination: Guidance on Clause 4', https://www.impress.press/wp content/uploads/2023/02/Impress-Standards-Code.pdf. Accessed 23 October 2025.

Institute for Public Policy Research (2023), 'UK on track for lowest ever benefit levels by 2030 warns IPPR, as it urges renewed purpose for social security', IPPR, 3 October, https://www.ippr.org/media-office/uk-on-track-for-lowest-ever-benefit-levels-by-2030-warns-ippr-as-it-urges-renewed-purpose-for-social-security. Accessed 9 July 2025.

'Is there a moral case for cutting welfare?' (2025), *Moral Maze*, London: BBC Radio 4, 12 March.

Islam, Faisal (2023), 'The Inside story of the mini-budget disaster', BBC, 25 September, https://www.bbc.com/news/business-66897881. Accessed 9 July 2025.

Iyengar, Shanto (1991), *Is Anyone Responsible? How Television Frames Political Issues*, Chicago: University of Chicago Press.

Jackson, Lucy (2024), 'Fury as Isabel Oakeshott claims benefit claimants are "parasites"', *The National*, 1 November, https://www.thenational.scot/news/24695882.isabel-oakeshott-claims-benefits-claimants-parasites/. Accessed 9 July 2025.

Jennings, Ben (2025), 'Ben Jennings on Labour plans to cut disability benefits rather than impose a wealth tax', *The Guardian*, 12 March, https://www.theguardian.com/commentisfree/picture/2025/mar/12/ben-jennings-labour-disability-benefits-wealth-tax-cartoon. Accessed 10 July 2025.

Jensen, Tracey (2014), 'Welfare commonsense, poverty porn and doxosophy', *Sociological Research Online*, 19(3), pp. 277–83.

Joseph Rowntree Foundation (2025), *UK Poverty 2024: The Essential Guide to Understanding Poverty in the UK*, https://www.jrf.org.uk/uk-poverty-2024-the-essential-guide-to-understanding-poverty-in-the-uk. Accessed 10 July 2025.

Kamal, Rashida (2022), 'Quitting is just half the story: The truth behind the "Great Resignation"', *The Guardian*, 4 January, https://www.theguardian.com/business/2022/jan/04/great-resignation-quitting-us-unemployment-economy. Accessed 9 July 2025.

Kendall, Liz (2024), 'Get Britain working speech', Gov.UK, 23 July, https://www.gov.uk/government/speeches/getting-britain-working. Accessed 9 July 2025.

Kilshaw, Susie (2005), *Impotent Warriors: Gulf War Syndrome, Vulnerability and Masculinity*, New York: Berghahn Books.

Knapton, Sarah (2022), 'Long COVID not to blame for the "great resignation"', *Telegraph*, 10 October, https://www.telegraph.co.uk/news/2022/10/09/long-covid-not-blame-long-term-sick-who-have-quit-jobs-recent/. Accessed 9 July 2025.

Lavrakas, Paul J. (2008), *Encyclopedia of Survey Research Methods*, London: Sage.

Lawford, Melissa and Butcher, Ben (2024), 'The English town where children grow up doomed to worklessness', *The Telegraph*, 24 March, https://www.telegraph.co.uk/business/2024/03/24/middlesbrough-children-grow-up-doomed-worklessness/. Accessed 9 July 2025.

Lawton, Katherine and Neal, Jonathan (2025), 'Not everyone needs to be diagnosed with depression and anxiety says Tony Blair as he tells Brits to "stop medicalising the ups and downs of life" ', *MailOnline*, 13 January, https://www.dailymail.co.uk/news/article-14276897/Stop-medicalising-life-Tony-Blair-mental-health.html. Accessed 9 July 2025.

Leaker, Debra (2009), 'Economic inactivity', *Economic & Labour Market Review*, 3, pp. 42–46.

LeBesco, Kathleen (2010), 'Neoliberalism, public health, and the moral perils of fatness', *Critical Public Health*, 21, pp. 153–64, https://www.tandfonline.com/doi/abs/10.1080/09581596.2010.529422. Accessed 15 October 2025.

Lewis, Oscar (1966), *La Vida*, London: Random House.

Lilley, Peter (1992), 'Speech to Conservative Party conference', YouTube, https://www.youtube.com/watch?v=FOx8q3eGq3g. Accessed 10 July 2025.

Littlejohn, Richard (2024), 'Why are we importing cleaners from Ecuador when 9 million Brits are "economically inactive?"' *MailOnline*, 19 February, https://www.dailymail.co.uk/debate/article-13100929/RICHARD-LITTLEJOHN-importing-cleaners-Ecuador-9million-Brits-economically-inactive.html. Accessed 10 July 2025.

Lytton, Charlotte (2024), 'How Britain's sick note culture made us the West's most workshy nation', *The Telegraph*, 19 April, https://www.telegraph.co.uk/news/2024/04/19/how-britains-sick-note-culture-made-us-the-wests-most-works/. Accessed 9 July 2025.

Macrotrends.net (2025), 'UK population (1950–2025)', https://www.macrotrends.net/global-metrics/countries/gbr/united-kingdom/population. Accessed 10 July 2025.

MailOnline (2011), 'House rules', *Daily Mail*, 6 June, https://www.dailymail.co.uk/home/article-1388145/House-Rules.html. Accessed 10 July 2025.

malingerer, *Cambridge Dictionary* (2025), https://dictionary.cambridge.org/dictionary/english/malingerer. Accessed 10 July 2025.

Malthus, Thomas (1967), *Essay on Principle of Population 1798*, New York: Readex Microprint.

Mann, Kirk and Roseneil, Sasha (1994), ' "Some mothers do 'ave 'em": Backlash and the gender politics of the underclass debate', *Journal of Gender Studies*, 3(3), pp. 317–31.

Matthews, Glenna (1989), *'Just a Housewife': The Rise and Fall of Domesticity in America*, Oxford: Oxford University Press.

Mayring, Philipp (2014), 'Qualitative content analysis: Theoretical background and procedures', in A. Bikner-Ahsbahs, C. Knipping and N. Presmeg (eds), *Approaches to Qualitative Research in Mathematics Education: Examples of Methodology and Methods*, Dordrecht: Springer Netherlands, pp. 365–80.

McCulloch, Adam (2025), 'UK is only advanced economy where economic inactivity is increasing', *Personnel Today*, 20 March, https://www.personneltoday.com/hr/uk-is-only-advanced-economy-where-economic-inactivity-is-increasing/. Accessed 10 July 2025.

McIntosh, Marjorie Keniston (2011), *Poor Relief in England: 1350–1600*, Cambridge: Cambridge University Press.

McKinstry, Leo (2023), 'Balanced, shrewd and effective route to prosperity: Spring Budget 2023', *The Express*, 16 March, pp. 12–13.

McKinstry, Leo (2024), 'The welfare state has become a bloated monster. Can Keir Starmer really tame it?' *MailOnline*, 24 November, https://www.dailymail.co.uk/news/article-14121389/LEO-MCKINSTRY-welfare-state-bloated-monster-Keir-Starmer-really-tame-it.html. Accessed 10 July 2025.

Merriman, Sam (2024), 'Sicknote Britain even sicker than thought: Number on long-term sickness benefits "underestimated by 250,000"', *MailOnline*, 29 October, https://www.dailymail.co.uk/health/article-14015973/Sicknote-Britain-long-term-benefits-underestimated-250-000.html. Accessed 9 July 2025.

Meta (2025), 'Hateful conduct', Meta, 7 January, https://transparency.meta.com/en-gb/policies/community-standards/hateful-conduct/. Accessed 10 July 2025.

Milburn, Alan (2024a), *Pathways to Work Commission Report: July 2024*, Barnsley: Barnsley Metropolitan Borough Council.

Milburn, Alan (2024b), 'How to solve Britain's most toxic issue: Get millions back to work', *The Times*, 23 July, https://www.thetimes.com/uk/politics/article/how-to-solve-britains-most-toxic-issue-get-millions-back-to-work-f9s92mms7. Accessed 10 July 2025.

Mind (n.d.), 'Autism and mental health', https://www.mind.org.uk/information-support/tips-for-everyday-living/autism-and-mental-health/#:~:text=Research%20suggests%20that%20many%20autistic,how%20best%20to%20support%20you. Accessed 15 October 2025.

Ministry of Defence (2012), 'Gulf veterans' illnesses', Gov.UK, 12 December, https://www.gov.uk/guidance/gulf-veterans-illnesses. Accessed 10 July 2025.

Mittman, Gloria, Schrank, Beatte and Steiner-Hofbauer, Verena (2023), 'Portrayal of autism in mainstream media – A scoping review about representation, stigmatisation and effects on consumers in fiction and non-fiction media', *Current Psychology*, 48, pp. 8008–17, https://doi.org/10.1007/s12144-023-04959-6.

Morrison, James (2016), *Familiar Strangers, Juvenile Panic and the British Press: The Decline of Social Trust*, Abingdon: Routledge.

Morrison, James (2019), *Scroungers: Moral Panics and Media Myths*, London: Bloomsbury.

Morrison, James (2022), *The Left Behind: Reimagining Britain's Socially Excluded*, London: Pluto Press.

Morrison, James (2025), 'Labour says benefit reforms are a moral mission: It looks more like moral panic', *The Conversation*, 19 March, https://theconversation.com/labour-says-benefit-reforms-are-a-moral-mission-it-looks-more-like-moral-panic-252404. Accessed 10 July 2025.

Mostert, Mark P. (2002), 'Useless eaters: Disability as genocidal marker in Nazi Germany', *The Journal of Special Education*, 36(3), pp. 157–70, https://journals.sagepub.com/doi/abs/10.1177/00224669020360030601.

Mujagić, Mersina (2018), 'Dangerous waters metaphor in news discourse on refugee crisis', *Metaphorik. de*, 28, pp. 99–131.

Murphy, Louise (2024), 'A U-shaped legacy: Taking stock of trends in economic inactivity in 2024', Resolution Foundation, 23 March, https://www.resolutionfoundation.org/publications/a-u-shaped-legacy/. Accessed 9 July 2025.

Murphy, Rhian, Dennes, Matt, White, Emmie and Vizard, Tim (2022), 'Reasons for workers aged over 50 years leaving employment since the start of the coronavirus pandemic: Wave 2', Office for National Statistics, 27 September, https://www.ons.gov.uk/employmentandlabourmarket/peopleinwork/employmentandemployeetypes/articles/reasonsforworkersagedover50yearsleavingemploymentsincethestartofthecoronaviruspandemic/wave2. Accessed 9 July 2025.

Murray, Charles (1990), 'Underclass', in C. and F. Field, *The Emerging British Underclass*, London: IEA Health and Welfare Unit.

National Union of Journalists (2022), *Reporting Poverty: A Guide for Media Professionals*, https://www.nuj.org.uk/resource-report/reporting-poverty-a-guide-for-media-professionals.html. Accessed 10 July 2025.

National Union of Journalists (n.d.), *Code of Conduct*, https://www.nuj.org.uk, https://www.nuj.org.uk/about-us/rules-and-guidance/code-of-conduct.html. Accessed 25 July 2025.

Nevett, Joshua (2025), 'Some on benefits are "taking the mickey", says minister', BBC, 7 February, https://www.bbc.co.uk/news/articles/cq5gpyv4dnwo. Accessed 10 July 2025.

Nevett, Joshua and Catt, Helen (2025), 'Starmer says benefit system unfair and indefensible', BBC, 11 March, https://www.bbc.co.uk/news/articles/c0kgpyz3mmpo. Accessed 10 July 2025.

Nielsen, Kim E. (2012), *A Disability History of the United States*, Boston: Beacon Press.

O'Brien, Lotti (2025), 'New figures show just how reliant Rachel Reeves is on pensioners over 70', *Express*, 13 March, https://www.express.co.uk/news/uk/2026562/rachel-reeves-pension-income-tax. Accessed 10 July 2025.

Office for Budget Responsibility (2023), 'Why has working-age inactivity risen since the pandemic?', https://obr.uk/box/why-has-working-age-inactivity-risen-since-the-pandemic/. Accessed 9 July 2025.

Office for National Statistics (2024a), 'Population estimates for the UK, England, Wales, Scotland and Northern Ireland: mid-2023', 8 October, https://www.ons.gov.uk; https://www.ons.gov.uk/peoplepopulationandcommunity/populationandmigration/populationestimates/bulletins/annualmidyearpopulationestimates/mid2023. Accessed 10 July 2025.

Office for National Statistics (2024b), 'Births in England and Wales: 2023', Office for National Statistics, 28 October, https://www.ons.gov.uk/peoplepopulationandcommunity/birthsdeathsandmarriages/livebirths/bulletins/birthsummarytablesenglandandwales/2023. Accessed 10 July 2025.

Office for National Statistics (2025b), 'Labour market overview, UK: March 2025', Office for National Statistics, 20 March, https://www.ons.gov.uk/employmentandlabourmarket/peopleinwork/employmentandemployeetypes/bulletins/uklabourmarket/march2025. Accessed 21 October 2025.

Office of Communications (2024), 'Section three: Crime, disorder, hatred and abuse', Office of Communications Broadcast Standards, 22 February, https://www.ofcom.org.uk/tv-radio-and-on-demand/broadcast-standards/section-three-crime-disorder-hatred-abuse. Accessed 10 July, 2025.

Osborne, George (2012), 'Speech to Conservative Party conference', *New Statesman*, 8 October, https://www.newstatesman.com/blogs/politics/2012/10/george-osbornes-speech-conservative-conference-full-text. Accessed 10 July 2025.

Osborne, George (2013), 'Chancellor's speech on changes to the tax and benefits system', Gov.UK, 2 April, https://www.gov.uk/government/speeches/chancellor-speech-on-changes-to-the-tax-and-benefit-system#:~:text=Some%20have%20said%20it's%20the,that%20creates%20real%2C%20lasting%20jobs. Accessed 23 October 2025.

Pagano, Maggie (2024), 'Get the over-50s back to work to boost Britain's wealth, says Maggie Pagano', *This is Money*, 21 July, https://www.thisismoney.co.uk/money/comment/article-13656769/Looking-job-follow-Robert-Niros-lead-says-MAGGIE-PAGANO.html. Accessed 10 July 2025.

Parkinson, Justin (2007), 'What does "British jobs" pledge mean?', BBC, 16 November, http://news.bbc.co.uk/1/hi/uk_politics/7097837.stm. Accessed 10 July 2025.

Parris, Matthew (2023), 'Mental health crisis may not be all it seems', *The Times*, 4 August, https://www.thetimes.com/article/mental-health-crisis-may-not-be-all-it-seems-btn6q5627. Accessed 9 July 2025.

Partington, Richard (2023), 'UK is worst performer in G7 for workforce participation since COVID', *The Guardian*, 13 April, https://www.theguardian.com/business/2023/apr/13/uk-worst-performer-g7-workforce-participation-since-covid. Accessed 9 July 2025.

Pearson, Geoffrey (1983), *Hooligan: A History of Respectable Fears*, Berlin: Springer.

Petrillo, Maria, Zhang, Jingwen and Bennett, Matt (2024), *Valuing Carers 2021/22: The Value of Unpaid Care in the UK*, Carers UK, November, https://www.carersuk.org/media/mfbmjbno/valuing_carers_uk_v3_web.pdf. Accessed 10 July 2025.

Pfeil, Ulrike and Zaphiris, Panayiotis (2010), 'Applying qualitative content analysis to study online support communities', *Universal Access in the Information Society*, 9(1), pp. 1–16.

Phillips, Sarah (2009), '"There are no invalids in the USSR!": A missing Soviet chapter in the new disability history', *Disability Studies Quarterly*, 29(3), https://dsq-sds.org/article/id/494/. Accessed 10 July 2025.

Ping Chan, Szu, Nolsoe, Eir and Lawford, Melissa (2024), 'The looming crisis that Hunt's Budget failed to address', *The Telegraph*, 7 March, https://www.telegraph.co.uk/business/2024/03/07/budget-2024-mass-migration-growth-workforce-crisis-worsens/#:~:text=Even%20as%20Hunt%20doubled%20down,taken%20into%20a%20new%20bracket. Accessed 10 July 2025.

Political Thinking with Nick Robinson (2024), 'The Liz Kendall One', BBC, 27 July, https://www.bbc.co.uk/sounds/play/m0021h4k. Accessed 9 July 2025.

Politics Live (2025), *BBC2*, London, 5 March.

Powell, Andrew (2024), 'Economic update: Inactivity due to illness reaches record', House of Commons Library, 25 April, https://commonslibrary.parliament.uk/economic-update-inactivity-due-to-illness-reaches-record/. Accessed 9 July 2025.

Preston, Jeremy (2023), 'Times Letters', *The Times*, 6 August.

Pring, John (2025), 'Snap survey reveals disabled people's "fear and desperation" ahead of likely cuts to benefits', *Disability News Service*, 30 January, https://www.disabilitynewsservice.com/snap-survey-reveals-disabled-peoples-fear-and-desperation-ahead-of-likely-cuts-to-benefits/. Accessed 9 July 2025.

Purnell, James (2008), 'Speech to Progress Challenge series', Progressive Britain, 19 June, https://archive.progressivebritain.org/2008/06/19/james-purnells-speech/. Accessed 28 July 2025.

Putnam, Robert D. (1994), 'Social capital and public affairs', *Bulletin of the American Academy of Arts and Sciences*, 47(8), pp. 5–19.

Quinio, Valentine (2023), 'Has economic inactivity gone up everywhere in the country since the pandemic hit?' Centre for Cities, 15 February, https://www.centreforcities.org/blog/has-economic-inactivity-gone-up-everywhere-in-the-country-since-the-pandemic-hit/. Accessed 9 July 2025.

Rainer, Charlotte, Treloar, Nick, Abdinasir, Kadra and Edwards, Priya (2024), *A Dual Crisis: The Hidden Link Between Poverty and Children's Mental Health*, Centre for Mental Health, https://cypmhc.org.uk/wp-content/uploads/2024/07/CentreforMH_ADualCrisis.final_.pdf. Accessed 14 October 2025.

Reilly, Jonathan (2022), 'Blame game: Jet2 boss blames airport chaos on "lazy Brits who live off benefits and sit on arses" ', *The Sun*, 2 June, https://www.thesun.co.uk/travel/18766701/jet2-boss-airport-lazy-brits/. Accessed 10 July 2025.

The Rest is Politics (2025), Goalhanger Podcasts, London, 16 January.

Ring, Katya, McCurry, Holly, Colthorpe, Rosanna and Rawlings, Joshua (2024), 'Trends in labour market inactivity for caring purposes', Office for Budget Responsibility, 11 January, https://articles.obr.uk/trends-in-labour-market-inactivity-for-caring-purposes/index.html. Accessed 9 July 2025.

Robertson, Una A. (1997), *The Illustrated History of the Housewife, 1650–1950*, Stroud: Sutton Publishing.

Robertson, Una A. (2000), *Coming out of the Kitchen: Women Beyond the Home*, Stroud: Sutton Publishing.

Rodger, James (2024), 'Rishi Sunak under fire over new DWP powers which "demonise" people on benefits', *Birmingham Mail*, 19 April, https://www.birminghammail.co.uk/news/cost-of-living/rishi-sunak-under-fire-over-29028016. Accessed 10 July 2025.

Roffe, D. and Roffe, C. (1995), 'Madness and care in the community: A medieval perspective', *British Medical Journal*, 311, https://doi.org/10.1136/bmj.311.7021.1708.

Row-Heyveld, Lindsey (2018), *Dissembling Disability in Early Modern English Drama*, Berlin: Springer.

Rowlands, Terry, Waddell, Neal and McKenna, Bernard (2016), 'Are we there yet? A technique to determine theoretical saturation', *Journal of Computer Information Systems*, 56(1), pp. 40–47.

Ryan, Frances (2025), 'Labour mollifies the rich, targets disabled people and claims moral justification', *The Guardian*, 10 March, https://www.theguardian.com/commentisfree/2025/mar/10/disabled-people-labour-benefits-system. Accessed 10 July 2025.

Schifferes, Steve and Roberts, Richard (2015), *The Media and Financial Crisis*, New York: Routledge.

Schweik, Susan M. (2009), *The Ugly Laws: Disability in Public*, New York: New York University Press.

Scottish Express (2023), 'Let's get Britain working for a prosperous future', 15 March, p. 12.

The Scottish Government (2016), *A New Future for Social Security: Consultation on Social Security in Scotland*, https://consult.gov.scot/social-security/social-security-in-scotland/supporting_documents/Consultation%20on%20social%20security%20in%20Scotland%20%20full%20version.pdf. Accessed 10 July 2025.

The Scottish Government (2023), 'Carers census, Scotland, 2022–23', The Scottish Government, 12 December, https://www.gov.scot/publications/carers-census-scotland-2022-23/pages/caring-roles/. Accessed 9 July 2025.

Sempick, Joe and Becker, Saul (2013), *Young Adult Carers at School: Experiences and Perceptions of Caring and Education*, London: Carers Trust.

Slater, T. (2014), 'The myth of "Broken Britain": Welfare reform and the production of ignorance', *Antipode*, 46(4), pp. 948–69.

Smith, David (2023), 'Back-to-work sweeteners won't cure labour market ailments on their own', *Sunday Times*, 15 March, p. 37.

Social Security Scotland (2024), *Our Charter*, https://www.socialsecurity.gov.scot/about/our-charter. Accessed 10 July 2025.

Sommerlad, Joe and Gregory, Andy (2023), 'How did Chancellor Jeremy Hunt make his money?', *The Independent,* 23 November, https://www.independent.co.uk/news/uk/politics/jeremy-hunt-chancellor-net-worth-b2452218.html. Accessed 15 October 2025.

Squires, Peter and Stephen, Dawn (2005), *Rougher Justice: Antisocial Behaviour and Young People*, Cambridge: Willan.

Starmer, Keir (2024a), 'Keir Starmer speech at Labour Party Conference 2024', Labour, 24 September, https://labour.org.uk/updates/press-releases/keir-starmer-speech-at-labour-party-conference-2024/. Accessed 23 July 2025.

Starmer, Keir (2024b), 'Keir Starmer: Jobs are about dignity and pride … not just paying the bills', *MailOnline*, 23 November, https://www.dailymail.co.uk/debate/article-14118885/SIR-KEIR-STARMER-Jobs-dignity-pride-not-just-paying-bills.html. Accessed 9 July 2025.

Stearn, Emily (2024), 'Get a sick note for £25 – by just filling out a form: Anger over online firms offering same-day letters with "no appointment necessary"', *MailOnline*, 19 April, https://www.dailymail.co.uk/health/article-13327839/sick-note-anger-online-day-letters-appointments.html. Accessed 10 July 2025.

Stewart, Mo (2020), 'What price preventable harm: social policies designed to disregard human need', Centre for Welfare Reform, https://www.mostewartresearch.co.uk/wp-content/uploads/2020/10/What-Price-Preventable-Harm-Oct-2020-1.pdf. Accessed 23 October 2025.

Stone, Deborah (1986), *The Disabled State*, Philadelphia: Temple University Press.

Sunak, Rishi (2024), 'Prime minister's speech on welfare', Gov.UK, 19 April, https://www.gov.uk/government/speeches/prime-ministers-speech-on-welfare-19-april-2024. Accessed 9 July 2025.

Swinford, Steven (2023), 'Learn work skills or face benefits cut, jobless told', *The Times*, 11 February, pp. 1–2.

Tapsfield, James (2024), 'If people refuse to work they WILL lose their benefits, insists Labour as Starmer's vows to crack down on huge welfare bill is branded a "hollow promise" ', *MailOnline*, 24 November, https://www.dailymail.co.uk/news/article-14119947/Cabinet-minister-young-people-benefits-jobs-training-Starmer-welfare.html. Accessed 10 July 2025.

Taylor, Charlotte (2022), 'The affordances of metaphor for diachronic corpora & discourse analysis: Water metaphors and migration', *International Journal of Corpus Linguistics*, 27(4), pp. 451–79.

The Telegraph (2023), 'The benefits of the nuclear family cannot be ignored', *The Telegraph*, 31 August, https://www.telegraph.co.uk/news/2022/08/31/benefits-nuclear-family-cannot-ignored/. Accessed 26 July 2025.

The Telegraph (2024a), 'Fighting sick-note culture', *The Telegraph*, 20 April, https://www.telegraph.co.uk/opinion/2024/04/20/rishi-sunak-speech-out-of-work-pip-sickness-benefit-nhs/. Accessed 10 July 2025.

The Telegraph (2024b), 'Labour isn't working', *The Telegraph*, 26 November, p. 17.

The Telegraph (2025), 'The Telegraph community guidelines', *The Telegraph*, 8 May, https://www.telegraph.co.uk/about-us/community-guidelines/. Accessed 10 July 2025.

Thompson, Edward P. (1968), *The Making of the English Working Class*, London: Penguin.

The Times (2024a), 'The Times view on growing worklessness: British disease', *The Times*, 14 August, https://www.thetimes.com/comment/the-times-view/article/the-times-view-on-growing-worklessness-british-disease-w529j5qsg#:~:text=Economic%20inactivity%20in%20the%20working%2Dage%20population%20continues%20its%20alarming%20rise&text=In%20the%201970s%20it,from%20another%20malady%3A%20economic%20inactivity. Accessed 9 July 2025.

The Times (2024b), 'The Times view on encouraging employment: Mountain to climb', *The Times*, 25 November, https://www.thetimes.com/comment/the-times-view/article/the-times-view-on-encouraging-employment-mountain-to-climb-bk5s278zk. Accessed 10 July 2025.

Today (2025a), BBC Radio 4, London, 5 March.

Today (2025b), BBC Radio 4, London, 10 March.

Trading Economics (2025), 'United Kingdom Inactivity Rate', https://tradingeconomics.com/united-kingdom/inactivity-rate#:~:text=Markets,percent. Accessed 10 July 2025.

Trouillot, Michel-Rolph (2015), *Silencing the Past: Power and the Production of History*, Boston: Beacon Press.

Tuchman, Gaye (1972), 'Objectivity as strategic ritual: An examination of newsmen's notions of objectivity', *American Journal of Sociology*, 77(4), pp. 660–79.

Turn2Us (2025a), *Reporting on Social Security: A Toolkit for Media Professionals*, https://www.turn2us.org.uk/getmedia/67dda446-8f44-43ae-8120-49dca57235e5/Turn2us-Media-Guide.pdf. Accessed 10 July 2025.

Turn2Us (2025b), *Talking about Social Security: A Guide for Parliamentarians*, https://www.turn2us.org.uk/getmedia/193e78e0-5fd7-4077-9b43-ba8b85af2743/Turn2us-MP-Guide.pdf. Accessed 10 July 2025.

Turner, David M. (2012), *Disability in Eighteenth-Century England*, New York: Routledge, https://www.taylorfrancis.com/books/mono/10.4324/9780203117545/disability-eighteenth-century-england-david-turner. Accessed 10 July 2025.

UK Research and Innovation (2025), 'UKRI Creating opportunities: rethinking economic (in) activity', UKRI, 2 December, https://www.ukri.org/opportunity/ukri-creating-opportunities-rethinking-economic-inactivity/. Accessed 10 July 2025.

UK Statistics Authority (2025), 'Office for National Statistics follow-up correspondence to the Lords Economic Affairs Committee's inquiry on preparing for an ageing society', https://uksa.statisticsauthority.gov.uk/org/office-for-national-statistics/#:~:text=International%20comparisons%20of%20economic%20inactivity,any%20of%20its%20other%20inquiries. Accessed 10 July 2025.

Ullrich, Peter and Keller, Reiner (2014), 'Comparing discourse between cultures: A discursive approach to movement knowledge', in B. Baumgarten, P. Daphi and P. Ullrich (eds), *Conceptualizing Culture in Social Movement Research*, pp. 113–39, London: Palgrave Macmillan.

Vries, Robert de, Baumberg Geiger, Ben, Scullion, Lisa, Summers, Kate, Edmiston, Daniel, Ingold, Jo, Robertshaw, David and Young, David (2021), *Solidarity in a Crisis? Trends in Attitudes to Benefits during COVID-19*, https://62608d89-fc73-4896-861c-0e03416f9922.usrfiles.com/ugd/62608d_ffc54112b28141fdb85a9e9474120452.pdf. Accessed 10 July 2025.

Wadsworth, Jonathan and Machin, Stephen (2023), 'Should the UK Government Get Active about Economic Inactivity?' *Economics Observatory*, 26 May, https://www.economicsobservatory.com/should-the-uk-government-get-active-about-economic-inactivity#:~:text=The%20first%20point%20to%20make,in%20the%20aggregate%20inactivity%20rate. Accessed 10 July 2025.

Wallace, Tim (2023), 'British over 55s least likely to keep working in G7 in setback for Hunt', *The Telegraph*, 13 July, https://www.telegraph.co.uk/business/2023/07/13/british-over-55s-least-likely-to-keep-working-in-g7/. Accessed 9 July 2025.

Warner, Jeremy (2023), 'The scandalous shame of workshy Britain', *The Telegraph*, 4 February, https://www.telegraph.co.uk/business/2023/02/04/scandalous-shame-workshy-britain/. Accessed 9 July 2025.

Warner, Jeremy (2024), 'Stagnating Britain faces ruin without radical action', *The Telegraph*, 17 February, https://www.telegraph.co.uk/business/2024/02/17/uk-economy-recession-work shy-britain/. Accessed 10 July 2025.

Weeks, Kathi (2011), *The Problem with Work: Feminism, Marxism, Antiwork Politics, and Postwork Imaginaries*, Durham: Duke University Press.

Wells, Whitney, Xue, Baowen, Lacey, Rebecca and McMunn, Anne (2024), 'Differences by ethnicity in the association between unpaid caring and health trajectories over 10 years in the UK Household Longitudinal Study', *Journal of Epidemiology and Community Health*, online first, https://doi.org/10.1136/jech-2024-222633.

Welshman, John (2007), *From Transmitted Deprivation to Social Exclusion: Policy, Poverty and Parenting*, Bristol: Policy Press.

Welshman, John (2013), *Underclass: A History of the Excluded: 1880–2000*, London: Hambledon Continuum.

Wheatley, Edward (2010), 'Humoring the sighted: The comic embodiment of blindness', *Stumbling Blocks Before the Blind*, Michigan: University of Michigan Press, pp. 90–128.

Whitfield, Graeme (2024), 'More than a quarter of North East workforce classed as "economically inactive" ', *ChronicleLive*, 13 February, https://www.chroniclelive.co.uk/news/north-east-news/more-quarter-north-east-workforce-28626323. Accessed 10 July 2025.

Wilcock, David (2024), 'Calling people without jobs "economically inactive" is "terrible" because they are "real human beings" says Work and Pensions Secretary Liz Kendall', *MailOnline*, 14 November, https://www.dailymail.co.uk/news/article-14082301/Calling-people-without-jobs-economically-inactive-terrible-real-human-beings-says-Work-Pensi ons-Secretary-Liz-Kendall.html. Accessed 9 July 2025.

Willetts, David (1992), 'Theories and explanations of the underclass', in David J. Smith (ed.), *Understanding the Underclass*, London: Policy Studies Institute.

Willetts, David (2024), 'Young people urgently need more mental health support, but current policy is skewed against them', *ConservativeHome*, 27 February, https://conservativehome.com/2024/02/27/david-willetts-young-people-urgently-need-more-mental-health-support-yet-current-policy-is-skewed-against-them/. Accessed 9 July 2025.

Williams, Karl (2023), *Where are the Workers? A New Diagnosis of Economic Inactivity in Britain*, London: Centre for Policy Studies.

Wilski, Andrzej (2023), 'Times Letters', *The Times*, 6 August.

Wintour, Patrick (2022), 'British "idlers": How a 2021 attack on UK's work ethic could haunt Liz Truss', *The Guardian*, 30 July, https://www.theguardian.com/politics/2022/jul/30/british-idlers-how-a-2012-attack-on-uks-work-ethic-could-haunt-liz-truss. Accessed 9 July 2025.

Wodak, Ruth (2001), 'The discourse-historical approach', in R. Wodak and M. Meyer (eds), *Methods of Critical Discourse Analysis*, London: Sage, pp. 63–94.

Wodak, Ruth (2015), 'Critical discourse analysis, discourse-historical approach', *The International Encyclopedia of Language and Social Interaction*, 3, pp. 1–14.

Woods, Judith and Eijsberg, Meike (2025), '"They get benefits for nothing": The town that sums up Britain's youth worklessness crisis', *The Telegraph*, 17 March, https://www.telegraph.co.uk/news/2025/03/17/a-grim-trip-to-the-epicentre-of-britains-youth-worklessness/#:~:text='They%20get%20benefits%20for%20doing,up%20Britain's%20youth%20worklessness%20crisis. Accessed 10 July 2025.

Work Foundation (2024), 'Sick workers four times more likely to leave work if they have no job flexibility', Lancaster University Management School, 5 December, https://www.lancaster.ac.uk/work-foundation/news/sick-workers-four-times-more-likely-to-leave-work-if-they-have-no-job-flexibility. Accessed 10 July 2025.

World Economic Forum (2023), 'These countries have the highest childcare costs in the world', World Economic Forum, 19 July, https://www.weforum.org/stories/2023/07/highest-childcare-costs-by-country/#:~:text=Highest%20childcare%20costs%20by%20country,income%2C%20according%20to%20OECD%20figures.&text=In%20Czechia%2C%20net%20childcare%20costs,US%20the%20share%20is%2032%25. Accessed 10 July 2025.

X (n.d.), 'The X rules', https://help.x.com/en/rules-and-policies/x-rules#:~:text=Illegal%20or%20Certain%20Regulated%20Goods,of%20regulated%20goods%20or%20services. Accessed 10 July 2025.

www.ingramcontent.com/pod-product-compliance
Lightning Source LLC
LaVergne TN
LVHW080314130626
841179LV00002B/3